Becoming American, Being Indian

The Anthropology of Contemporary Issues

A Series Edited by Roger Sanjek

A full list of titles in the series appears at the end of this book.

Becoming American, Being Indian

An Immigrant Community in New York City

MADHULIKA S. KHANDELWAL

CORNELL UNIVERSITY PRESS

Ithaca & London

First published 2002 by Cornell University Press
First printing, Cornell Paperbacks, 2002

Printed in the United States of America

Library of Congress Cataloging-in-Publication Data

Khandelwal, Madhulika S. (Madhulika Shankar), 1957–
  Becoming American, being Indian : an immigrant community in New York
City / Madhulika S. Khandelwal.
    p. cm. — (The anthropology of contemporary issues)
Includes bibliographical references and index.
  ISBN 0-8014-4043-2 (acid-free paper) — ISBN 0-8014-8807-9 (pbk. :
acid-free paper)
  1. East Indian Americans—New York (State)—New York—Ethnic identity.
2. East Indian Americans—New York (State)—New York—Cultural
assimilation. 3. East Indian Americans—New York (State)—New
York—Social conditions. 4. Asian Americans—New York (State)—New
York—Ethnic identity. 5. Asian Americans—New York (State)—New
York—Social conditions. 6. Immigrants—New York (State)—New
York—Social conditions. 7. Queens (New York, N.Y.)—Ethnic relations.
8. Queens (New York, N.Y.)—Social conditions. 9. New York (N.Y.)—
Ethnic relations. 10. New York (N.Y.)—Social conditions. I. Title.
II. Series.
  F128.9.E2 K47 2002
  305.891'4110747—dc21
                                    2002005849

Cornell University Press strives to use environmentally responsible suppliers and materials to the fullest extent possible in the publishing of its books. Such materials include vegetable-based, low-VOC inks and acid-free papers that are recycled, totally chlorine-free, or partly composed of non-wood fibers. For further information, visit our website at www.cornellpress.cornell.edu.

Cloth printing 10 9 8 7 6 5 4 3 2 1
Paperback printing 10 9 8 7 6 5 4 3 2 1

To
my parents, the Shankar Saxenas,
and my parents-in-law, the Khandelwals,
for their integrity, courage, and caring

Contents

Preface

In 1986 I came to New York City to conduct doctoral research on Indian immigrants. Quite new to both the United States and the city, I navigated through various neighborhoods, boroughs, subway routes, and libraries to piece together a research methodology for studying this largest concentration of Indians in the country. I noticed scores of activities occurring every month. I also observed rapid demographic change. I was eager to record the growth and change in this population over time, and to analyze issues simmering among its multiple subgroups.

Having taught American history at an Indian university, I knew this new country's general contours, but now had an opportunity to observe Americans on a daily basis. I had moved from India—whose longstanding diversity of cultures, religions, social groups, and philosophies is proverbial—to the multiethnic and multicultural United States, whose relatively short history has been shaped by waves of immigrants. I now became increasingly conscious of Indian versus American ways of approaching "difference." I observed Indian immigrants trying to re-create Indian settings in New York, but in the American ethnic context, and thus fashioning an "ethnic" Indian American life. I was also convinced that immigration studies should focus on the voices and perspectives of immigrants themselves. With this objective in mind, I conducted oral history interviews over the next decade with about one hundred and fifty Indian immigrants in New York City. These data, together with my ongoing participant observation of their activities, form the basis of this research.

In 1987 I serendipitously visited the Asian/American Center at Queens College, City University of New York, and met its director, Roger Sanjek, an anthropologist, and a team of scholars from diverse cultural backgrounds and disciplines studying grassroots politics, intergroup relations, and demographic change in Queens. Joining this "New Immigrants and Old Americans" project soon thereafter profoundly shaped my own research. I added a comparative perspective, looked more closely at multicultural settings, and shared findings with researchers studying Taiwanese, Korean, and Latin American immigrants, as well as established African American and white populations. My training as a historian benefited greatly from exchange with these anthropologists and sociologists. As a team, we visited local schools, businesses, houses of worship, and cultural events.

These academic and personal experiences also provided the foundation for my commitment to pan–Asian American studies in the following years. I continued as a research historian at the Asian/American Center until 1997 and, following completion of my doctoral thesis in 1991, extended my ethnographic research in Queens and shared my findings with community-based and progressive organizations, municipal and social-service agencies, and journalists. My teaching at Queens College and other colleges and universities also brought me into contact with scores of South Asian students and organizations, experiences that further enriched my work. This book reflects a decade of community-oriented research.

Queens contains the largest concentration of immigrants from India in the United States, but also substantial immigrant populations from China, Taiwan, South Korea, the Dominican Republic, Colombia, Ecuador, Russia, Pakistan, Bangladesh, and other countries. In that borough I focused on four multiethnic, multiracial areas: Flushing, the first neighborhood to which Indians moved; Jackson Heights, with its prominent South Asian business concentration; Richmond Hill, a setting for intergroup relations between Indian immigrants from India and Guyana; and eastern Queens, a site of emerging South Asian participation in local politics. As both a researcher and a Queens resident from 1987 to 1997, my social visits and participation in religious and cultural events yielded additional insights about the immigrant community I was studying. My shopping trips to Indian businesses produced enlightening conversations with storeowners and workers. I used my frequent taxi rides to and from airports to converse with South Asian cabdrivers. I learned about the complexity and human face of immigration from middle-class homemakers who generously allowed me to attend religious activities in their homes, and from working-class women who invited me to join their part-time work assembling belts, a "better job" in their view than that of a professor.

Most of my conversations were in English, Hindi, Urdu, and Punjabi or some combination thereof. In translating some of them into English for this book, I tried to preserve their South Asian flavor. The statements originally in English are presented almost verbatim, and the distinctive South Asian conversational English is still discernible. Some names of people interviewed have been replaced by assigned names to protect their anonymity. I remain deeply grateful to all the respondents and informants for being so open with their views. However, this book is not a comprehensive account of all Indian experiences in New York City; it illustrates the main patterns and trajectories with selected examples from diverse Indian lives. My observations reflect the conditions existing at the time of recording them; the use of past tense in the text has no bearing on whether those facts continue to be true or not.

Early in my work I met Parmatma Saran and Maxine Fisher, who in the 1980s had published studies that captured well the formative cohort of post-1965 professional immigrants, the beginnings of associations and religious institutions, and the conditions for immigrants up to the mid-1970s. In my oral history interviews I retraced this earlier period through 1987, and I covered the next dozen years through interviews and participant observation, and by following the ethnic and mainstream media. Early on Professor Anand Mohan at Queens College offered useful advice. Johanna Lessinger, who was also researching New York's Indian community, and I shared ideas, and I benefited from her work on newsstand workers and transnational activities. By the mid-1990s I was part of an "invisible college" of South Asian academics and activists in New York and elsewhere, including the historian Sucheta Mazumdar, the sociologist Margaret Abraham, the poet Meena Alexander, and the journalist Somini Sengupta. Their work is amply represented in this volume's references. I also thank Anuradha Advani, Sarita Ahuja, Morshed Alam, Geeta Bhatt, Sayu Bhojwani, Nilanjana Chatterjee, Sachi Dastidar, Shefali Dastidar, Akhtar Khan, Sarita Khurana, Rekha Malhotra, Basdeo Mangru, Arthur Pais, Tito Sinha, and others in my "intimate circle of South Asian New Yorkers," for generously sharing their friendships and views with me.

Meanwhile, the cordial relationships established at the Asian/American Center continued. From time to time Roger and Lani Sanjek would reconvene our original team to celebrate a visit to New York, a wedding, or completion of a book; for their friendship over the years, I also thank Hsiangshui Chen, Kyeyoung Park, Ruby Danta, Milagros Ricourt, Steven Gregory, Elena Acosta, Priti Prakash, Lamgen Leon, Lori Kitazono, and Wu Hong. In my later years at the center I worked with Jack Tchen, Joe Doyle, Margo Machida, and Joanne Balek, and an extended Queens College circle of various departments and centers. I also cherish the friendship and insights of far-flung Asian American studies colleagues Marilyn Alquizola, Yen Espiritu, Lane Hirabayashi, Evelyn Hu-DeHart, Peter Kiang, Robert Lee, Yvonne Lau, Gail Nomura, Gary Okihiro, and Steve Sumida. In New York,

Margaret Fung and Stan Mark at the Asian American Legal Defense and Education Fund, Cao O at the Asian American Federation, Steve Zeitlin at Citylore, Amanda Dargan at the Queens Council on the Arts, and Kamala Motihar at Asian Indian Women in America were also sources of inspiration.

Among those whose faith and support sustained the writing of this book, my foremost thanks go to Roger Sanjek for his vision, commitment, and untiring work. Writing the main draft was made possible by my "Boulder community" of Evelyn Hu-DeHart, Lane Hirabayashi, Steve Medina, Karen Moreira, and Ana Scheffield of the Department of Ethnic studies at the University of Colorado at Boulder, who provided a nurturing academic environment; and fellow devotees at the Siddha Yoga Meditation Center of Boulder, a source of affection and spiritual support. The book was completed at the University of Massachusetts at Boston, where colleagues in the Asian American Studies program and the College of Public and Community Service were supportive and inspiring. I am indebted to Peter Kiang for his commitment and generosity. My thanks go to Dean Ismael Ramirez-Soto for his vision and insights, and to Zong Guo Xia for helping with the maps in the book. In Boston, as in Boulder, I enjoyed the support of many spiritual seekers at the Siddha Yoga Meditation Center. Deep appreciation goes to my husband, Sanjiv Khandelwal, for his friendship. And, for continuous guidance and boundless grace, I offer my gratitude to my Guru, Swamis Muktananda and Chidvilasananda.

Becoming American, Being Indian

Introduction

In Bombay, our neighbors were Gujaratis, Punjabis, and South
Indians. Here, they are Chinese, Koreans, and Hispanics. We continued our family traditions amidst diversity there, and we will do
the same here. I do not see much change in our life in the United
States. Maintaining our traditions was the most important goal for
us there [in India], and it continues to be the most important here.
Here we just have to try harder.

Indian resident of Queens

Indians in the United States, like other immigrants, are often assumed to
be a single ethnic group and to behave in a standardized "ethnic" fashion.[1]
Yet the words above offer a window into the mindset of an immigrant population that, even before arriving in multicultural urban America, lived in a
culturally diverse homeland. This book documents the changing circumstances of Indian immigrants in New York City from the 1960s through the
1990s and highlights internal and external forces in the formation of an
American ethnic group. The following pages examine closely the interplay
between ethnic consciousness and such factors as class, gender, generation,
American politics, and Indian cultural traditions.

The well-educated Indian immigrants arriving in the 1960s and early
1970s were imbued with an Indian national identity and sophisticated pan-
Indian culture that translated readily into a unitary ethnic consciousness.
Coming from the middle and upper classes of urban India, their exposure
to Western ways of life was already substantial. Many held professional occupations and made a rapid and successful entry into American society. In
New York in those decades their numbers and socioeconomic diversity
were too limited to sustain a separate and more internally diverse existence.
Since the mid-1970s, however, the demographic profile of New York City's
Indian population has altered dramatically. The rapid growth in numbers—
from a few thousand in 1970 to over 170,000 by 2000—has been matched
by greater socioeconomic diversity.[2] As more Indian immigrants arrived

every year, they occupied a wider spectrum in the city's economy. And with growing numbers, they re-created their varied homeland traditions of family, religion, and regional culture, increasing both activities and organizational resources for Indian life in the New York area. Those processes of change are seen most readily in Queens, the major site of Indian residential concentration.

While living dispersed among non-Indians in Queens and elsewhere in the New York metropolitan area, Indian immigrants have created spatial microcosms of urban Indian commerce and cultural activity amidst American settings. From these "Indian" spaces in a Western country, they have established intricate networks not only with their home country but also with overseas Indian communities. The local and the global, the national and the transnational, the American and the Indian—all are intermeshed for Indian immigrants in New York. Moreover, the process of becoming an American ethnic group has operated at the same time that being Indian, with heightened consciousness of Indian identities and the re-creation of diverse Indian traditions, has become both more possible and strikingly more evident.

Diversity

India's cultural diversity is proverbial. The country contains practitioners of all the major world religions, an amazing array of regional languages and cultures, and subcultural identities based on dialect, religious sect, and caste (see map 1). Paradoxically, pursuing one's own particular culture has been so integral to Indian life that many regard this as a common signifier of "Indianness" (Ramanujan 1990). The recognition of cultural diversity has also been an important ideological aspect of nation-building in independent India, as in the Nehruvian elaboration of "Unity in Diversity," an early nationalist slogan.

The first wave of post-1965 Indian immigrants brought this high valuing of diversity to the United States. Coming mainly from urban areas all over their homeland, they themselves embodied a wide range of India's diversity. Even in the mid-1970s, when their numbers were still relatively limited, they demonstrated a commitment to maintaining their diverse identities. As Maxine Fisher noted of that time, "New York Indians [are] an ethnic group composed of ethnic groups; and the latter [are] in turn, in many cases, still in some sense ethnically heterogeneous. . . . This situation, though dizzying to contemplate, and the bane of government agencies concerned with ethnic groups, derives quite naturally from the possibility of multiple identities" (1980:4).

[2]

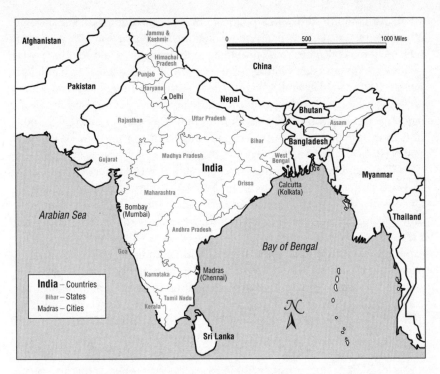

Map 1. Map of India

The expression of regional and religious diversity would strengthen over the next two decades. As continuing immigration brought more Indian immigrants to the city, the growing numbers supported activities pertaining to even narrower identities of *jati* (endogamous marital group, or "caste") and religious sect. Indian diversity was thus accompanied by established concepts of "difference" that were at variance with American understanding of nationality and other forms of diversity. For example, though accustomed to living amidst culturally, religiously, and linguistically diverse populations, Indians were unfamiliar with North American notions of race and ethnicity. Uncertainty about these American ideas and how they applied to themselves impeded their participation in the existing political system of the United States.

The racial classification of Indians in the United States has varied historically. In the early twentieth century, some Indians claimed a "Caucasian" origin to qualify for citizenship; unsuccessful, they were deemed nonwhite by the Supreme Court (Mazumdar 1989). As a result of Indian lobbying, in 1980 the U.S. Census assigned them a separate group identity as "Asian Indian" within the "racial" category "Asian and Pacific Islanders" (Fisher

[3]

1980). Still, and despite some political efforts to include Asian Indians and other South Asians in a pan-Asian category, their place in the American racial schema continues to be problematic to themselves and to others, who generally equate "Asian" with East Asians, or the "yellow race" (Khandelwal 1996b, 1998; Shankar and Srikanth 1998). Although India has its own hier-archical social structure, the determination of minority status by caste or re-ligion in contemporary India has a different history and intellectual founda-tion from the pseudobiological racial categorizations used in the United States (Robb 1995; Sanjek 1994a).

Indian immigrants nevertheless encountered racial categorization daily in work and residential settings in New York City. As most Indians in Queens lived in mixed neighborhoods, they interacted with people of different racial and ethnic backgrounds, including other immigrants from Asia, Latin America, and the Caribbean, as well as whites and blacks. (This experience distinguished them from suburban Indians and from those in many other parts of the United States, whose neighbors were primarily white.) Still, many Indian immigrants continue to be uncertain about their "race." Indians come in all skin colors, from fairest to darkest, and have different facial features. Indian college students, in particular, struggle with the idea of an exclusive racial identity. When asked, some respond that they are white because of their Aryan origins; others, understanding race in terms of skin color, consider themselves brown; others now accept an "Asian American" racial identity; others assert they are "Indian" or "South Asian"; still others, to the vexation of some established Americans, reject the significance of race altogether. Thus, according to varying political and economic interests, Indian immigrants may see themselves as white (al-though fewer and fewer do so); identify with other racial minorities; per-ceive themselves as a self-contained minority group, neither white, black, or "Asian"; or maintain that they are "color blind." This variation highlights the role of both external social and political forces and human agency in shap-ing the racialization process (Omi and Winant 1986; Kibria 1996).

Although not all Indians may identify, or identify fully, with a single racial category, they are too large a population to be ignored in New York City's multicultural politics. Accordingly, politicians have urged them to partici-pate as a group in local and national American politics; as one part of the of-ficial "Asian and Pacific Islander" census category, their community leaders have been invited to join other Asian groups in public activities such as an Asian American Awareness Month, and to serve on Asian American advi-sory councils of elected officials.[3]

Nor has ethnicity in its American form been immediately intelligible to Indian immigrants. As Chandra Jayawardena (1980, 430) concluded, the publicly expressed consciousness described as ethnicity can be understood only "in terms of particular political, class, and social conflicts." Ethnic, like racial, formation should be considered a process that commences with a population's arrival in the United States, and their interaction with a model of ethnicity is determined by their new society. The current American model of multiculturalism and a multiethnic society is based on the premise that all ethnic groups are equal in the eyes of the state. This model assumes that each ethnic group is organized as a unit, with only one culture per group. By accepting this political ideology of an internally homogeneous ethnicity, some established Indian leaders became participants in the celebration of American multicultural democracy, but a growing number within their own "ethnic" population, like those in other minority communities, suffered invisible and unacknowledged economic need. As a result of their status as "successful" immigrants, these Indian ethnic leaders distanced themselves from their less privileged compatriots and rejoiced in their "model minority" image. In their desire to participate in the current American model of multiculturalism, they became the accepted ethnic representatives of the Indian community.

However, to fit fully within American multicultural politics these Indian leaders had to define a unitary Indian ethnic culture. Given the wide range of Indian subcultural variety, this was not a simple task. Regional cultures in India, indeed, competed with an overarching national culture, which was often equated with the numerically predominant Hinduism. In the intricate dynamics of ethnic cultural politics in America, some aspects of Indian culture were highlighted symbolically and others dropped. Like Indian migrants in other countries (see Vertovec 1995; Baumann 1996), community leaders made efforts to present a reified (and simplified) version of Indian culture that accorded with American notions of ethnic identity.

In his landmark *Ethnic Groups and Boundaries,* Frederick Barth insisted that it is "the ethnic boundary that defines the group, not the cultural stuff that it encloses" (1969, 204). With regard to Indian immigrants, however, the multiple varieties of "cultural stuff" within their national boundary have only compounded confusion over the meaning of ethnicity (Steinberg 1981; van der Veer 1995). Moreover, although the principal subjects of this book are Indian nationals, a number of them came from countries to which Indians had previously emigrated, including Guyana, Trinidad, Mauritius, Kenya, Uganda, South Africa, Britain, Canada, Fiji, and Hong Kong. This Indian diaspora challenges even more a simplified notion of ethnicity that equates nation and culture. One stream of this diaspora—the descendants of nineteenth-century migrants to Guyana and Trinidad—met up in Queens with the direct flow of immigrants from India, compounding the issues of who bore "Indian" identity, and what Indian ethnic culture might be.

In their attempt to define Indian ethnic identity, some Indian immigrant

[5]

leaders made Indian nationality or birth a criterion for Indian ethnicity in the United States. The doomed nature of this nation-bound approach to ethnicity was apparent by the 1990s in New York City, where growing numbers of diaspora Indians now resided. In addition, immigrants from other South Asian countries such as Pakistan and Bangladesh, and emerging young progressives who chose to call themselves South Asians and organized on this basis, now shared the ethnic arena with the established "Indian" immigrant leaders. The wider diasporic South Asian population shared many cultural traditions and practices with "direct" Indian immigrants. Moreover, for the younger, U.S.-reared generation, identification with the Indian nation or with birth there was not the primary basis of their "Indian" or "South Asian" ethnic identity in the United States. Many young progressives preferred deliberately to transcend the boundaries of nation, religion, and region in order to arrive at a broader, composite South Asian solidarity.

Stratification

Although Indians in the United States are perceived as a successful immigrant group, epitomized by highly educated professionals, a longitudinal view over the decades since the 1960s reveals a continual widening of social-class differences within the group. This trend has been most pronounced in New York City.

Indian immigrants of the 1960s and 1970s, products of a "brain drain" emigration, were a highly educated cohort who took advantage of an expansive American economy and built well-paying professional careers (Visweswaran 1997). But thereafter the spectrum began to widen as the pioneer immigrants sponsored relatives from India who lacked elite educational backgrounds. In addition, as American economic conditions changed, opportunities for newly arriving immigrants, including professionals, became less rewarding, and by the 1990s the Indian population was a multilayered community, with affluent professionals and businesspersons at the top and an increasing number of middle-and working-class immigrants in lower strata.

Growing economic diversity led to the formation of well-recognized social-class distinctions in the Indian community. Most post-1965 immigrants to the United States fitted broadly into a white-collar, middle-class continuum. But a growing number of those arriving in the 1980s and 1990s did not fare as well, and a sizable number among them were even clearly downwardly mobile. Over time, the class profile of the Indian community has come to resemble more closely that of other Third World immigrant groups in New York City.

[6]

Indians believed in the American immigrant saga that all people in the United States, if only they worked hard, could become wealthy. It is testimony to the power of this myth that individual successes were ascribed to boundless opportunities in America, and failures were ascribed to individual irresponsibility or were merely ignored as exceptions. Aspirations for upward mobility were so strong that Indian immigrants in lower-scale occupations refused to believe that they belonged to the working class. Correspondingly, the favored rank of Indian immigrants who had entered American middle and upper echelons found it hard to admit that Indians actually might exist in dire poverty in the United States.

By the 1990s this multilayered community was distributed across the New York metropolitan area—from the urban receiving areas of initial settlement and (for some) continuing residence in west and central Queens (including Flushing, Jackson Heights, Richmond Hill) to the single-family homes in the eastern half of the borough, from the suburban counties on Long Island and in Westchester and New Jersey to a professional and college-student elite in Manhattan (see map 2). Class differentiation was more and more evident in the extent and quality of educational attainments, both at the primary and secondary levels and at universities, and in the variety of occupations Indians held. The established leadership of wealthy professionals and businesspersons who used their resources to represent their ethnic group in American multicultural politics consisted with few exceptions of immigrant males (described by the young South Asian left as "bourgeois"); they subscribed to the traditional Indian hierarchy and were rooted in the politics and conditions of their home country. Their favored issues reflected their class interests, although they presented those issues on behalf of the entire ethnic community. They directed much effort to preserving Indian cultural heritage as they defined it in the United States, and to organizing Indian professionals against occupational discrimination. Issues affecting working-class Indians, disempowered women, or U.S.-reared youth were not on their agenda.

This class-based, home-country-inspired elite leadership built none of the intergroup coalitions necessary for effective participation in the multiethnic politics of New York City and the United States. Indeed, these Indian leaders felt alienated from racialized minorities who seemed comparatively disadvantaged. Within the Indian American population, however, they faced increasing challenges from a new, alternative leadership of women, younger-generation Indians, and emergent progressives. Although this new leadership was diverse in itself, it was united in rejection of the established immigrant generation's politics. In the 1990s, with calls for ethnic and racial justice, equality across gender and sexuality-based lines, and transcendence of religious and South Asian nationality

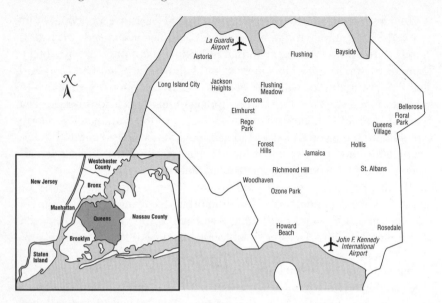

Map 2. Neighborhoods in Queens, New York City

differences, a new, progressive politics was creating a stir among Indians in New York City.

New York City and Queens

Indian immigrants all over the United States consider New York City's Indians different from themselves: "Living in New York is like living in India," they say. Indians living in London, Toronto, and Hong Kong, however, see parallels between their overseas communities and the one in New York. People arriving from India find the cosmopolitanism of New York reminiscent of that of Indian cities. To a significant degree, this book is not only about Indian immigrants but also about the particular urban context of New York City as it shapes this immigrant population.

The focus on New York City has three main facets. First is the cosmopolitan nature of the city, which historically has accommodated diverse cultures, although the range of its diversity has never been greater than today. As one Indian immigrant respondent put it, New York reminds him of his own position between national and international spaces, hanging in the middle and yet connected to both. A second facet is New York City's economy, which offers multiple opportunities for upward mobility as well as multiple survival strategies (Sanjek 1998). Indians are aware of New York

[8]

City's place in immigrant imagery as a gateway to the American dream (see Park 1997 on Korean immigrants), and they directly experience the impact of New York's changing economy on their own widening socioeconomic spectrum.

The third facet is New York's geography—its division into multiple boroughs and, for Indians, the centrality of Queens (see map 2). Since the late 1960s new Indian immigrants have arrived first in Queens neighborhoods and have by and large continued to live there. Indian immigrants share Queens neighborhoods with immigrants from many nations in Asia, the Caribbean, and Latin America, and over four decades these neighborhoods have become intensely multiethnic and multicultural. Although certain places may be called "Little India" because of clusters of businesses, the ethnic boundaries of these spaces are crossed daily by members of non-Indian groups. Moreover, Indians are in fact spread widely all over Queens, among scores of named neighborhoods and some two million residents. These multiethnic and multineighborhood realities are in fact impediments to Indians' viewing any one neighborhood as theirs.

By the 1990s Queens contained dozens of houses of worship where Indian immigrants practiced different faiths, and multiple sites where they organized a wide array of cultural activities, all widely dispersed. Indians in Queens were engaged in many different occupations; they ranged from professionals and successful business owners to working-class and entry-level employees. And in contrast to the economically well-integrated Indians whose social activities have continued in Manhattan, many Queens Indians had serious social and economic needs.

Indians in the United States

Although past and current Indian migration to the United States has been motivated primarily by the search for economic opportunity and a better life, the earliest Indians to set foot in what is now the United States were merchants and sailors who traveled on East India Company ships to colonial America. Among the several visits of the nineteenth century, perhaps the best remembered is that of a young Indian monk, Swami Vivekananda, who attended the Parliament of World Religions in Chicago in 1893 and surprised his American audience by giving a speech in English (Barrows 1893; Richardson 1988, 85–94). As a result of his visit, a network of Vedanta Societies were established all over the United States.

The first Indian community in the United States was established in the early twentieth century, when thousands of Sikhs from Punjab arrived on the West Coast. They were part of a large global Indian labor migration extending through the nineteenth century, and their arrival in America coincided with that of other Asian groups. Primarily males, they worked in mining and railroad-building, eventually settling as farmers in California and British Columbia. The Punjabis formed exclusive communities where they maintained their religious and cultural traditions, though many men did marry Mexican women.[4]

In addition to these California Sikhs, small numbers of Indian merchants, professionals, and students were scattered across the country before the 1960s. Although they created associations such as the Indian League of America, overall they integrated remarkably well into the mainstream as their education, knowledge of English, and high incomes brought regular contact with white Americans. These Indians often developed friendships with Americans interested in Indian history and culture, and many married white American women (Gordon 1989; Mazumdar 1989). Several of these Indians wrote about the Indian independence struggle, relations between India and the United States, and their own lives. Dr. Haridas T. Mazumdar, who migrated to the United States in 1920 and worked as an engineer for U.S. Steel in Pennsylvania, later compiled a booklet in which, as "One of Uncle Sam's Many Children," he praised the United States and its democracy (1986, dedication).

Indian immigration to the United States largely ceased when the 1924 Immigration Act effectively barred new arrivals from Asia. A year earlier, in *United States v. Thind,* the Supreme Court had ruled Indians ineligible for naturalization as U.S. citizens, on the ground that they did not fall under the common meaning of "white." In 1946, following World War II, India was granted an annual immigration quota of 100, but more important, after 1952 Indians could become U.S. citizens. Indian immigrant Dalip Singh Saund did so and was subsequently elected to the California legislature for three terms. The trickle of Indian immigration increased to a few thousand skilled persons in the 1950s.

The 1965 Immigration Act was the next turning point for Indian immigration. With the removal of national-origin quotas, each country in the Eastern Hemisphere could send up to 20,000 persons annually. Soon the bulk of American immigration was arriving from Asia, Latin America, and the Caribbean rather than Europe. Their particular postcolonial knowledge of English and high educational levels distinguished Indian immigrants and enabled a secure professional trajectory in the 1960s and 1970s. Given the urban background of this wave of immigrants, it is not surprising that few knew about or identified with the earlier Sikh immigrants in rural California. It was with the next generation, the children of the post-1965 immigrants, that this history was retrieved and revered.[5] Table 1 summarizes the crucial Immigration Act of 1965 and subsequent legislation,

Table 1. Immigration Laws, 1965–1990

The Immigration and Nationality Act of 1965 established a preference system emphasizing family reunification and occupational skills:
    First preference: unmarried sons and daughters of U.S. citizens
    Second preference: spouse and unmarried sons and daughters of aliens admitted for
      legal residence
    Third preference: professionals, scientists, and artists of exceptional abilities
    Fourth preference: married sons and daughters of U.S. citizens
    Fifth preference: brothers and sisters of U.S. citizens
    Sixth preference: skilled and unskilled workers for which U.S. labor is in short supply
    Seventh preference: refugees

The 1986 Immigration Reform and Control Act legalized the undocumented immigrants who had resided continuously in the United States since January 1, 1982, and those employed as seasonal agricultural workers for at least ninety days during the year ending May 1, 1986.

The 1990 Immigration Act maintained family reunification provisions but increased employment visas for highly skilled workers. This act also provided legalization for dependents of undocumented immigrants who had received an amnesty under the 1986 act.

---

which have influenced Indian immigration to the United States in important ways.

Plan of the Book

The following chapters explore developments and important themes in the lives of Indian immigrants in New York City from 1965 through 2000. Chapter 1 presents the spatial landscape of South Asian New York and traces movements and concentrations of Indians in the city with a particular focus on the borough of Queens. Chapter 2 covers various cultural activities of Indian immigrants and highlights the formation of an ethnic culture in the American multicultural context. Chapter 3 surveys the range of religions practiced by Indian immigrants in New York with special emphasis on responses to immigrant conditions. Chapter 4 discusses how, from the 1960s to the 1990s, Indian immigrants changed from a professional middle-class population to one with diverse occupations and intensifying social stratification. Chapter 5 outlines changes in immigrant family structure and analyzes the role of gender in community issues. Chapter 6 focuses on the emergence of two different generations, elders and youth, among Indian New Yorkers and highlights their distinctive issues and perspectives. Chapter 7 traces patterns of South Asian community organization that led to a contestation for ethnic leadership in the 1990s.

[1]

The Landscape of South Asian New York

From the 1960s through the 1990s a continuous stream of immigrants replenished the Indian population of New York City, and, as new arrivals increasingly chose Queens over other boroughs, the city's residential concentration of Indians shifted from Manhattan to Queens. These developments produced both the concentrations and dispersal of the Queens Indian community described in this chapter. By the 1990s, besides having the largest urban concentration of Indians in the United States, Queens also housed the widest range of Indian immigrant cultural activities and economic diversity.

This chapter outlines three successive trajectories of Indian immigrants in New York City. The first was the initial and continuing dispersal outward from Manhattan into New York's boroughs and suburbs, and increasingly into Queens (see table 2). The second was the arrival of new immigrants directly in Queens neighborhoods that became receiving areas for Indians, four of which are profiled here: Flushing, Jackson Heights, Richmond Hill, and eastern Queens. As new immigrants continued to arrive in these core areas, the more established ones left them for better housing in suburban areas. In the third trajectory, reflecting the interplay between ethnicity and class, suburban Indians frequently traveled back to these Queens core areas for various ethnic resources—the Indian businesses, houses of worship, and cultural centers located here in diverse areas that were also occupied by other new immigrants and established Americans (see Sanjek 1998). These three trajectories produced the landscape of Indian life in late-twentieth-century New York.

Table 2. Asian Indians in New York City
Boroughs, 1990 and 2000

	1990	2000
Bronx	11,051	15,258
Brooklyn	15,641	25,404
Manhattan	7,395	14,630
Queens	56,601	109,114
Staten Island	3,902	6,493
TOTAL	94,590	170,899

Sources: Demographic Profiles, New York City Department of City Planning, 1992; U.S. Census 2000.

Indians in Manhattan and Beyond

In the 1960s a few thousand Indians at most lived in New York City. They
consisted of students, small numbers of professionals and businesspersons,
and Indian nationals posted at such official institutions as the Indian consulate, India's official airline, Air India, and the Indian delegation at the
United Nations. The durations of stay in the United States varied among
these Indians. Those on government postings and some students returned
to India, while others settled permanently in this country. Professionals and
businesspersons stayed the longest, practicing remarkably Western
lifestyles in their newly formed families.

This Indian population consisted primarily of males, some of whom
began families by bringing their spouses to the United States. They were
concentrated in Manhattan, although students lived mainly around university campuses, and professionals were spread out in other parts of the borough. *India Abroad*, a newspaper established in 1970, at first carried advertisements for businesses and accommodations primarily in Manhattan; the
few Indians who lived in other boroughs and in suburbs traveled to Manhattan for ethnic resources or activities.

The small number of Indian restaurants and the stores where Indian groceries were available were also located in Manhattan. The restaurants included Natraj, at 112 West 42nd Street; Shalimar, at 39 East 29th Street;
New Pakistan-India Inn, on 8th Avenue and 110th Street; and Tandoor, on
Lexington Avenue and 92nd Street (*India Abroad* 10/2/70). Indians who
lived in New York in the 1960s recall purchasing Indian food and clothing at
Kalustyan's, on 29th Street and Lexington Avenue. Owned by an Armenian,
this store was the best-known business serving New York's Indian population in those years. One woman who arrived in 1967 also mentioned shopping for Indian textiles at Modlin Fabrics, at 240 West Street; a man who

[13]

had lived in New York City since 1968 remembered going to Canal Street, in Lower Manhattan, to buy electronics from Indian merchants.

Films were a popular form of entertainment for Indians in New York as early as the 1960s. Besides special showings at Columbia University, a theater on 57th Street and Seventh Avenue held regular screenings of Indian movies. A large number of Indians—quite noticeable to passersby—gathered every weekend at this theater to see films supplied by distributors in India. In the late 1960s several Indians started to import films for the New York City audience, and *India Abroad* featured advertisements for these movies at various venues. This trend continued until the invasion of videocassettes for home rental overtook it in the 1980s. Indian movies shown on large screens resurfaced in the 1990s, but by then these were shown in theaters in Queens and Long Island, the sites of the new concentrations of Indians in New York.

Indian cultural performances were also organized in Manhattan in the 1960s when renowned artists, particularly classical musicians and dancers, visited the United States. Cherishing these special and rare events, Indians were joined by Americans interested in Indian culture and arts. The visiting artists often developed close relations with both Indian immigrants and Americans and established lasting friendships. One woman, then a student leader in New York, remembered hosting leading Indian artists, working enthusiastically with her friends and receiving assistance from the Indian consulate. She stated that the visiting artists boosted the immigrants' pride in India's cultural heritage.

Indian student clubs at New York universities were also important in organizing Indian cultural activities. Students presented films, seminars, and lectures and sponsored music and dance concerts. The Indian Students Association of Columbia University was particularly well known for organizing these events. The social contacts established among these Indians and with American friends provided a foundation for long-lasting relationships. The student-based networks also provided job and housing information and helped promote the interracial friendships of Indian students who remained in the United States. In contrast, nonstudent immigrants from India had to make fresh starts on their own.[1]

Prakash, who lived in a student dormitory for four years, and for another year in an apartment in Manhattan, completed his doctoral program in the 1960s and took a professorial appointment in a New York college. He soon married an Indian and moved to a single-family house on Long Island (which comprises Nassau and Suffolk Counties). Suresh moved from a Manhattan apartment to a private home in Westchester County within a few years of starting his legal practice in the early 1970s. New waves of students and other transient Indians replaced them in Manhattan, and their lives continued to be well integrated with mainstream American careers or institutions of higher education.

Meanwhile a new ethnic community began to form in Queens, made up primarily of immigrants arriving directly from India and who established their households in that borough. Naresh came to New York City in 1966. He obtained an executive job in a Manhattan firm but quickly decided to reside in Flushing, Queens. At that time he knew of no other Indians living in this neighborhood.

> All Indians then lived in Manhattan. However, accommodation in Manhattan was becoming expensive. . . . When my employer told me that some cheaper apartments were available in Queens, I took a ride to Flushing and liked the area. I was satisfied with Flushing because the Number 7 subway line provided an easy commute to Manhattan where I worked, and the apartment rents were quite cheap. We paid $140 for an apartment of a size adequate for me, my wife, and our two young children. At that time, every third plot in Flushing was vacant and there were fewer apartment buildings. . . . Then more and more Indians began to arrive.

Naresh had arrived in New York with no prior contacts. Early Queens residents like him, however, became trailblazers for Indians coming later, who chose to live in Queens neighborhoods such as Flushing, Elmhurst, and Corona. Often the newer immigrants stayed initially as guests of Indians already living in Queens. Later they moved into their own households, which often were located in the same neighborhood.

In 1969 Malti, an Indian woman, arrived in New York City with her husband.

> When we decided to leave India for New York, we knew only one Indian who lived in Queens with his family. He was my husband's brother's acquaintance. We had never met him, but at that time he was our only hope. My husband's brother introduced us to him, and, after exchanging a couple of letters, it was decided that we would initially stay with him in New York. He came to receive us at the airport and hosted us at his apartment for a few months. He helped us start our immigrant lives in New York. In a few months, when my husband felt comfortable in his new job, we got our own apartment in a nearby building. This building had many other Indian tenants.

Until the late 1960s no businesses in Queens sold Indian food or clothing, and Indian residents of Queens did their shopping for home-country food in Manhattan despite the inconvenience of carrying large bags of groceries by public transportation. In response to the rapidly growing Indian population, a few businesses began to appear in Queens. In 1970 G. L. Soni, an engineer living with his family in Elmhurst, started an Indian grocery store, which he called House of Spices, on Broadway in Elmhurst.

> I had come to the United States as a graduate student in engineering and had never run a business before. One day I saw a store available for renting in our neighborhood. So I consulted my brother and we decided to open this business. We saw that the Indian population was growing in Queens, but the decision was not a calculated business move. It was a spontaneous decision. We knew of many Indian families who lived in Queens but had to travel far for their groceries to Manhattan. The business arose out of necessity rather than a projection of Indian population.

House of Spices grew from a single store into a nationwide chain of retail and wholesale Indian groceries under the brand name Laxmi Products.

Indians such as Naresh and Soni were part of the transformation of Queens through immigration. Before the late 1970s, predominantly white neighborhoods such as Flushing and Elmhurst were perceived almost as small towns in "the outer boroughs." As immigrants from Asia, Latin America, and the Caribbean moved into these areas, this image changed. The immigrants also revitalized dormant or declining neighborhood economies. Indeed, the impact of the continuing post-1965 immigration is readily evident in many parts of Queens (Chen 1992; Sanjek 1998).

Since the 1960s Indians have distributed themselves widely throughout Queens (see table 3). Demographically they were more widely dispersed than Chinese or Koreans, the other preponderant Asian immigrant groups in the borough, who were more concentrated in areas such as Flushing, Bayside, and Elmhurst (New York City Department of City Planning 1992). Newly arriving Indian immigrants settled in the earliest receiving areas such as Flushing and Elmhurst, but they also moved elsewhere. In 1980 large numbers of Indians resided in Flushing and Elmhurst, but their growing presence was also being felt in neighborhoods such as Astoria, Jackson Heights, Forest Hills, and Fresh Meadows. By 1990, eleven out of the fourteen Census Bureau Community Districts in Queens had over 2,500 Indians, and five recorded numbers over 5,000. This dispersal continued into the 1990s, and in 2000, eleven of the community districts showed over 5,000 Indian residents each. Through these decades, Flushing and Elmhurst continued to house significant numbers of Indians, but between 1990 and 2000, new growth was palpable in areas such as Richmond Hill and eastern Queens. Jackson Heights, containing the "Little India" shopping area on 74th Street, was not a leading residential district, and its Indian residents were primarily a northward extension of the Elmhurst-Corona concentration.

[16]

Table 3. Indians in Queens Community Districts, 1980–2000

Community District	1980	1990	2000
1 Astoria, Long Island City	2,355	3,860	7,798
2 Sunnyside, Woodside	1,288	2,770	5,553
3 Jackson Heights, North Carona	1,649	3,941	7,382
4 Elmhurst, South Carona	4,404	7,653	9,577
5 Ridgewood, Glendale, Maspeth	326	820	1,291
6 Forest Hills, Rego Park	2,095	3,898	5,948
7 Flushing, Bay Terrace	4,592	7,200	11,100
8 Fresh Meadows, Briarwood	1,814	5,091	9,958
9 Woodhaven, Richmond Hill	926	3,837	13,919
10 Ozone Park, Howard Beach	752	4,630	12,491
11 Bayside, Douglaston, Little Neck	731	1,221	2,221
12 Jamaica, St. Albans, Hollis	1,562	5,291	7,135
13 Queens Village, Rosedale	1,139	5,786	13,884
14 The Rockaways, Broad Channel	424	628	775

Source: New York City Department of City Planning, 1996, and New York City Department of City Planning's website www.nyc.gov/html/dcp/html/popstart.html.

Core Areas and Suburbs

Flushing and Elmhurst became receiving areas because they had ample accommodations in apartment buildings, and accessible linkage by subway to Manhattan (Peterson 1987). Indian immigrants preferred apartment housing in "one-fare" zones like these neighborhoods, where they could walk to a subway station, rather than in a "two-fare" zone, where they had to take a bus to reach the subway. In addition, the location in the borough containing New York's two major airports, John F. Kennedy and La Guardia, made air travel convenient. Indians not only used these airports for their own travel but also often received and sent off visitors there from their home country. Indian traditions continued of hosting visitors in one's own home, escorting them on local sightseeing and shopping, and accompanying guests to and from airports. A constant flow of visitors from India became a regular feature in the lives of Indians in Queens, with women expected to cook and clean for guests.

From the 1970s onward these core areas received waves of Indian immigrants and developed a range of resources for this growing population. Ethnic businesses emerged; houses of worship of different religions appeared in temporary as well as permanent locations; association meetings and cultural events were held each week. These Queens neighborhoods became sites to which Indians from other areas, including the suburbs, traveled from far and near to utilize these resources. Even Indians overseas or elsewhere in the United States knew about Queens and these named core areas.

[17]

Still, the core neighborhoods were little more than temporary residential stopping points for some immigrants who hoped to move into better housing in the suburbs. The transient nature of residences in Queens for the more successful Indian immigrants reflected class differences. While working-class Indians remained in outer-city (see Gans 1962) Queens neighborhoods, professional and upper-middle-class Indians preferred to live in upper-scale suburbs with few other Indians. Post-1965 Indian immigrants perceived suburban life to be a significant part of their American Dream, achievable by, as well as emblematic of, their economic success (compare Park 1997). Whereas the core areas represented one's arrival in the United States, a suburban single-family home signified one's success in the new country.

Many middle-class, professional immigrants of the 1960s and 1970s who later lived in suburban areas had spent their first years in the core areas of Queens commuting to Manhattan workplaces by subway; their children attended local Queens public schools. As one man reminisced,

> No matter how often I come back to Flushing—in a month or a few months—something changes in the meanwhile. Even the faces of people change every few years. New ones seem to be arriving all the time. When we lived here in 1970, many blocks had old stores, movie theaters, and gas stations. There were fewer apartment buildings, but housing was easily available at reasonable rents. There were one or two Indian stores and no temples. The place is bursting now; it's like being in some part of India.

Those who arrived in the 1980s and 1990s, however, encountered an altered stage for Indian life in Queens, one replete with established and new ethnic resources. Not only did ethnic businesses, houses of worship, and cultural activities proliferate, but class differentiation widened. While sizable numbers of professionals continued to arrive, a growing number of them, as well as less-educated immigrants, started off in lower-middle-class to working-class employment, engaged in such occupations as store clerk, cabdriver, or small business proprietor. Some, indeed, were unemployed. Striving for upward mobility was more arduous for them than for the earlier Indian immigrants. Immigrants now stayed longer in rented apartments in Queens receiving areas. If, or when, they moved, it was more frequently to cooperative apartments or smaller private homes in or near the core neighborhoods.

The continuing process of moving in and out of these core areas highlights class formation and division in the Indian community. The waves of newer immigrants produced more crowded streets, frequent turnover in

Queens businesses, and living standards visibly lower than those in suburban areas. Even though the suburban Indian immigrants returned frequently to the core areas for ethnic resources, they looked upon them as the denser, dirtier, and poorer side of Indian life in the United States. Nostalgia for earlier days in these neighborhoods was coupled with maintaining distance from them.

Beyond Queens, smaller numbers of Indians were scattered in the other boroughs of New York City, the neighboring suburban counties of Nassau, Suffolk, Westchester, and Rockland, and in Connecticut and New Jersey (see map 2). In 1990, approximately 59 percent of New York City's Indian population lived in Queens; this lead was maintained in 2000 when it recorded 63 percent of the city's Indian population. By comparison, other boroughs had much smaller portions; Manhattan, for example, had about 8 percent in both 1990 and 2000 (see table 2). Many of the Indians in the other four boroughs maintained links with the Queens core areas.

Manhattan's share of the city's Indian population had fallen from 14 percent in 1980 to 8 percent in 1990 and 2000, but Indian immigrants still viewed this borough as a place of prestige and economic centrality. A considerable number of Indians worked in Manhattan. In the 1990s, besides professionals and businesspersons, Indian cabdrivers, newsstand workers, and restaurant and store employees commuted to jobs there. As in the 1960s, Manhattan's residential Indian population was dominated by university and medical school students, yuppies, a small number of affluent businesspersons, and diplomats working at the United Nations or the Indian consulate. By the 1990s there was also a growing presence of working-class Indian, Bangladeshi, and Pakistani immigrants in Manhattan's Lower East Side and Washington Heights neighborhoods. Many of these were single men who had arrived in New York City beginning in the late 1980s, and who lowered their housing costs by sharing accommodations with other immigrant men.

In the 1980s several businesses that catered to Indian immigrants moved from Manhattan to Queens. Large stores such as India Sari Palace reopened on 74th Street in Jackson Heights, and the State Bank of India, the largest Indian banking institution, opened a branch in Flushing. The cluster of Indian businesses that remained in Manhattan on Lexington Avenue along 28th and 29th Streets, and called "Little India," reflected the characteristics of Indian life in Manhattan. Since the 1960s this handful of Indian businesses had expanded, but it remained smaller than the 74th Street concentration of Indian businesses in Queens. For Manhattan's Indian population, as well as for Americans interested in Indian cuisine, this indeed was "Little India." The majority of New York's Indian immigrant community, however, preferred the wider range of Indian businesses in Queens.

[19]

Several Indian restaurants catering to a mixed clientele of Indians and Americans also existed near the United Nations and university campuses. In the 1990s an increasing number of small Indian restaurants scattered throughout midtown and downtown served the South Asians working in Manhattan, with much of their business consisting in deliveries to offices. A row of Indian restaurants run by Bangladeshi immigrants also emerged along Sixth Street, in the East Village, in the 1980s. Several owners of these restaurants claimed they could attract more American customers by calling their businesses "Indian." One said, "If we call them Bangladeshi, only Bangladeshi immigrants will come. Americans don't know about our food; they come only to eat Indian food. So we serve them South Asian food— and call it Indian—so that they do not get confused." In contrast, restaurants in Queens that catered to Bangladeshis or Pakistanis explicitly named their businesses to indicate this fact.[2]

In Queens, Indian restaurants served many more South Asian families than single male customers. Although in general few Indians or Americans from Manhattan visited Queens for Indian shopping, exceptions included the young Indian Americans and other Americans who were aficionados of things Indian, and who ventured occasionally to 74th Street in Jackson Heights. Their main motivation, much like that of suburban Indians, was the Indian shopping district there, including the Jackson Diner, an eatery well publicized in ethnic restaurant reviews. Most South Asian businesses in Queens, however, including the majority of restaurants, served only South Asians.

Eastward from Queens, the Indian population on Long Island gradually thinned. By 1990, 11,875 Indians lived in Nassau County and 5,648 in Suffolk. Many Indian professionals commuted by car on the Long Island Expressway and Grand Central Parkway or by train on the Long Island Rail Road to jobs in New York City. In the late 1980s and 1990s increasing numbers of nonprofessional Indian immigrants also arrived in Long Island towns, often via family reunification visas. Still other Indians, mainly from Queens, traveled to Long Island to working-class jobs there, usually commuting by carpool in private vans or by public buses. Thus, amidst the predominantly upper-middle-class Indian residents of Long Island, working-class Indians established a growing presence. Although Long Island was considered a "better" extension of Queens, accessible to those who could afford large private houses and higher taxes, the boundary between Queens and Long Island was permeable, both metaphorically and literally.

By the 1990s this outward movement from Queens created a congeries of small Indian concentrations in Nassau and Suffolk Counties. Following the suburban-bound Indian immigrants who chose Long Island as their home, clusters of ethnic businesses, houses of worship, and cultural centers emerged in towns such as Hicksville and Hempstead. Some merchants who had owned retail businesses in Flushing, Elmhurst, or Jackson Heights relocated to Long Island, where the smaller clientele was balanced by wealthier customers and less competition. Films from Bombay were shown to full houses of South Asians at such Long Island movie theaters as Village 7 Cinema and Hicksville Twin Theater. Up to 15,000 South Asians of all generations, including Indians, Pakistanis, Bangladeshis, Sri Lankans, Guyanese, and Trinidadians, gathered several times a year at the Nassau Coliseum to watch musicians and film stars from Bombay's movie industry perform in "megashows."

Smaller numbers of Indian immigrant professionals lived in Westchester, Rockland, and other upstate New York counties. Their residential pattern was determined by proximity to workplaces in corporate offices, universities, or medical establishments. For everyday Indian groceries, Indians in these areas traveled to the one or two local Indian stores that carried a limited variety of essentials. For major shopping, they traveled to Queens.

In adjoining New Jersey, the number of Indians grew from 29,500 in 1980 to 79,440 in 1990 to 169,180 in 2000, with concentrations in such towns as Edison, Elizabeth, and Jersey City, where the growth in numbers of businesses and ethnic resources now rivaled that in Queens. Indians often traveled between these two areas to visit relatives or attend special events. Many Indian immigrants who worked in Manhattan now preferred to live in New Jersey and commute by train or bus.

Four Queens Neighborhoods

Several Queens neighborhoods with high concentrations of Indian immigrants present distinct characteristics and dynamics. In downtown Flushing, although Indians were the first Asian group to arrive in significant numbers, they were soon overshadowed by what has been called "New York's second Chinatown" and Flushing Koreatown (Chen 1992; New York City Department of City Planning 1993; Smith 1995; Park 1997). The Indian population in Flushing has continued to be primarily residential, with few businesses and little involvement in local politics. In Jackson Heights the 74th Street commercial area is the most prominent Indian ethnic site in the nation, and known internationally. Richmond Hill, a neighborhood in southwest Queens, houses populations of North Indian Punjabis and Indo-Guyanese immigrants, an intersection of two streams of Indian diaspora immigrants. In Queens Village and Floral Park, in eastern Queens, an Indian immigrant presence dominated by South Indian Malayalees grew rapidly in the late 1980s and 1990s, and moves were made to attain local political power.

Flushing

The first wave of Indian immigrants arrived in Flushing in the 1960s, most commuting to professional jobs in Manhattan on the Number 7 subway line. By the mid-1970s Flushing was perceived as a core neighborhood for New York City Indians, and this status was affirmed by the opening of a Hindu temple, set amidst residential streets, on Bowne Street in 1977. The founding secretary of this temple, Dr. A. Alagappan, explained that the site was selected because of the substantial number of Indian residents in the neighborhood. The founders knew that a larger space was available in a suburban area, but they wanted to establish a temple in the area then most accessible to Indian immigrants.

Businesses also opened to serve this growing residential population. The first Indian food store, Kalpana, opened on Main Street in 1970 and was a daily stop for many local Indians. Within a few years this one store expanded into a block-long complex of businesses selling groceries, saris, clothing, and other items. Mrs. Parekh, the owner of Kalpana, estimated that when her store opened there were about a thousand Indian families in the Flushing area. "We were catering to a rapidly growing local Indian population which required Indian businesses within its walking distance. The decision to open multiple stores on the same block was based on this growth." A Flushing branch of the Elmhurst-based House of Spices also appeared. Despite the growth of this cluster of businesses, to Indian immigrants Flushing remained primarily a residential neighborhood.

From the 1960s through the 1990s, Flushing became more and more a transient neighborhood for newly arrived Indian immigrants. Earlier arrivals moved out from Flushing apartment buildings to more expensive and commodious housing in suburban areas. They continued to return to the neighborhood for shopping, dropping off and picking up their children at Indian-language and cultural classes, or attending religious services. Many former Flushingites combined these ethnic activities in visits there and reserved Jackson Heights shopping for special occasions. The outward movement of Indians from this receiving area, however, mitigated any Indian involvement in neighborhood politics. Indians perceived Flushing as a cultural hub but were more interested in pursuing their dreams of upward mobility in suburbs. Flushing did not become their ethnic neighborhood.

In the 1980s Chinese and Koreans began to concentrate their Queens-based business and political activities in this neighborhood (Chen 1992; Park 1997). Flushing's Chinese population grew from 6,700 in 1980 to

20,352 in 1990 and 41,777 in 2000, while Koreans jumped from 3,794 in 1980 to 17,803 in 1990 and 27,113 in 2000. The number of Indians, in contrast, grew only from 4,592 in 1980 to 7,200 in 1990 and 11,100 in 2000. By the 1990s many New Yorkers referred to Flushing as Chinatown or Koreatown. Chinese and Koreans also took seats on the local community and school boards (Smith 1995; Dugger 1996). By comparison, Indian participation in Flushing's civic and political life was negligible.

As elsewhere in Queens, during the 1990s Flushing continued to receive immigrants of diverse origin: between 1990 and 1994 more than 4,000 Chinese, 1,770 Koreans, and 1,430 Indians settled there, along with smaller numbers from the former Soviet Union, Colombia, Afghanistan, the Dominican Republic, and Pakistan (New York City Department of City Planning 1996). As when Indians first arrived in the 1960s, public transportation connections and reasonable apartment accommodations continued to attract new immigrants.

The growing presence of other South Asians such as Pakistanis and Afghans intensified the cultural and religious diversity already present in Flushing. A Hindu center combining worship and social gatherings was founded in 1990 on Kissena Boulevard, just a few blocks from the older Hindu temple on Bowne Street. Adjoining this center, a large mosque with imposing Islamic architecture opened in 1995 on Geranium Avenue. This mosque was affiliated with the Muslim Center of New York and served Muslims from India and Pakistan. A number of smaller mosques in Flushing operated in rented locations, while larger ones opened for Afghan immigrants (Husain 1997). A Sikh *gurdwara* (temple, or "abode of the guru") nearby, on Parsons Avenue, was renovated to accommodate its growing congregation. In 1995 a Sai center—organized by Hindu followers of Sai Baba, a twentieth-century saint—opened in 1995 on Robinson Avenue, only blocks from these other houses of worship.

The first Hindu temple, on Bowne Street, expanded in terms of both facilities and attendance (Hanson 1997). After several years of fundraising, in 1997 it added a new Kalyan Mantapam auditorium and community center. Worshippers at this South Indian–style temple included immigrants from all parts of India who found it a convenient place to visit and participated in its busy calendar of ceremonies. The most public event here was an annual parade organized for the festival of Ganesh Chaturthi, in which devotees accompanied the deity's chariot along Flushing streets surrounding the temple. In the mid-1990s, however, the Ganesha parade was much smaller than the Chinese New Year parade, which had become the emblematic event in Flushing's Asian ethnic politics.

Scores of other Indian activities were organized every weekend in Flushing, in rented spaces such as the Colden Center for the Performing Arts at

Queens College, the Queens Botanical Garden, and school auditoriums. These locations, not owned by Indian organizations or individuals, were less prestigious venues than the houses of worship. Here groups of Indian participants, often dressed in traditional Indian dress, engaged in cultural performances, leaving only a fleeting trace of Indian life on the location or among non-Indian onlookers. In comparison to other ethnic groups, Indian participation in the Queens Festival, held each June in Flushing Meadows–Corona Park during the 1980s and 1990s, was not well organized; whereas Chinese or Koreans considered the pavilion assigned to them a reflection of their communal presence in Queens, less enthusiasm and energy were visible in the Indian pavilion, where activities were organized by only one organization rather than a coalition (Chen 1992, 232–245; Park 1997, 163–171). This large city park, however, was used at other times for ethnic events by Indian cultural organizations. In the 1990s it became the site for several South Asian Muslim festivals.

One other important ethnic space in Flushing, the Gujarati Samaj, a location for festivals, religious events, film showings, parties, and lectures, opened in 1990. Although this center belonged to a Gujarati organization (composed of immigrants from the Indian state of Gujarat), it was used by other Indian organizations as well. In its first few years it was made available for, among other activities, religious ceremonies sponsored by a Bengali organization, dances attended by Indian American youth, a *garba*, or Gujarati folk dance, open to all, and a panel of scholars of India.

By the 1980s the Indian-owned stores near Kalpana, including India Bazaar, Sabzi Mandi, Patel Brothers, and Japan Sari House, occupied an entire block. Since then they have extended another block southward. In addition to business, these stores served as information exchanges, with advertisements, newspapers, and posters near their entrances. Families strolled by on the street, spoke South Asian languages in comfort, and shopped. Increased numbers of shoppers and featured sale items usually indicated an approaching festival. The new stores added in the 1990s included Afghan, Pakistani, and one Iranian business. New store signs stressed religious identity as more salient than South Asian nationality. Words such as *halal* (meat cut in accordance with methods prescribed by Islam) or phrases written in *nastaleeq* (Arabic/Persian/Urdu script) appealed to Muslim immigrants from across nations such as Afghanistan, Bangladesh, India, Iran, and Pakistan (Husain 1997).

In the drive to succeed in business, Shan Groceries was open twenty-four hours a day and enticed customers by offering discounts on telephone calls to South Asian countries. Other shops sought to lure customers by featuring low prices for milk, an item heavily consumed by South Asians. Bargaining for lower prices, a practice in South Asia, was common. New stores with names such as Pak American Money Transfer and New York International Telephone Center also indicated a widening ethnic and socioeconomic patronage. Newly arrived immigrants in Flushing were no longer from India's urban middle classes. Many now hailed from small towns or even villages in India, Pakistan, and Afghanistan. Their background and class were apparent from their dress, language, and consumer practices.

The housing situation in Flushing also revealed increasing stratification among the Indian population. Some of the earlier arrivals who moved out to the suburbs in the late 1960s and 1970s had invested in real estate in Flushing, especially in condominiums, which they lent to relatives or rented. Less well-established immigrants arriving in the 1980s had moved from rented apartments to single-family homes close to downtown Flushing, and in turn rented out one or two floors of their own houses to more recent arrivals. By the 1990s larger, extended-family groups might share a single-family home, and several single men might share an apartment. Rental and real estate sales information was advertised in ethnic newspapers or in flyers posted in stores and religious institutions. Housing information also traveled through ethnic networks by word of mouth.

Jackson Heights

In the 1980s the two blocks of 74th Street between Roosevelt Avenue and 37th Avenue in Jackson Heights, and a few blocks around it, emerged as the prime Indian ethnic space in the tristate area. Businesses in this area were patronized by Indians from Queens as well as visitors from other parts of the United States or elsewhere in the world. Whereas the wide dispersal of Indian immigrants in New York prevented any residential space from being noted for an Indian presence, Indian commercial areas were widely perceived as centers of the city's Indian community (Khandelwal 1995).

The Indian business presence on 74th Street began in 1976, when an appliance and electronics store called Sam & Raj moved there. One of its original owners, Subhash Kapadia, explained: "We had a sense that this area was an important one for Indian immigrants. Queens was the favorite borough of Indians, and several subway routes intersected near 74th Street. But we had no conception that our business would pioneer such a large expansion of Indian businesses on this street."

The 74th Street location was just north of Elmhurst, the neighborhood with the largest Indian population in Queens. From the late 1960s Elmhurst, like Flushing, was a prime receiving area for Indian immigrants. After the Indian grocery store House of Spices opened on Broadway in 1970, more businesses sprang up on the same street. Nearby, Shaheen's, well known for its sweets and fast-food service, first opened on Woodside

[25]

Avenue and then moved to its present location on Broadway and 73rd Street in 1977. A number of houses of worship, including a mosque in nearby Corona, and a Jain temple, the Hindu Geeta Temple, and Satyanarayan Temple in Elmhurst, became part of the local landscape. However, unlike 74th Street in Jackson Heights, Indian businesses in Elmhurst were patronized primarily by local residents. Despite the smaller number of Indian residents in Jackson Heights than in Elmhurst, Indians eventually came to see Elmhurst as merely a southward extension of their commercial concentration in Jackson Heights.

For two decades the expansion of South Asian businesses on 74th Street was emblematic of the growing Indian community in Queens. This concentration of businesses became known to Indians all over the United States. Its merchants conducted a substantial business with Indians in other states through mail orders, and many expanded beyond Jackson Heights, opening chains of stores in Indian shopping clusters in other cities. On 74th Street itself, businesses such as Raj Jewels of London and Singapore Emporium indicated the global network linking Queens to other parts of the world. To Indian visitors from beyond New York City, Jackson Heights was reminiscent of Southall in London or a shopping bazaar in India. Half-seriously, many repeated that instead of Jackson Heights it should be called "Jai Kishan" Heights, after a popular Hindu god and a common male first name.

On 74th Street, "Indianness," as distinct from American lifeways, was visible and audible in stores purveying saris, jewelry, food, music, and movies. Although India has multiple regional cuisines, restaurant food is generally either North or South Indian. In the 1980s two Indian restaurants each represented these different categories, Delhi Palace being the North Indian restaurant and Udupi Palace specializing in South Indian cuisine. Video rental shops featured movies in Malayalam, Telugu, Tamil, Bengali, Punjabi, and the majority language, Hindi. Grocery stores sold ingredients for various South Asian cuisines; shelves in the same store carried sambhar masala (a spice mixture) for South Indian food next to Punjabi pickles and Afghan bread. Middle Eastern and Southeast Asian customers also shopped for rice and spices. The transcendence of regional and national boundaries was signaled by a new pan–South Asian cultural identity, with "Indo-Pak-Bangla" commonly used on store signs. The motivation for this cultural crossover was clearly to maximize business. No Pakistani-owned business on 74th Street could maintain an exclusive appeal to fellow nationals, and several were known to feature sales before the Indian festivals of Diwali and Holi. Only in the 1990s did open identification of Pakistani and Bangladeshi ownership begin to surface.

In addition to retail stores, offices of immigration lawyers, travel agents, and astrologers were found on 74th Street. The number of South Asian businesses grew from 71 in 1990 to 104 in 1996. Intensified commercial development was also evident. Surrounded by apartment buildings to the north and west, Latin American businesses to the east, and an extensive multiethnic commercial presence on Roosevelt Avenue and in Elmhurst to the south, the Indian 74th Street area could not expand beyond the few blocks it occupied in 1990. Instead, commercial growth occurred through the construction of Indian-financed minimalls, with more than one business now sharing a single storefront, or through the replacement of one of the few remaining non-Indian businesses with an Indian one. In 1998 the established firm Patel Brothers reopened in a space previously occupied by Woolworth, and the Jackson Diner in a former Keyfood supermarket, both expanding their commercial space. In the course of the 1990s Indo Us Books, the only bookstore on 74th Street, moved from a small storefront to a large store across the street, and then into the space vacated by Patel Brothers. In its expanded new space, in addition to books and magazines it carried a wide range of articles for domestic worship.

Some qualitative changes in business ambiance were also apparent. Between 1990 and 1996 the number of clothing stores increased from 18 to 22, jewelers from 5 to 11, electronics and appliance stores from 9 to 12, grocery stores from 6 to 14, and restaurants from 8 to 17. Other South Asian businesses also opened: immigration law offices, dentists, a "smoke shop," a barber shop, a bookstore, more fast-food restaurants, more small sari and jewelry shops, and the Eagle movie theater, owned by a Pakistani immigrant. Street vendors also appeared and increased in number over the years. Increasingly, upper-middle-class and affluent Indians living in the suburbs avoided Jackson Heights. Objecting to "parking problems" or a "lowering of class," they now visited it only to escort an Indian or American guest to a restaurant or to shop for a family party or a wedding. For everyday grocery shopping or video rental, the newer business clusters on Long Island or in Westchester had ample parking and no "quality" problems.

Merchants on 74th Street in the 1990s, unlike the pioneer merchants of the 1970s and 1980s, most of whom were highly educated, were drawn by the lure of profits in an increasingly oversaturated ethnic market. They came from later, more diverse immigrant waves and included Bangladeshis and Pakistanis as well as Indians. Before 1990 store signs were in English, the common language of the pan-Indian upper classes; no written display of Indian regional or separate national South Asian identities was visible. By the mid-1990s many businesses declared themselves Bangladeshi, Pakistani, or Afghan. Some stores included Bangla or Punjabi signs in addition to English, and music stores sold audio- and videocassettes from Pakistan as well as India. Hiring Bangladeshi sales clerks in established stores represented a response to the changing clientele. Overall, many more customers,

[27]

whatever their ethnic or national background, were now from the lower-middle and working classes.

Many pioneer merchants sensed early on this economic change in 74th Street's customer profile, and its likely adverse impact on business. In conversations in the late 1980s they complained about the scarcity of parking spots, littering by customers, and the sea of flyers by business canvassers, and also about muggings, burglaries, and traffic tickets and towings, all in addition to dwindling retail sales. While some turned more to mail and wholesale orders, others resorted to big storewide "sales" or permitted a decline in the quality of their stock. To combat competition from new restaurants offering cheap lunch and dinner buffets, the upscale restaurants put energy into catering for parties or moved to the suburbs. Some pioneer merchants, however, maintained their businesses for sentimental reasons, and either diversified into new economic sectors or increased their wholesale marketing. But one disgruntled merchant who had built a fortune in Indian groceries observed: "We cannot survive in a retail market where businesses compete for a price difference of a few cents and the customers bargain for lowering the price by a few dollars. People now come to Jackson Heights not for serious shopping but for an outing. If one person has to buy an item, ten accompany him or her. They cruise in and out of stores, comparing prices. Eventually, they may eat a cheap meal for the entire family, buy groceries, and leave."

Such frustration was less evident among recent merchants, but the high turnover in businesses was unmistakable. Some merchants who had followed the pioneers of the 1970s sold their businesses or moved at the end of their leases. A stark indication of the new customer profile was the appearance on grocery and food stores of signs announcing: "Food Stamps Accepted Here."

Surrounding the 74th Street business district was a residential area where white Americans of Irish, Jewish, and Italian ancestry were the established but numerically declining population, and were now living among diverse Latin American and Asian immigrants. Many of them were elderly; their friends and neighbors had died or moved; their children had established their households elsewhere. Most had moved into the area in the 1940s and 1950s and had confronted anti-Italian or anti-Semitic prejudice. In the 1980s and 1990s, however, some of these white Americans were alarmed by what seemed to them inroads of "foreign" cultures in "their" neighborhoods. Their desire to counter the changes accompanying the arrival of Indian businesses was coupled with efforts to document the early twentieth-century history of Jackson Heights, a time, ironically, when they were then unwelcome, and to extol its distinctive garden apartments (Karatzas 1990).

Emerging tensions between Indians and established whites centered on "quality of life" issues—the litter, traffic, and crowded streets resulting from the numbers of South Asian shoppers. Local white leaders contended that Indian merchants should share these civic concerns. (In fact, many did.) Indian merchants assumed that by remaining nonconfrontational and by paying taxes regularly they had been acting as "good citizens." A gap became evident between white and Indian perceptions of neighborhood civic responsibilities.

In 1989 and 1990 these issues were the subject of a series of meetings organized by white Jackson Heights resident groups. Indian merchant representatives were invited to participate. In these dialogues the merchants' own set of issues came to the fore. Most merchants were not residents of Jackson Heights, and they voiced their difficulties in operating businesses in the area. Besides parking and traffic problems, there had been a spate of burglaries and muggings on 74th Street, and cars had been vandalized, perhaps because of a common perception that Indian shoppers traveled with large amounts of cash and valuables. To deal with these problems, in 1989 the Indian business owners formed their own organization, the Jackson Heights Merchants Association. It represented their concerns to neighborhood associations and civic authorities and sought remedies through tightened security and cleaner streets.

Intergroup tensions reached a high point in November 1990, when a mainly white organization, the Jackson Heights Beautification Group, scheduled a rally to protest the filth and traffic in the neighborhood, which they blamed upon Indians. Although the purpose of the rally was street cleanliness and other civic concerns, some signs were clearly anti-Indian. Before the rally began, the New York City Human Rights Division's Crisis Prevention Unit intervened to tone down the "biased" sloganeering. The officials insisted that they had no difficulty with the basic purpose of the rally, but that the organizers should have sought cooperation and participation from Indian merchants.

The rally prompted both local residents and Indian merchants to seek more communication with each other to deal with problems through dialogue and negotiation. Abraham Mammen, owner of two 74th Street restaurants, was given a seat on the Jackson Heights Beautification Group board. Indian merchant leaders and white residents also met with officers from the local police precinct and Community Board 3, covering Jackson Heights. In 1993 an Indian police officer, Ravi Malhotra, one of fourteen police officers in the New York City police force who spoke Hindi, was assigned to the 74th Street area. A *New York Times* story described him as an Indian man who "became a peacemaker between Indian immigrants and other residents" (Holloway 1995). Members of a more liberal Jackson

Heights group, the Cultural Awareness Council, also held discussions with Indian, Korean, Chinese, African American, and Latin American leaders.

The Jackson Heights Merchants Association continued to maintain contact with the local police precinct, community board, Human Rights Commission unit, and mayor's office. In 1992 the secretary of the Jackson Heights Merchants Association informed the Indian press of a plan to designate 74th Street as "Little India" and to add distinctive architectural markers. They hoped that as in the cases of Chinatown and Little Italy, this move would put the neighborhood on New York's ethnic map as a tourist attraction (*India Abroad* 8/14/92). Later that year the association invited Mayor David Dinkins to its celebration of the Indian festival of Diwali. In his speech the mayor referred to the plan to designate the 74th Street area as "Little India." In the audience, one white American carried a placard protesting: "Mayor Dinkins: Wrong. I live here. This is my American home. Not 'Little India'" (*India Abroad* 10/30/92).

In the 1990s many Indians perceived 74th Street as part of the chain of diasporic Indian locations in such cities as Hong Kong, London, and Toronto. Developments in the wider Queens community—increasing socioeconomic diversity, unemployment and underemployment, and youth gangs—were also visible on its blocks (Melwani 1996). Although the liaisons established by the Jackson Heights Merchants Association with city officials, the local police precinct, and the community board continued, as the business district changed, the older merchant leaders were less effective in creating new channels of communication with their own co-ethnic merchants who had arrived during this decade.

Richmond Hill

Growing numbers of subcontinental Indian immigrants arrived in the southwestern Queens neighborhood of Richmond Hill in the late 1980s and through the 1990s. During the 1980s this neighborhood was already becoming home to an increasing number of Caribbean and Latin American immigrants, particularly Guyanese, Trinidadians, Dominicans, and Jamaicans (New York City Department of City Planning 1996). Two distinct Indian immigrant populations came to Richmond Hill: one from the state of Punjab in India, and the other from Guyana, consisting of "twice migrants" whose ancestors had migrated there from India in the nineteenth and early twentieth centuries (Mangru 1987, 1993; Depoo 1993; Kale 1995). Between 1980 and 2000 the Indian population of Community District 9 increased from 926 to 13,919, mainly in Richmond Hill. Although most of these immigrants were undoubtedly of Guyanese and Trinidadian origin, it is difficult to determine precise numbers from the published census figures.

In Brooklyn, Guyanese immigrants tended to be of African ancestry, but those in southern Queens neighborhoods (Richmond Hill, South Ozone Park, Jamaica-Hillcrest) were largely of Indian descent (see Gosine 1990a, 1990b; Depoo 1993). By 1990 Richmond Hill was the core area for these Indo-Caribbeans, with residences, houses of worship, and businesses along Liberty Avenue between Lefferts Boulevard and the Van Wyck Expressway. The Indian flavor was evident in the Hindu temples, Muslim mosques, homes with *jhandis* (flags placed outside Indian homes in Guyana and Trinidad as a mark of identity), and businesses carrying ethnic items. To immigrants from India, however, these houses of worship, homes, and businesses were readily identifiable as Guyanese. Thus two streams of Indian immigrants, separated by a century of migration and/or remigration, now met on the streets of Richmond Hill.

The communities, however, remained distant from each other, largely as a result of mutual ignorance. Guyanese wondered why many of them shared the surname Singh with Punjabi Sikhs from India. (The name is commonly used by Sikh men as a mark of religious identity, but it can also denote jati, or kin-group membership, in northern India.) Punjabi Indians were curious about the nineteenth-century labor migrations that had taken Indians to plantations in the British Caribbean; few among them had any prior knowledge of this history. "They call themselves Indian too, and practice many Indian traditions. But they are very different from us," remarked a puzzled Punjabi immigrant. When the Guyanese Phagwah parade traveled through the neighborhood to celebrate the festival of Holi (called Phagwah in the North Indian region whence many Indo-Guyanese emigrated), Punjabi families came out of their homes to join the rows of spectators. Apart from such events or chance individual encounters, the two communities had little interaction.

A Sikh gurdwara on 95th Street in Richmond Hill was the focal point for the new Punjabi community. Founded by the Sikh Cultural Society of New York in 1972 (Williams 1988), this gurdwara had preceded significant Punjabi population growth in the neighborhood. In the gurdwara's early years, Sikhs from the entire New York metropolitan area had traveled there to attend religious services. In accordance with tradition, the Richmond Hill gurdwara offered meals, lodging, and other services to visitors, and to the continuing stream of Sikh immigrants it served as house of worship, community center, and entry point to a new country. In 1994 a Sikh cabdriver explained:

I have the highest regard for that place. The guru's home is also my home abroad. When I first arrived in New York, I did not know anyone. I had no relative or acquaintance. This gurdwara gave me shelter for a week. It was like a blessing—I was among my own people, but without any obligation. It is a place of worship, so you have to follow their rules—no drinking or smoking. I know many wealthy people who have stayed here. There is no discrimination and everyone is equal. What more can one ask for?

As increasing numbers of nonprofessional Punjabi immigrants arrived, many found work in Richmond Hill in automobile-related occupations—trucking, driving taxis, operating gas stations, and working in auto-repair shops. In the early 1990s these businesses proliferated, along with Punjabi restaurants and grocery stores. The Richmond Hill gurdwara continued to be the central focus for this community, but some of the new Punjabi families attended newer Sikh or even Hindu houses of worship as well. The Punjabi presence in the neighborhood was underscored in 1993, when the Jackson Heights–based immigration attorney Kuldeep Singh Kasuri opened a second office on Lefferts Boulevard in Richmond Hill.

Eastern Queens

In the late 1980s the neighborhoods of Queens Village and Floral Park, in eastern Queens, began receiving an increased flow of Indian immigrants. A few professional families had moved to these quiet neighborhoods at the border of Queens and Nassau County in the early 1970s, but by the 1990s many more middle-class Indian immigrants had settled there. These areas were less expensive than Long Island suburban communities, and were within financial reach for the later wave of Indian immigrants. Between 1980 and 1990 the Indian population of Community District 13 (Queens Village–Rosedale) jumped from 1,562 to 5,786. The numbers continued to grow during the 1990s, and by 2000, Indians, including some Indo-Guyanese, numbered 13,884. They were the most numerous new ethnic group arriving in these neighborhoods (New York City Department of Planning 1996; for 2000 data, see www.nyc.gov/html/dcp/html/popstart.html).

Most Indian residents of eastern Queens had initially lived in rented apartments in Flushing or Elmhurst, leaving those core areas to purchase their first American homes in Floral Park and Queens Village. The same trend held for Guyanese families moving from Richmond Hill. All these recent immigrants regarded eastern Queens as cleaner and offering better housing than the core areas they had left, but as still close enough to the core areas to permit easy travel to them for visits and ethnic resources. Eastern Queens, moreover, was well served by city buses. During the 1990s a new cluster of ethnic businesses emerged in eastern Queens to serve this growing Indian population.

A distinct pattern of chain migration, with new arrivals joining established relatives, also emerged in eastern Queens among Malayalam-speaking South Indians from the state of Kerala. A large portion of Malayalee immigrants were Syrian Christians, and new Indian churches and congregations emerged in this area. In the early 1980s the Malayalees also formed a Kerala Cultural Association of North America (KCANA), which began with about thirty members. The primary goal of this organization was to assist Keralite parents in transmitting their language and culture to their children. The KCANA organized cultural events, offered classes in Malayalam, and served as a network for member families. In the 1990s the enlarged KCANA became involved in politics in Kerala, taking an active interest in development projects there (Nair 1997). Eastern Queens was by now the meeting ground for Malayalees spread throughout the New York metropolitan area.

When Indian immigrants started moving into this area, most established residents were white Americans. Indians were the first, and most prominent, group of people of color in this part of Queens, and racial incidents targeting Indians had occurred since the early 1970s. In a meeting in 1996 of a new organization, Indian/South Asians of Eastern Queens (ISAEQ), several persons recalled incidents in which the windows in their homes had been broken by vandals or their children had been beaten up in school because of their color (Nair 1997). Most Indians had resigned themselves to these incidents, but a few activists now took on the challenge of influencing local government agencies. With the goal of representing Indian residents, Sachi Dastidar, a college professor, was appointed to Community Board 13 in 1991, and in 1996 became the first Indian member of School Board 26. Dastidar had been a longtime member of the mainly white Northern Bellerose Civic Association, a homeowner group, and with Morshed Alam, a Bangladeshi immigrant also elected to School Board 26 in 1996, served on the executive board of the Eastern Queens Democratic Club.

Conclusion

The demographic shift of Indians from Manhattan to Queens beginning in the 1970s intensified over the next two decades. Manhattan, the workplace destination for many, continued to be a symbol of American preeminence, but neighborhoods in Queens now became receiving areas for immigrants, and 74th Street in Jackson Heights was widely perceived as the center of Indian ethnic life. Indian immigrants, however, readily moved out of these receiving areas to other Queens neighborhoods, or to homes in the suburbs, when they could afford it. The dream of owning one's own home was ardently pursued, and it was more prestigious to live in largely-white suburban Long Island or New Jersey than in Queens neighborhoods with high densities of diverse immigrants. These moves from apartment housing in core areas to single-family homes in the suburbs also demarcated class divisions within the Indian immigrant community.

Cultural diversity among Indians became steadily more apparent in social and cultural activities, as well as in the neighborhood concentrations of Punjabis in Richmond Hill and Keralites in eastern Queens. However, a countertrend of crossing South Asian national boundaries was also apparent by the 1990s as Pakistani and Bangladeshi immigrants increasingly shared neighborhoods, occupational niches, and commercial concentrations with Indians of the same social class. Immigrants from India also encountered immigrants of Indian descent from Guyana and Trinidad in Queens, and sometimes shared the same neighborhoods.

Politically, pan-Indian ethnic organizing was obstructed by the demographics of the South Asian New York landscape. The merchants on 74th Street, the best-known Indian area, did not live in Jackson Heights and traveled there from suburban homes. Despite substantial numbers in Elmhurst and Flushing, the Indian population was spread all over the borough. And by the time Indian immigrants naturalized and could vote, many had moved to suburban neighborhoods, where their presence was even more diluted.

[2]

Transplanting Indian Culture

Culture symbolizes both group identity and survival for Indian immigrants. The high priority placed on transplanting their cultural traditions to foreign soil is also connected to a deeply rooted belief in the indestructibility of Indian culture—even removed from the home country in which it arose, it must and will have a life of its own (Khandelwal 1997c). Thus, Indians have made major efforts to celebrate their cultural traditions in the United States and to transmit them to the next generation. For many, moreover, there is also a widespread sentiment that the biggest problem they face with Americans is that "they do not understand our culture." This perception produces a desire, particularly among Indian leaders, to educate others about their traditions and to gain acceptance for them in America. Their own children are often included in the category "others" because, to many adult immigrants, they do not seem to embrace Indian culture as their parents do. Similar concerns are found in most immigrant groups, but their intensity in the Indian community is remarkable.

Attempts to address these concerns involve questions about what elements of South Asian culture should be transmitted in the United States, what the relationship should be between national Indian culture and the various subcultures that form it, and what methods are most suitable to transplant cultural traditions. This chapter discusses several key Indian cultural elements—food, dress, language, arts, entertainment, media, festivals, and celebrations—and their modes of expression and transmission in New York. It also highlights the impact of the American context on shaping these immigrants' version of their culture.

The postcolonial experience of Indians transcends simplistic binaries of

Eastern versus Western culture, creating complex crossovers in cultural expression. Although they inherit established notions of hierarchy from Indian culture, these notions interact with the demands of urban life, and both at home in India and as immigrants, Indians often follow traditional practices while creating new ones for themselves in contemporary society. Indeed, they may sometimes even use tradition to secure a modern, individualistic identity for themselves. Moreover, although cultural hierarchy is obvious in India, there is no exclusive opposition between classical and folk culture, either in India or outside it. Indian folk dance and music may be performed by the highest classes without condescension. Indian cultural practices may be viewed simultaneously as "traditional," popular, and sophisticated, and also as instrumental in gaining access to mainstream American life.

The efforts to transplant Indian culture to a foreign country are not immune from American influences and local conditions. The rationale for celebrating Indian festivals in New York may be rooted in Indian culture, but the programs, arrangements, and messages reflect the immigrant context. The Indian movie concerts that draw thousands several times a year are a product of overseas Indian cultural realities that do not exist in India itself. Major festivals and parades seeking to represent India also define this version of ethnic culture as one more component of an expanding American multicultural scenario. The political goal of such activities—gaining recognition for Indian culture in the United States—is also apparent in the conscious outreach to American politicians in particular, and to American audiences in general.

Bruce Kapferer (1988) argues that culture plays an important part in the formation of an ethnic group, but an analysis of the various cultural expressions of Indian immigrants demonstrates that by the 1990s there was no single Indian ethnic culture in New York; indeed the cultural diversity of India had defiantly strengthened itself since the 1960s to counter any homogenizing forces. This diversity encompassed regional, religious, and caste traditions, as well as cultural expressions generated by new tensions of class, generation, and gender. By the 1990s all these variations had emerged with full force in Indian cultural activities in Queens.

Preserving cultural tradition has marked Indian immigrant activities continuously since the 1960s, but a distinct pattern is discernible from the mid-1970s through the 1990s. By the later period, many Indian cultures could be identified in Queens, each oriented to a distinct regional, class, religious, and generational clientele. Though based in this borough, these activities drew upon networks extending to elsewhere in the city and its suburbs, and to other parts of the country, overseas Indian communities, and India. This busy calendar of Indian cultural activities, most of them concentrated in

Queens, thus linked New York to a worldwide chain of Indian diasporic centers in London, Toronto, Guyana, and elsewhere. However, to elite Indians in Manhattan and suburbia, Indian life in Queens symbolized a lower social stratum than their own. Upper-class Indians came to avoid Queens and, to their minds, its lower-class Indian popular culture. These sophisticated Indian New Yorkers attended Indian cultural activities in Manhattan's Lincoln Center and universities, alongside white Americans. A decided cultural gap existed between them and the expressions of Indian ethnic culture that were apparent in Queens.

Food

Regardless of class, Indians preferred home-cooked meals prepared by women. Indian gastronomic culture was intimately bound up with the social relations of Indian families, which in large part centered on preparing and eating meals. As a result, even though restaurants were part of Indian life in Queens, eating in restaurants was not as popular as among other Asian immigrant groups such as Chinese or Koreans. Visits to restaurants were reserved for special occasions or parties. And because of the continuing primacy of cooking at home, the cultural diversity of Indian food traditions prevailed in homes and was sustained in the Indian grocery stores that supplied their varied ingredients.

The cuisines of India correspond to the dimensions of cultural diversity—region, religion, caste, and class. In addition to recipes and cooking styles, ingredients themselves vary by region. But even when a family lives in a large Indian city, its home-prepared food continues the tradition of its ancestral cuisine. These traditions are maintained by the women of the family, who, because of still-prevalent arranged marriages, usually come from the same caste as their husbands. In India, preparing meals remains so exclusively the responsibility of women that it is unusual to encounter men in kitchens. This is considered women's space, and cooking appetizing traditional food is a woman's most appreciated talent. Indian men also expect women to prepare food in large quantities for ceremonial occasions and social gatherings.

Indian immigrants brought their food-related traditions to New York. They were often heard defining their culture in terms of their regional or religious foodways: "In our culture, we eat [a particular dish]" or "In our community, food is prepared [in a particular way]." Indian parents expected their U.S.-reared children to appreciate home-cooked food more than a meal eaten out. One young Indian American complained that her mother wanted her to eat at home in the morning before leaving for the day. "Every day she persuades me to have breakfast at home. And here I am, busy getting ready for school. I would rather stop somewhere on my way for coffee. I don't know why she wants me to sit at the dining table and eat her home-prepared breakfast." Her mother responded, "I don't understand the sense in spending money outside when there is food at home. On one hand, she says continuously that she doesn't have money, and then she throws money away like this. This reason of saving time is a mere excuse. Do you think she will save time by buying breakfast from outside? It's so American to drink and eat while you are driving." Despite such disagreements, most young Indian Americans were well aware of their mothers' cooking talents and asked them to prepare Indian meals on special occasions.

A large part of India's people live their entire lives without tasting animal products (including, for most, eggs); many who are not vegetarians eat meat only outside the home. Vegetarianism is so widespread in India that any large gathering or restaurant may serve only vegetarian food or may carry separate sections of food for vegetarians and nonvegetarians. Indian vegetarianism is associated with Hinduism, although the religion does not require such a practice and although many Hindus do consume nonvegetarian food. Traditional Indian philosophy, however, laid out rules of nutrition that emphasized vegetarian foods for both spiritual and physical well-being. It is therefore common for even nonvegetarian Hindus to practice vegetarianism on certain religious days in the Hindu calendar. Meat items, even eggs, cannot enter most Hindu kitchens, and most restaurants in India are solely vegetarian.

Although some Hindu immigrants in the United States have abandoned pure vegetarianism, many others conform to tradition. Some immigrants who have become more religious here are also dedicated vegetarians. Indian immigrants, however, find it difficult to explain their food habits to Americans. "They think that we must be eating grass and boiled vegetables only, and many feel sorry for us. If only they knew the variety of vegetarian foods available in India, they would envy us." As one immigrant put it, "For Americans, vegetarianism is a fad, like a new age sort of thing, which you delve into over periods of time. They ask, 'How long have you been a vegetarian?' and are shocked to find that I haven't eaten meat all my life."

Vegetarian Indians do consume milk, cheese, and butter and avoid only the flesh of animals, including fish and seafood. One man has struggled to find an explanation of his vegetarianism that Americans could understand. "Will it be right to say that we value living beings and don't want to take a life for our food? The problem is that they have no concept of *ahimsa* [nonviolence], which is the basis of Indian vegetarianism. And in India, vegetarianism is so integral to our lives that we are never taught why we practice it. We just grew up as vegetarians."

In a number of pan-Asian organizational events in New York City, Indians regularly refrained from refreshments or meals that had any nonvegetarian ingredients, including sauces and broths. In some instances this practice was both an inconvenience to the vegetarian Indian and embarrassing to the host. Often, awkward situations also arose on trips, although domestic and international airplane flights more easily provided the option of requesting a vegetarian special meal. Still, according to one Indian immigrant woman, maintaining vegetarianism was not particularly difficult in New York. "There is such a large variety of foods available here. There are salads, pastas, breads, Middle Eastern food, and, then of course, we have pizzas. It *is* more difficult to be eating out a lot when you are a vegetarian, but it is easy with home cooking. Now almost every ingredient necessary for Indian cooking is available in New York, thanks to the grocery stores. Even the quality of spices and other packaged foods that we get here is better than what we get in India."

Before the establishment of Indian stores in Queens in the early 1970s, Indian immigrants had to make do with American grocery stores or travel to Kalustyan's, on Lexington Avenue in Manhattan. House of Spices, the first Indian grocery in Queens, opened in Elmhurst in 1970, and as the Indian population grew, other stores appeared in Flushing and later in Jackson Heights. Indians from beyond New York combined visits to the city with shopping at these stores, purchasing bulk supplies of basmati rice and Indian vegetables not available at their local Indian grocery, or not at New York prices. The retail food businesses in Queens eventually became quite competitive, and stores offered a fuller range of ethnic ingredients to their Indian customers. By the 1980s "Indo-Pak-Bangla" stores carried an array of spices, lentils, flours, sweets, snacks, fresh vegetables, cans and jars of spicy pickles, frozen items, and prepared packaged foods. The variety available in each category also increased. To the delight of Indian customers, stores carried mustard greens and fresh fenugreek in their produce sections, and cases of mangoes imported from Mexico, Haiti, or Florida during the summer. Perplexingly to the occasional American customer, these stores contained only limited offerings of Indian curry powder. One store owner explained: "You ask any Indian, and they don't even know what curry powder is. Instead, every Indian kitchen carries a range of spices that are used differently according to the dishes. Curry powder is for Americans who do not know how to prepare Indian food. They want a short cut so that they do not have to buy different spices and learn their uses."

To maximize their business, groceries in Queens also carried videocassettes of Indian movies for rental, and ritual items for upcoming festivals. They also served as information exchange centers. Their walls were plastered with large colored posters of concerts and other cultural events, often with tickets available right there, and they sold Indian newspapers and magazines and made space available for flyers announcing job openings and real estate offerings.

Often it was grocery stores that reminded immigrants about events on their religious calendars and provided information about performing rituals. As an Indian woman in one store walked to the counter to pay for her groceries, she looked hard at a display of *rakhis*, the decorative bands that Hindu women tie on their brothers' wrists every year for the Raksha Bandhan festival. She exclaimed, "Oh, I forgot that the festival is almost here! Life is so busy in this country, you forget everything. When exactly is the festival? I have to send these rakhis to my brother in India." The Indian groceries buzzed with special energy around major festivals, selling sweets and ritual paraphernalia. Special sales were announced around festival times, or at store openings and anniversaries. Here immigrants also spoke in their own languages and could behave in ways reminiscent of home. When a customer complained to a proprietor that an Indian vegetable item was not fresh, he responded, "We often forget here that we are not in India. All these things are so easily available to us now that we can afford to complain about their quality. The new immigrants do not know that ten, fifteen years ago, hardly any of these things were available in this country. Only *we* know what routes they travel to reach here."

The influence of immigrant life in America was also obvious in these stores. A single grocery carried a wider range of cooking pastes and powders—for Gujarati, Punjabi, South Indian, and other cuisines—than would be available in a single store in any part of India. Out of commercial necessity, grocery stores were perhaps the most powerful promoters of pan-Indian and pan–South Asian unity; a jar of pickles or a bag of rice might be used by immigrants from India, Bangladesh, Pakistan, or Sri Lanka. And in response to the fast pace of American life, each store had a frozen-food section of packets of green peas, fried onions, chunks of *paneer* (cheese usually prepared at home in India), precooked *samosas* (fried patties with potato filling), *chapatis* and *parathas* (Indian breads), and other items. A store owner in Flushing exclaimed, "I have been in this country for many years, but I have not seen a group like us Indians where women prepare their bread every day from scratch. They work [outside the home] here and have no help in cooking and cleaning. The frozen foods are for this sector of Indian customers." Frozen foods were also convenient for single men who cooked for themselves, something they were not trained to do in India.

In the 1990s the growth of Indian grocery stores followed the demographic expansion of South Asian immigrants into more Queens neighborhoods and throughout the New York metropolitan area. Wholesalers such as House of Spices, Shaheen's, and Patel Brothers supplied products to retail stores here and throughout the United States. Despite competition from Indian businesses in Chicago and Houston, New York was the key distribution center for Indian food products. (House of Spices shipped its Laxmi brand-name items nationwide from a warehouse in Flushing.) Supplies were also imported from India and other countries, including wheat from Canada and rice from Thailand. Most stores everywhere carried jars of pickles from the London-based Indian company Patak's.

The Indian restaurants that opened in Queens after the 1970s, unlike those in Manhattan, served a primarily Indian clientele. The cluster located on 74th Street in Jackson Heights included the Jackson Diner, which replaced an American diner and served Indian cuisine. By the late 1980s similar restaurants had appeared all over Queens and Long Island. In its inaugural publicity one restaurant, Tandoor in Rego Park, described Queens as the "capital of Indians in America." These mid- to upscale restaurants based their trade on well-to-do customers, largely Indian, who, besides dining, hired restaurant space for weddings, birthdays, or parties. Patrons were not primarily residents of the neighborhood, but came from far and near.

Simultaneously a number of inexpensive eating places cropped up in the Queens neighborhoods receiving newly arrived immigrants. Their clientele (and workforce) were recent immigrants, including lower-middle- to working-class Indians, Bangladeshis, and Pakistanis. Meals were of the fast-food variety, with customers choosing from a limited range displayed in steam tables. (In the 1970s the only such South Asian restaurant in Jackson Heights and Elmhurst was Shaheen's, which operated a similar fast-food self-service outlet in Manhattan, on Lexington Avenue.) These "curry in a hurry" eateries carried both vegetarian and nonvegetarian items, cooked according to a standardized North Indian style that appealed as well to Pakistanis and Bangladeshis.

On 74th Street these fast-food restaurants emerged in quick succession in the late 1980s. Most offered dinner and lunch buffets and sold snacks such as samosas or *chat* dishes (a genre of snack with a medley of flavors). In the 1990s many such small restaurants opened in Elmhurst and Richmond Hill, street vendors selling *pan* (betel leaves wrapped around a mix of spices and nuts, and chewed) and fresh sugarcane juice appeared on 74th Street, and the first Bangladeshi restaurant, Mitali, opened there.

No new upscale Indian restaurant opened on 74th Street during the 1990s, although the Jackson Diner did move to a new, expanded location. Instead, the owners of the area's established Indian restaurants opened new restaurants in new locations. The owner of the Jackson Diner opened Diwan Palace in affluent Port Washington, on Long Island; and the owner of Delhi Palace opened a sophisticated restaurant in Floral Park, in eastern Queens, in 1996. Udupi Palace acquired a new owner and a new name,

Anand Bhavan, and changed its focus from South Indian to all-Indian food but maintained its vegetarian menu. The new owner, G. L. Soni, is an Indian food wholesaler who, as a side venture, sought to promote vegetarian cuisine in Queens; in the mid-1990s he also opened a vegetarian fast-food restaurant, Shamiana, in the South Asian business district in Flushing.

A number of Indian restaurants existed in Manhattan. Besides the inexpensive eating places in "Little India" on Lexington Avenue in the 20s, and the Bengali restaurant row on 6th Street, several upscale Indian restaurants such as Jewel of India, Shaan, and Chola were located in midtown Manhattan and near the United Nations and attracted a clientele of Indians and Americans. A restaurant in the SoHo area of Lower Manhattan named Baluchi, which specialized in food from northwest India and Central Asia, became popular with young Indian Americans and their American friends. Madras Place on Lexington Avenue, a vegetarian South Indian restaurant, announced to its mixed clientele, many of them Jewish, that its food was certified kosher by a rabbi.

As with other ethnic cuisines, Indian restaurant food varies considerably from home cooking. Indian restaurants in New York developed a standard menu, found nearly everywhere, consisting of Indian "appetizers," meat and vegetable curry dishes, rice and Indian breads, Indian lassi (a yogurt-based drink) or beer, American drinks, and Indian desserts. Deviations from Indian food habits were noticeable: in northern India, breads are part of the meal; in New York restaurants, breads were treated as a separate dish to be tried only by those familiar with them. Indian restaurateurs also trained their staff to exercise caution about spices and pepper-hot ingredients. Waiters asked American customers if they preferred their food hot, medium, or mild. One owner explained that since Americans were not used to Indian tastes, "I have seen situations where Indian food can send them sweating all over and running for the bathroom. That is not good for our business, so we try to accommodate them."

Among all New York Indians, the food next in popularity to their own was pizza, which also suited the vegetarian preference of many immigrants. Indian families patronized the Pizza Hut chain, but the first notable indication of the popularity of pizza was the large Indian clientele of a restaurant in Elmhurst called Singa's Pizza. This Greek-owned pizzeria, opened in 1967, sold a small eight-inch pie with various meat and vegetable toppings (including hot pepper) and became a favorite among Indian immigrants. Pizza was preferred as an inexpensive alternative to family dining in Indian restaurants and a timesaver versus cooking at home. Indian families who did not live in Queens made sure to pick up pizzas from Singa's when visiting the borough. Spurred by its popularity among Indians, Singa's opened other outlets in Flushing and Long Island City, neighborhoods with large

Indian populations; its opening in Flushing in the early 1990s was publicized in the Indian ethnic press. In the mid-1990s other pizzerias in Queens tried to succeed by using names similar to Singa's, but as one Indian customer explained, "We miss its special taste. I cannot say exactly why we like it so much, but somehow it has clicked with the Indian palate. Where else would you get such wonderful hot chili topping, and mango drink, to go with a pizza?"

Dress

Female Indian immigrants considered dress integral to their identity, and donning traditional dress was seen as preserving one's culture in the United States. Even highly educated women pursuing careers continue to wear traditional dress in urban India, although men of similar status long ago adopted Western attire. The forms of dress most popular with urban Indian women are the sari, the long wrapped and draped dresslike garment, worn throughout India, and the *salwar-kameez* or *kurta-pyjama*, a two-piece suit garment, sometimes also called Punjabi because of its region of origin. Whereas the sari can be considered the national dress of Indian women, the salwar-kameez, though originally from the north, has been adopted all over India as more comfortable attire than the sari. In some regions of South Asia, it is also worn by men.

Both forms of dress are worn by women as everyday clothing as well as on special occasions. Generally, everyday clothing is of inexpensive cotton or polyester fabric, while garments for special occasions are of silk with elaborate embroidery, and maybe interwoven with gold. Treasured women's clothing items are selected with immense care and sometimes use up the major part of a family's savings; they are bestowed with great affection on close family members. Expensive saris are considered works of art, each hand-woven with a distinctive design and color combination. Traditional schools of sari weaving have long existed at, among other places, Banaras in Uttar Pradesh, Chanderi in Madhya Pradesh, Kanjivaram in Tamilnadu, and Bangalore in Karnataka.

In the United States, Indians are one of the few immigrant groups whose women continue to wear their traditional dress. This practice is maintained by women of all class and education levels, although in workplaces some women alternatively wear Western styles as well. In the 1960s and 1970s Indian women wore saris they had brought from India or made from fabrics available locally; since then the range of saris from India available in the United States has increased considerably.

Traditional jewelry has also remained popular with Indian immigrant

[43]

women, and includes a wide array ranging from 22-karat gold jewelry to the glass bracelets called bangles, which women all over South Asia wear on their wrists. These items were increasingly available in Indian stores, particularly on 74th Street in Jackson Heights, where jewelers displayed gold jewelry in window showcases, and a wide choice of costume jewelry was also available.

The application of hand-applied henna paste designs, or *mehndi*, on women's hands and feet is common in northern South Asia, a tradition shared with Arab countries and Iran. Intricate designs are painted to celebrate occasions such as weddings. Although mehndi has never been as common in the United States as in South Asia, by the 1990s several Queens beauty salons offered mehndi application, particularly for a bride or female members of her wedding party. In the 1990s henna painting was also popularized in music videos—as the "painless tattoo"—by the American popular singer Madonna. Its display in multiethnic festivals became common, and, to the amusement of Indians, was called "body painting" by Americans.

Perhaps the most distinctive feature of adornment among Indian women in New York City was the colored dot, called *bindi*, on their foreheads. Bindi is such a common part of a woman's appearance in India that Indian immigrants were surprised when its use evoked curiosity in the United States. As with vegetarianism, Indians had a difficult time explaining it to Americans, and not many in fact were aware of its multiple rationales, ranging from esoteric philosophy to simple fashion.

Bindi can be worn in its pure form, red *kumkum* powder, by all Hindus, men and women, as a sign of auspiciousness, respect, and blessing on the part of the wearer. Thus, male devotees visiting a temple, or priests, may be seen wearing it. At the same time, bindi is a basic component of a Hindu woman's identity and appearance, transcending its religious origins and entering the realm of fashion. Indeed, stick-on bindis are commonly sold in India in different shapes and colors to match one's attire. In the United States bindis have become an ethnic marker for Indians. U.S.-reared Indian Americans consider them, along with saris and kurta-pyjama, part of Indian ethnic dress. In the 1980s an anti-Indian hate group in New Jersey focused on bindi in calling itself "the Dotbusters." Elsewhere Indians were described as the "dot-head" Americans (Gosine 1990b).

Indian immigrant women who were homemakers wore traditional dress at all times. Many professional women also continued to wear saris in their American workplaces. An Indian professor who had worn saris ever since she arrived in the United States in the early 1970s explained, "I cannot imagine myself in Western clothing. I feel so comfortable in a sari, as if I am with my own self. My dress is an extension of my cultural self, my Indian identity. Other considerations, like standing out among Americans, do not bother me." However, in response to covert social pressure in their work-place, some career women turned to Western dress. According to one of them, "One cannot wear an Indian dress in an office like mine. If you do so, your colleagues will admire you or even give you compliments, but as a result they consider you an outsider who will never be treated equally. They know I am Indian, and they have seen me in Indian dress in social situations, but not at work."

An Indian professional woman who worked in Manhattan explained, "It is basically your individual decision. You decide if you can wear Indian dress to work or not. It is an everyday cultural dilemma: Will my Indian dress be accepted today, will it be comfortable, will it stand out too much, whom am I meeting today, should I bring out my American professionalism or my traditional side, etc. etc." But an Indian physician from Queens stated that she had to wear Western clothes at work. "By the time I complete my day's work, I am dying to get back in my Indian clothes. As soon as I reach home, I throw my Western clothes off—they are so stressful—and change into something Indian that is comfortable. It is like switching into a different world."

Like many professional women, working-class Indian women perceived Western clothes as a workplace uniform to be worn by women who, like men, worked outside the home. A woman who arrived in New York in the mid-1990s from a small Indian town, where she had never worked outside her house, wore an inexpensive polyester shirt and trousers to her job as a cashier in a Queens store. Attributing this change to her immigration, she said, "See, I have to wear these men's clothes here. It is okay because I am doing a man's job here. Our clothes do not fit in this American culture. To feel Indian, we can wear our own clothes when we are not on the job."

In Queens, Indian women's clothing became increasingly visible at the neighborhood level. It was common to see several women in Indian dress walking together, helping each other cross streets, with young children in strollers, riding buses or subways, and shopping in stores. The widening of the class spectrum was also apparent to fellow South Asians from the quality and style of dress, whether Indian or Western, of poorer Indian women.

A few older men continued to wear their traditional Indian garments out of choice. On a cold weekend in December 1994, a group of Sikh men of varying ages was conversing on a Flushing street. One, in his early twenties, apparently had arrived in the United States recently, and stood shivering in a light silk suit no doubt tailored for him in India. The other, older men were dressed in salwar-kameez outfits under heavy overcoats. One older man told the youth, "Son, this is not the time to show off your new silk suit. I told you how cold it is going to be here today. If you catch a cold or become sick, nobody will take care of you in this country. Here you have to take care of yourself. All the money your family spent on making this suit for America will go down the drain in one doctor's visit here. There will be other occasions when you can use this suit!"

It is unlikely that traditional dress among Indians will continue among their U.S.-born children. Its use among women was more common, but occasionally young men did wear traditional kurta-pyjama, considering it national or ethnic dress. Younger Indian American women took more readily to kurta-pyjama outfits than to saris, which many did not know how to wrap around themselves properly (see also Narayan 2000). Weddings remained the prime occasion for wearing traditional clothes. Families of brides and grooms spent substantial sums on outfits for the couple and immediate family members. Many jewelry and clothing stores on 74th Street cultivated this market, bringing the latest fashions from India and displaying them in elaborate showcases. Indian immigrants, however, preferred to shop for most of their Indian clothes during vacations in India; for Indian women in particular, visits home were opportunities to refurbish their wardrobes. They enjoyed the wider choice available in India and used readily accessible tailoring services in preference to the ready-made garments sold in the United States.

Language

Knowledge of English is a characteristic skill of postcolonial Indian immigrants to the United States, which distinguishes them from most other Asian or Latino immigrants. Their efforts to maintain their Indian languages are combined with a practiced use of English, particularly in occupational and educational settings. However, comfort levels in using this language varied among Indians in New York, and fluency in English within this new American ethnic group often coincided with position in the class hierarchy.

English is widely used in cities throughout India. It is most prevalent among the middle and upper classes of urban Indians educated in English-medium schools. Among the urban lower classes and in small towns, knowledge of English shrinks to the use of phrases intermixed with Indian languages, and it is nearly nonexistent in rural India. Still, English plays an important role as the official medium of communication in bureaucratic, business, and formal settings. But it is seldom used in preference to indigenous languages, called "mother tongues" in India, in any cultural, religious, or regional in-group setting. It remains a symbol of high status and is associated with sophistication and privilege.

The widespread knowledge of English among post-1965 Indian immigrants reflected their class backgrounds. Although in the 1960s and the 1970s about three-fourths of the population of India was illiterate, most Indian immigrants to the United States in those decades had received higher education in English-medium Indian universities. Their English-language skills and education undoubtedly provided them with an advantage over other immigrants in gaining professional jobs once in the United States. For other post-1965 Asian immigrant groups such as Koreans, despite high levels of education, more downward mobility occurred (see Min 1996; Park 1997).

Indian immigrants arriving in the 1960s and 1970s came from different language groups in India, but all knew English and used it with other Indians and with American friends (Sridhar 1988, 1997). Use of their diverse mother tongues, and with them the shared experience of their distinctive regional cultures, was then submerged by a pan-Indian culture, only to surface occasionally in small, homogeneous social settings. Studies that pointed to the wide use of English among Indian immigrants as a major factor in establishing them as "assimilative" or "model" immigrants reflected the sociolinguistic realities of the 1960s and 1970s (Saran and Eames 1980), and this pattern continued in suburban or upper-class Manhattan arenas.

With growing numbers, a widening class spectrum, and increasing cultural diversity among Indians in Queens, a more complex range of language-use patterns became evident in the 1980s and 1990s (Sridhar 1997). The enhanced demographic base for speaking regional languages accelerated the use of different mother tongues. English was now seen more as a skill required at work. The wider use of Indian languages was evident in immigrant associational activities. In the 1970s and the 1980s a number of groups such as the Bharathi Society, named after the Tamil litterateur Subramaniam Bharathi, and the Tagore Society, honoring Bengali writer and Nobel Prize winner Rabindra Nath Tagore, were formed by highly educated immigrants to promote their regional literatures. Other, more popularly based associations included literary activities within a more comprehensive celebration of their regional cultures. Cultural events presented by these organizations invited literary figures from India as featured guests, but dance and musical performances by established artists or groups of children were more typical. Informally, Indian languages flourished in families as before, but also in now-widened social networks, and in newly established cultural classes for children. For example, a Queens group called Adabi Sangam (Literary Confluence) brought together local writers in Hindi, Punjabi, and Urdu, all closely related Indian languages, to read their work; these meetings were held monthly in homes and became the basis for social networks among speakers of these languages.

By the 1990s, the status of Hindi, India's official language, which is spoken across most of North India, had changed in New York City from that of a widely used common language in India to that of one among many languages used by Indian immigrants. Although the use of spoken Hindi grew in New York as a result of the growing number of Hindi-speaking immigrants, its numerical dominance here was far less than in India, and its formal role had contracted. An organization called Vishwa Hindi Samiti (World Hindi Organization) strove to enlist Indians across the United States interested in written and literary Hindi, but its resources were meager, and its membership was confined to scholars and writers who received little recognition in the United States.

The Indian tradition of maintaining one's native languages at home despite migration continues in the United States. Regional languages such as Gujarati and Punjabi are maintained by large numbers of immigrants in the United States, who also support their mother-tongue publications (Center for India Studies 2000, 44). Several Punjabi newspapers reached Queens from long-established communities in Vancouver, Canada, and California. A Gujarati weekly from India, *Gujarat Samachar,* was printed in New York for readers in North America. Still, the most widely distributed Indian newspapers, *India Abroad* and *News India*, were English-language newspapers.

As in other immigrant groups, native-language use has declined among U.S.-reared children. Most understand their parents' language but have little practice in speaking it. Their facility also suffers because of their parents' knowledge of English, and few parents compel their children to speak their mother tongues exclusively at home. Reading and writing of Indian languages are even more unlikely unless children are registered in language classes. The language gap between immigrants and U.S.-reared Indian Americans has affected intergenerational communication. Even immigrants who speak English fluently consider their children's English "too American"; the children, in turn, object that their parents "have an Indian accent" and do not speak American English. Indian parents feel proud if their children learn their mother tongue; in contrast, U.S.-reared Indian Americans feel embarrassed by their parents' English.

The major extrafamilial exposure to Indian languages among U.S.-reared youth is through Indian movies and songs or on visits to India. Although Indian-language use overall has declined rapidly among the U.S.-reared youth, a select few words have entered a distinctive generational vocabulary. *Masala* is used for any medley of different elements or for a typical ethnic Indian situation. After filmmaker Mira Nair's *Mississippi Masala* became popular in the late 1980s, a number of young South Asians used the word *masala* in their movies, magazines, and websites. *Desi* (a native Indian or South Asian) is used as an adjective for food or dress or even behavioral patterns and individuals. By the late 1990s its use was so common that, quite unknown to many adult Indian immigrants, it was used by U.S.-reared Indians as a defining term for all South Asians (Mukhi 2000; Prashad 2000b).

English-language use among Indians who had grown up in India varies according to the social class of their families, and a growing number of immigrants arrive with limited English proficiency (DeCamp 1991). Although their younger children acquire spoken English quickly, reading and writing in English requires attentive teaching. Compared to East Asian or Hispanic students, this group's distinctive linguistic needs are seldom accommodated by established bilingual education programs. Because of the prevalence of English as an official language in India and their own experience, elite Indian community leaders do not champion bilingual education for Indians in the United States.

The link between language use and class became evident during the 1990s in a series of public interactions on the Indian television channel ITV, aired in Indian immigrant concentrations in Queens, Brooklyn, and New Jersey. ITV was watched by thousands of South Asian immigrant families, mainly for its entertainment fare, which included programs about Indian film stars and several movies each day. But it also carried live call-in shows on community issues. Initially these were held in English, but, presumably in response to a growing audience not comfortable in English, eventually some were conducted in Hindi. However, even on community programs in English, many callers spoke in Hindi. On one program about women's issues, a female caller said in Hindi that the discussion was so valuable that the entire program should switch to Hindi. The host responded by insisting that this was an English-language program, and that if the caller did not speak English, she should watch the Hindi-language programming. The caller reacted by saying that she did know English, but that in order to reach a larger group of immigrants, such discussions should not be limited to English-speakers only. Her comment provoked a discussion among the panelists about the necessity of speaking English in the United States. In the mid-1990s ITV began to air programs in Hindi, or a combination of English and Hindi, from India's state-owned television network, Doordarshan; this move brought daily newscasts in Hindi to Indians in Queens.

Media

The Indian population is geographically scattered, but it is connected through various cultural networks, a principal one being the ethnic mass media. Most media published or broadcast in English transcend any regional or language loyalties. Most of the Indian ethnic media focus on news and film-based popular entertainment from India, but they have also become a virtual community forum for cultural expression in New York and the United States.

The first Indian newspaper of the post-1965 period, *India Abroad*, was founded in New York in 1970 by several professionals, immigrants who envisaged it as a networking mechanism for their growing population. Soon it took professional form under the editorship of Gopal Raju, one of the original founders, who led its operations into the late 1990s. In these decades, *India Abroad* expanded from a biweekly newsletter of a few pages into a forty-page weekly newspaper that reached Indian households all over North America and other parts of the world. While its primary focus remained news from India, its sections on local community news, commercial advertisements, and matrimonials all expanded. For Indian immigrants, it served the dual purposes of providing news from the home country and creating a shared media space with other overseas Indians.

In the 1980s, the leading competitor to *India Abroad* was *News India*, a newspaper started in New York by editor John Perry. *News India* also built a readership in the United States and made alliances with newspapers of India. In terms of content and focus, however, it did not differ significantly from *India Abroad*. Other Indian newspapers published from New York were *India Monitor*, *India Post*, and *Asia Online*, and a host of smaller Pakistani and Bangladeshi newspapers read by some Indians who shared languages with these groups.

Some Canadian newspapers printed partly in Punjabi and partly in English arrived in local stores from Toronto and Vancouver. *Gujarat Samachar*, a daily newspaper published in the Indian state of Gujarat, was reprinted in New York City. These mother-tongue newspapers met some of the diverse language needs within the New York Indian population. English newspapers such as *India Current* and *India Post*, printed on the West Coast, however, enjoyed limited readership in New York. In striking contrast to the multiple dailies in Chinese and Korean published in Queens, there was no daily Indian newspaper in New York in any mother tongue. In the 1990s *India Today*, a leading weekly magazine in India, reached out to middle-class Indians in the United States by starting a North American supplement in its international edition.

Bharat Vani, or "Voice of India," the first Indian radio program in New York, began in 1975. Its founder and primary anchor, Brij Lal, continued to run the program through the 1990s without major changes in style or format. Its content included news, community announcements, interviews with Indian immigrants, and film music. Bharat Vani aired for a few hours on weekend mornings and enjoyed consistent support from early Indian immigrants, who had listened to it for decades. On its twenty-first anniversary in 1996, it featured a number of community organizations led by well-known Indian immigrant leaders. It was lesser known among later immigrants, who were more familiar with ethnic television.

Vision of Asia, the first Indian television program in New York City, was started in 1976 by a couple, Dr. Vishwanath and his wife Mrs. Satya Vishwanath. Its few hours of airtime on Sunday comprised news and film segments, and for two decades it shared a channel with other ethnic television programs. In the late 1980s several other Indian television programs copied the *Vision of Asia* format, notably *Eye on Asia*, an hour-long program, which earned high Nielsen ratings; although its main focus was news, it interspersed features, short interviews, location shootings, and news of Indian films. Meanwhile, *Vision of Asia* expanded into its own cable channel, ITV, accessible to viewers in Queens, Brooklyn, and parts of New Jersey. ITV soon became a twenty-four-hour channel showing several Indian movies a day, and programs appealing to Pakistani and Guyanese immigrants, as well as regional Indian groups. In the mid-1990s it added a community news segment and offered live call-in programs. These steps made its anchors, Karl Khandalwala, Renu Lobo, and Bindu Kohli, into household names. The impact of widening social class among Indians and other South Asians could be felt in the menu of ITV programs of the later 1990s. Initially ITV carried some ITV-Gold programs, which could be viewed only through its paid channel, and eventually the entire channel was available only through payment to a local cable company.

In the 1990s a few new magazines were established by young Indian professionals, including *The Indian American* and *Masala*. In spite of professional marketing and high-quality production, however, they failed to sustain themselves. A different kind of effort was undertaken by a few young immigrant professionals who started the monthly magazine *Little India*, aimed at the tristate area. Instead of subscriptions, *Little India* was supported by advertisements and was available free at businesses and houses of worship. Each issue of *Little India* carried well-researched feature stories on three or four topics. Politically, *Little India* was a progressive entry into the Indian ethnic media, with its reporters drawing attention to immigration politics, lower-class immigrants as well as successful entrepreneurs, the younger generation, and women. In 1995 and 1997 *Little India* held conferences to discuss Indian immigrant issues, with younger-generation Indians prominent at both. In the late 1990s, *Little India* started an Internet version of its magazine. A more recent addition to the Indian press was a weekly, *India in New York*, started in 1997 as an offshoot of *India Abroad* and devoted to analyses and reporting of events in New York in the broader context of the city and other ethnic groups. In the mid-1990s South Asian writers also formed the South Asian Journalists Association, which brought together journalists in both the ethnic and mainstream media.

Arts and Entertainment

In the 1990s public performances of music, dance, and theater were a prominent part of the booming Indian cultural life in New York. Thousands of Indians traveled each weekend to attend events ranging from the classical arts to popular entertainment, in settings ranging from formal concerts before thousands to informal social gatherings of a few score. Most of these cultural activities were held in Queens, particularly the smaller, less formal events, which have been of increasing incidence in that borough since the 1970s.

In efforts to bring what they saw as the best of Indian culture to the United States, some upper-class Indian immigrants in the 1960s had presented classical music and dance concerts in Manhattan. These events found enthusiastic support from American admirers of Indian culture, who often provided the resources for organizing the performances. In that decade, select Indian films, including those of world-renowned director Satyajit Ray, were also shown at international film festivals. Concerts by classical artists such as Pandit Ravi Shankar were held in prestigious venues like Lincoln Center and Carnegie Hall. Indian immigrants, then relatively few in number, were gratified to see Americans appreciating their culture. Compared to these presentations of its "national" culture, India's various religious, regional, and popular arts were not yet visible in New York City.

In the 1960s Indian artistic performers rarely included any who had actually immigrated to the United States, and the noted Indian maestros traveled back and forth between the two countries. In the United States, several performers of Indian classical arts were in fact Americans, some of whom had studied in India. They were accepted by Indian immigrants at that time as skilled and capable representatives of India's arts. This pattern was eventually challenged by performers from within the growing Indian immigrant population, however. One white American woman who was trained in the classical Indian dance form *Bharatnatyam* described this reversal.

> I had spent many years in South India learning the intricacies of the dance. I would come back to New York and perform Bharatnatyam for Americans and Indians. Over the years I got to know many Indian immigrant families, and they loved to see my performances. I could explain for them many parts of the dance that they did not know, and I could learn a lot of things like Indian cook-

ing or Indian-language words from them. There was so much sharing. They admired the fact that even though I was American I had adopted their culture. But then, almost suddenly around the mid-1970s, things began to change with this new population in Queens. Now there were so many Indians, and many artists among them, that they had no patience for me. Besides, organizers of cultural events in Manhattan now had Indian artists to perform Indian arts. Why would they hire me, an American, for those performances? My public performances of Indian dance have declined ever since. There is nothing much left in that part of my life, except for a strong interest in Indian culture, which I try to sustain by visiting Indian restaurants and Indian concerts in Manhattan. Queens, the center of Indians, is too far and alien to me.

In Queens, the new immigrant population included artists who devoted part- or full-time attention to Indian performance arts. Although performers from India continued to visit New York, local artists had new opportunities to practice their talents. The growing number of Indian regional organizations and religious institutions sponsored cultural performances at their events. In addition, many Indian parents wanted their children to receive training in these arts. Besides performing, a number of immigrant artists, particularly women, turned to teaching. In the 1980s, among others, Rachna Sarang, of the well-known Sarang Sisters duo, gave classes in the *Kathak* classical dance tradition at the Flushing Hindu temple. And Indian music and dance classes were taught at Shikshayatan, a school in Flushing headed by another Indian woman, Purnima Desai. These teacher-artists prepared their students to perform at events sponsored by Indian organizations, where, as a rule, one or two cultural pieces were included in programs. In addition, the schools themselves organized student concerts. From the 1970s through the 1990s both kinds of cultural performances occurred with increasing frequency.

In December 1990 Shikshayatan presented a day-long cultural program on a Sunday in a school auditorium in Richmond Hill. The event comprised a series of performances by students and speeches by invited guests. The schedule was clearly the result of the past year's work by the young Indian performers, and also reflected director Desai's support from Indian religious leaders, "dignitaries" from India, scholars, educators, community leaders, musicians, and artists. Two local white American elected officials also spoke. The souvenir journal for the program featured stories about Indian religious and cultural leaders, India's national heritage, and poems in Hindi.

Many Indian immigrant parents drove to the Queens core areas to drop off and pick up their children at cultural classes. Some parents, particularly those with strong personal interests in performance arts, may have had detailed knowledge of the content of the training received by their children. Most Indian parents, however, were content that their children received some kind of Indian cultural training. As one parent stated, "They teach our children about Indian culture, and keep them protected from bad influences of American life." Another, who lived in Westchester County, explained, "These facilities are not available where I live, so I drive every weekend into Flushing, where my daughter takes dance classes. It is no inconvenience to me. While she is in her class, I visit the temple and also pick up groceries from the Indian store. My wife and I are happy that she is learning about our culture. She will not take dancing as her career, but this is the best side activity for her because it keeps her busy and also teaches her about Indian culture at the same time."

The teacher-artists maintained their own circles of contact with other artists and cultural organizations. After its founding in 1981, the New York branch of Bharatiya Vidya Bhavan (Institute of Indian Culture), an organization that in India had championed a nationalist Indian culture for many decades, became key to New York's Indian cultural activities. Under its executive director, Dr. P. Jayaraman, widely respected by Indian community leaders, the Bhavan presented a yearly series of concerts and cultural performances by leading artists from India, as well as by local Indian and American performers. These programs, not exclusively classical, included Hindu devotional music, folk dance, and *qawwalis*, an Islamic Sufi song form. Bhavan programs were held in Manhattan in locations such as Lincoln Center and Town Hall, and attracted a middle- and upper-class Indian audience from all over the New York area; sponsors included Air India, local branches of the State Bank of India and Bank of India, and affluent businessmen. In the 1980s the Bhavan first operated in rented quarters in Woodside, Queens, but in the early 1990s it moved to a permanent space in Manhattan.

Despite such links between cultural activities in Manhattan and Queens, most Queens cultural activities were more informal, popular, and integral to Indian social life in the borough. Queens talents were displayed at religious and regional gatherings or on cable television programs. Aimed primarily at local audiences, these activities were publicized through ethnic media or flyers at houses of worship and 74th Street stores. The venues were rented school auditoriums or large tents in public parks. One typical smaller-size event was the Sur Sangam (Music Confluence), an informal group of Indian families who met every month to sing popular Indian music in members' homes, and in rented spaces for occasional special programs. Indian music and dance by professional and amateur performers were also common at wedding and birthday parties.

An overseas version of *bhangra*, a leading youth entertainment, was popularized primarily by South Asians in London, and melded Punjabi vocal music with Jamaican reggae and African American hip-hop. Radiating outward from England, bhangra dance and music reached the United States and Canada in the early 1990s, when many younger South Asians adopted it as a cultural expression of their ethnic identity (Gopinath 1995). Most did not understand the Punjabi lyrics, but they danced to rhythms of wide appeal. In the 1990s young Indian American disc jockeys played this music at Indian social gatherings in New York City (Farber 1997). A few even became well-enough known in this emerging cultural market to extend their activities beyond New York. Beginning with "bhangra party" contracts with nightclubs in Manhattan, they traveled to perform at South Asian events and parties in different parts of the United States. And through contacts in London, Toronto, New Delhi, and Bombay, some made reputations in the international recording business (Gehr 1993; Khurana and Gill-Murgai 1997).

As a dance/music form that crossed ethnic and even racial boundaries (non-Indians also attended), bhangra rapidly became the dominant cultural activity of young South Asian New Yorkers in the 1990s. Pan-Asian and American multicultural events began to incorporate it as the leading South Asian popular entertainment form. Bhangra's arrival in New York was confirmed when it was included in a Central Park Summer Stage concert in Manhattan in 1995. There the audience was an ethnic and racial mix, if dominated by young South Asians.

The leading popular entertainment form in India is movies, which pervade everyday life, politics, and music (Dickey 1993). Movies were also an important part of Indian cultural life in New York, although their role here grew and changed with the evolving immigrant (and technological) context. Only a few Indian films managed to reach New York audiences in the 1960s, but during the 1970s Indian distributors regularly started bringing Indian films for screenings at a theater in Manhattan. This trend ceased abruptly with the availability of films on videocassette in the 1980s. Now families could watch Indian movies on VCRs without going to a theater. At the same time the video invasion was also sweeping India, where popular movie stars beseeched the public to return to movie theaters and save India's film industry.

In New York, Indian stores stocked hundreds of films on videocassette and replenished them frequently with new releases. It became common for Indian immigrants to rent several videos on each visit to the grocery store. Unlike in India, however, where new movies are advertised on large street posters, in press reviews, and with film music recordings, in New York, Indians had little information about new movies. In Queens, store employees provided advice to customers making video rental selections. They called attention to star actors and star directors and explained, "This is good for viewing with the family," implying no explicit sexual scenes; "This has popular songs like . . ."; or "This is the best film of this actor so far." Such recommendations, bypassing published film reviews, generated an ongoing local word-of-mouth evaluation process in Queens. Video rentals were dominated by Bombay (or Bollywood) films in Hindi, but regional Indian films in Tamil, Telugu, Kannada, Malayalam, Bengali, Punjabi, and Gujarati were also available.

Bollywood's popular products are very different from the Indian "new wave" or "parallel cinema" art films of world-acclaimed filmmakers such as Satyajit Ray, M. S. Sathyu, and Mani Kaul, which flourished in the 1960s and 1970s. Such sophisticated and realistic films continue to reach other countries through international film festivals. Though appreciated by intellectuals in India and America, they have little appeal for the popular film market either in India or in New York, where they were screened in Manhattan art theaters but were unheard of in Queens video rental stores. When one Indian immigrant walked into an Indian grocery store and asked for a film that had received international awards, which he had read about in magazines, the owner, who had never heard of it, commented, "You should check the foreign film sections in American video stores for it. If it is so well known, then they must be carrying it. We don't have any market for it here."

In the 1990s, with a booming immigrant market, screenings of Indian movies in theaters returned to New York, but in Fresh Meadows in Queens, and Hicksville and Hempstead in Long Island, not in Manhattan. Several existing American theaters were bought by Indians or other South Asians who used them to show Indian movies. Though these theaters were reachable only by automobile, thousands of Indian, Pakistani, Bangladeshi, and Indo-Caribbean viewers arrived on weekends to watch the most recent blockbusters from Bombay. The atmosphere inside resembled that of theaters in India: the audiences, mixed in age and background, spontaneously burst into singing when popular songs were sung on screen and indulged in loud comments or whistling. In the lobbies, Indian samosas were sold along with popcorn. These theaters were also used for satellite telecasts of cricket matches, especially those between India and Pakistan.[1]

The newest movie venue was the Eagle Theater, on 74th Street in Jackson Heights, which opened in the mid-1990s. The Pakistani owner purchased and converted a deteriorated American pornographic movie house shut down for several years. Some local white residents objected. At a meeting at the Community Board office, one said, "They did not pay attention to my suggestion that some American movies should also be shown in this theater. Why should only Indian movies be shown in this American neighborhood?" An irate Indian merchant responded:

This is a useless debate. Sometime it is traffic problems, other times it is the curry smell from the Indian restaurants, and now it is the Indian movies shown in an Indian theater. Can I similarly ask why don't the local American theaters show Indian films? They never will, so we have to create our own theaters. And nobody appreciates the fact that a porno movie theater has been converted into one where families can watch films together. All that people talk about is a different culture because it threatens their own. Yes, movies are part of our culture, and we want to watch them in our own neighborhood with our own people.

The influence of Indian popular films was evident in various aspects of immigrant life. ITV cable television showed several Indian films each day and also featured song-videos from Indian films. Since every Bombay film uses at least five or six songs (sung by professional "playback" singers to whose vocals movie actors lip-synch), and because the success of a movie depends on the popularity of its music, videos of these songs were also for sale in Queens, as were audiocassettes. In the late 1980s CDs with improved sound quality offered still more choices for Indian film-music lovers, and DVDs made their entry in the 1990s. Cassettes and CDs of classical Indian music, *bhajans* (devotional songs), *ghazals* (Urdu poetry set to music), and bhangra (together called "non-filmi" or "private" music) were also available. Mass-produced in India, Singapore, Hong Kong, and Dubai, they were sold at far lower prices than U.S.-recorded music.

In 1989 two Indo-Guyanese immigrants started a radio station, RBC, to play Indian film music on a twenty-four-hour schedule. Interspersing music with trivia about the Indian movie world and music industry, live call-in programs and quizzes, and guest astrologers and immigration lawyers, RBC became popular among connoisseurs of this music. Programs featured top-ten countdowns of Indian film-music hits, requests with messages for friends and relatives, and live singing by listeners. RBC was broadcast from the Empire State Building in Manhattan—a fact repeated frequently throughout the day—but listeners who mentioned where they lived were usually from Queens or New Jersey (*India Abroad* 8/4/95). A typical call was from a cabdriver who said that RBC was his best companion while driving; the on-air host thanked him and appealed to all New York City cabdrivers (many of whom are South Asians) to listen to RBC. Commercials were generally for immigrant-owned businesses in Queens.

The most spectacular impact of the Indian movie scene on New York's South Asian community was experienced in the well-attended concerts featuring Bombay film stars and musical personalities, which were held during the 1980s in Madison Square Garden in Manhattan. In the next decade these shows moved to larger venues, beginning in 1990 with a concert featuring Indian movie star Amitabh Bachchan, held in the Giants Stadium in New Jersey. Although Bachchan had appeared before in New York, the organizers took the risk of filling a 50,000-seat stadium with his fans, despite the disappointing box-office performance of his recent movies. As one organizer stated, "At a recent charity premiere of *Agnipath* [a film] in Poona [in India], I was amazed to see 40,000 people wait for seven or eight hours to get a glimpse of the actor. . . . This will be the first major overseas Indian concert to be held in a stadium. Even though London has a bigger population from the Indian subcontinent than New York, they are yet to hold a concert in a stadium" (*India Abroad* 5/4/90). Full-page advertisements in Indian newspapers hailed a "Once-in-a-Life-Time Event!" with Amitabh, "the King," and a poster announced: "For the Benefit of AMITABH's Fans in Far Distance Places—We Bring LIVE SATELLITE BROADCAST on Large Movie Screen in the Following Cities: Atlanta, Chicago, Detroit, Dallas, Edmonton, Houston, Los Angeles, Miami, Montreal, San Francisco, Toronto, Vancouver." Not only did Amitabh's magic in songs and dialogues from his movies fill the stadium, but it began a new reign of "megashow" concerts in stadiums in which a host of Indian film stars performed for thousands.

In the 1990s, megashows featuring an array of male and female movie stars accompanied by popular singers were held every year. The Nassau Coliseum on Long Island, with a capacity of 18,000, became a favored location. In 1991 brothers Arun and Amit Govil presented the female movie star Rekha, billed as "the mysterious queen of the silver screen," and in 1993 two male actors, Aamir Khan and Salmaan Khan, appeared with three actresses and a host of musicians, in "Khan vs. Khan." Like Indian movies, these shows included songs, dances, and frequent changes of costume, some of which fans remembered from the stars' movies. The audiences included thousands of young South Asians, many of whom did not understand the songs or movie dialogues fully, but who shrieked and danced at the appearance of the stars.

Although movies are enormously popular in India, such megashows are not held there. Among Indian immigrants in New York, however, as with other overseas Indians in the United States and elsewhere, these concerts were enormously popular. Promoters catered to this audience with bigger shows every year (Sengupta 1995). Unlike classical Indian music and dance, which continued to draw a mix of Americans and Indians, the movie concerts were an overwhelmingly South Asian experience. Somini Sengupta (1994) noted at a 1994 concert held at the Nassau Coliseum, "The crowd here tonight . . . is not the multiracial mix of high culture connoisseurs who usually turn up at Indian classical music concerts and art exhibits. This is an almost exclusively South Asian audience letting loose among their own— singing along with their favorite songs and dancing in the aisles." Sophisticated Indians were conspicuous by their absence. As the *New Yorker* magazine (6/23/97, 48) put it,

> there are those who find the whole film-stage-show genre rather embarrassing. Upper-crust Indians despise it in the way Western highbrows despise Las Vegas kitsch. Only last week, at the Asia Society, the New Delhi fashion designer Rohit Bal said, "Indian movies are a completely warped, disgusting, vulgar part of the Indian sensibility." But any foreigner watching the Megastars is struck by how well Indian popular culture has resisted American influence when almost everywhere else in Asia Hollywood movies have won huge audiences.

If Bollywood's movie culture appealed to the popular South Asian taste in Queens and India's sophisticated art films did not, neither did the English-language literature created by elite Indian immigrants in the United States. Following the success of Bharati Mukherjee's short stories and novels, the 1990s witnessed an upsurge of such writers in the literary world, with Shashi Tharoor, Meena Alexander, Chitra Bannerjee Divakaruni, and Amitav Ghosh all drawing acclaim from highly educated Indians and Americans alike. These authors joined a similar growing number of Indian English-language writers in India and England, such as Salman Rushdie, Vikram Seth, and Arundhati Roy. However, their work hardly reached the middle and working classes of Indian immigrants in New York City.

A different pattern existed in Indian theater in New York. Not as popular as films, performances were limited, but frequently were in regional languages such as Bengali, Gujarati, or Marathi, which have a long theatrical tradition in India. These performances were sponsored by organizations with regional memberships, and announcements in Indian newspapers were published in both English and the regional languages. In comparison, Hindi theater was an infrequent event, with the rare performance boosted by popular movie actors like Shabana Azmi, Farooque Sheikh, Anupam Kher, or Naseeruddin Shah, who maintained a fondness for the stage.

Festivals and Celebrations

By the 1990s Indian cultural festivals in New York City filled an annual calendar of ever-increasing events. Some large festivals were organized by upper-class, first-wave immigrants to present national Indian culture to a diverse American public. Other events were expressions of more particularistic facets of Indian culture, meant primarily for Indian immigrants themselves or for segments of this population.

The celebration of national Indian culture in New York was characterized by an emergent prominence of Hinduism, India's majority religion, as a symbolic umbrella for Indian immigrants.[2] Although the organizers of large Indian festivals invariably promoted them as celebrations of pan-Indian and national culture, their Hindu religious tone was not far from the surface. An illustration of this phenomenon is the observation of Diwali, a Hindu festival, which has became widely acknowledged as *the* Indian festival in New York and the rest of the United States, and as an equivalent to holidays celebrated by other American ethnic groups.

Diwali, also called Deepawali, and meaning "a Row of Lamps," is a major Hindu festival celebrated in the fall according to the lunar calendar. Over centuries, legends and myths have been attached to this festival, among them the story of the residents of Ayodhya, in North India, greeting the return of their king, the Hindu deity Rama, after fourteen years of exile by lighting lamps and decorating their city with lights. Diwali also celebrates Laxmi, the goddess of wealth and abundance, whose blessings are sought for prosperity and happiness. In addition to the observation of rituals inside homes, buildings in India are decorated with lights on the evening of Diwali, children light fireworks, and gifts and sweets are exchanged with relatives and friends. Despite wide observance in India, Diwali is not celebrated equally by all Hindus in all regions and communities, and it is definitely not celebrated by non-Hindus. In the United States, however, it has become an ethnic festival for all Indians, regardless of religion or region; and other festivals have taken a secondary position, including the equally large and colorful Hindu festival of Holi, celebrated at the beginning of spring in India.[3]

Diwali's prominence, amidst a growing number of more particularistic Indian festivals in New York, points to the reification and packaging of culture in the process of ethnic group formation (Kapferer 1988; Vertovec 1995). In the United States, Indians keep the body of myths about Diwali for their own consumption and offer simple, often one-line answers to satisfy the curiosity of Americans, or even of their own children growing up in the United States: "It is the biggest Indian festival"; "It is the festival of lights since we decorate our houses and buildings with lights"; or, as one immigrant even stated, "It is like our Christmas." It is only in the immigrant context that such redefinitions are created and gain currency via acceptance by Americans and immigrants alike.

In this scramble for answers easily grasped by others, Diwali has come to be widely known as "the Indian New Year," the version of Diwali most prevalent among some Gujaratis and commercial castes in India. It is indeed the case that business communities in northern and western parts of India treat Diwali as the beginning of their business calendar, starting new account books, and beseeching the goddess Laxmi for success in the coming year. This fact is unknown to many other Hindus, however, and holds no such place in their festival calendar. In the United States, other Indian regional or caste communities have their own traditional "New Year," which they celebrate in regional associations or temples, and not in pan-Indian activities. However, as the identification of Diwali as the Indian New Year has gained ascendancy, Indians are often asked by Americans, "You celebrate your New Year on Diwali, don't you?"

In New York City, Diwali was in fact celebrated by Indians in many ways, from domestic rituals to large public cultural events. The most private were religious observances at home by families, and the most public, fairs attended by Indians from diverse backgrounds, along with sizable numbers of Americans. A common question among Hindu immigrant families became "What are you doing for Diwali?" Since Diwali was not a national holiday for all as it is in India, immigrants had to abbreviate Diwali celebrations drastically, especially if the actual date fell during the week. Immigrants also complained that in New York the fall weather was too cold for outdoor activities. Moreover, as they never failed to point out, "We are not allowed by the city laws to light lamps or candles all over the house, since it may cause fire." Within such limitations, more traditional immigrants performed *puja* (act of worship) for the goddess Laxmi at home, dressed in traditional costume, and prepared a special family meal. Almost all Hindus, including those who performed puja at home, also visited temples; in Queens most temples had special programs on the evening of Diwali.

Beyond religious observances, celebrations of Diwali occurred at dinners and parties organized in homes on the nearest weekend to Diwali. In the early 1990s an Indian promoter in New York even organized an overnight cruise so that affluent Indians could celebrate Diwali by dining and dancing on a ship that circled Manhattan. South Asian groceries and other businesses announced Diwali sales, and immigrants purchased boxes of sweets for friends or for offerings at home or temple ceremonies. Clubs and organizations of Indian/South Asian students in New York held annual parties around the time of Diwali, an opportunity to feature Indian music, food, dance, and fashion shows on their campuses. Diwali was also an occasion for gambling in some communities in India, and in New York this phenomenon translated into card games at home parties. In an interesting twist, one Atlantic City casino featured a "Diwali Festival—India's Festival of Lights" to which the public was invited: "Experience the intrigue of India at our two-day celebration of the Festival of Lights! Discover the customs and culture of the Crown Jewel of Asia with continuous entertainment featuring traditional singers and dancers, plus authentically prepared Indian cuisine, clothing and crafts!" (*India Abroad*, 10/21/94).

A Diwali celebration unique to Queens was the street procession staged

[61]

for the first time in 1994 by Hindu Indo-Guyanese immigrants in Richmond Hill. A motorcade of floats was accompanied by loud devotional music and Guyanese Arya Samaj leaders shouting "Laxmi Mata Ki Jai!" (Hail Mother Laxmi!), "Guyana Ki Jai!" (Hail Motherland Guyana!), and "New York Ki Jai!" (Hail New York City!). Organized by the Guyanese Arya Samaj, and with speeches by religious and civic leaders, the celebration honored deities traditionally associated with Diwali, such as Laxmi, as well as Swami Dayanand Saraswati, who founded the Arya Samaj reformist movement in nineteenth-century India (compare Vertovec 1995). Onlookers included a large number of Guyanese immigrants who were not members of Arya Samaj and did not know beforehand about the parade, and also immigrants from India for whom this Guyanese Diwali parade was an unexpected event.

The large annual Diwali fair at the South Street Seaport in Lower Manhattan was begun in the 1990s by the New York chapter of the national Association of Indians in America (AIA). This outdoor event quickly became the leading Indian cultural event in New York and the principal Indian entry on the city's multicultural calendar. By the mid-1990s it included a central stage featuring cultural programs and speeches by the mayor, the Indian ambassador to the United States, the Indian consul general, and top AIA leaders; stalls for Indian businesses and organizations; and fireworks by the American company Grucci. This Diwali fair exemplifies well how the New York immigrant context had shaped cultural life for Indians. It was scheduled on a weekend, usually a few weeks before the actual date of Diwali, to avoid the cold fall weather. Speeches by American and Indian dignitaries stressed cordial relations between the two countries, with AIA mediating this international exchange. The program of Indian dance and music and the display of Indian traditional arts and crafts had established AIA as the arbiter of what was considered Indian culture in America.

For the many Indian immigrants who attended, the event instilled cultural pride and served in an official sense to represent their culture to other Americans. They appreciated the high quality of its Indian cultural presentations, and its popularity grew each year. Not only large numbers of Indian immigrants but an increasing number of younger-generation South Asians saw it as their own major ethnic event. In addition to requests for display-area space from businesses and established groups, progressive South Asian organizations also applied. However, in the early 1990s, when Sakhi for South Asian Women, a group providing assistance to battered women, asked for space to display its materials, AIA turned it down. AIA's version of the Indian experience was the celebration of national culture, and not the social problems of an immigrant community or self-help agencies formed to highlight them. One Sakhi leader protested that AIA upheld a conservative view of Indian culture by presenting a Hindu wedding ceremony, thus reinforcing traditional gender roles (Bhattacharjee 1992, 1997b).

Since its founding in the late 1960s, AIA had considered itself a pan-Indian organization, but an emphasis on Hinduism, and not on the diversity of Indian culture, was apparent at its Diwali fair. Progressive South Asians had also opposed this religious focus. However, it is not clear that in celebrating Diwali AIA leaders were consciously promoting a sectarian view of Indian culture. Still, in so defining Indian culture through a public festival of Hindu origin, the AIA excluded other Indian traditions. The linkage of Indian culture with Hinduism became even stronger in the mid-1990s when AIA sponsored a Goddess Festival at the American Museum of Natural History in conjunction with Diwali. This event comprised talks on India and Indian immigrants, arts and crafts displays by artists from India, and Indian folk performances. Although promoting Hinduism was not its purpose, by calling it the Goddess Festival, and scheduling it to coincide with the Hindu Navaratri festival, the "nine nights of the Goddess" that precedes Diwali, AIA organizers again gave Indian culture a religious definition. The objections from progressive South Asians to its sectarian focus were not to Hindu ceremonies, which occurred without controversy in other parts of the city, but to the fact that AIA presented them to a mainstream New York audience as "Indian" cultural activities.

Other Hindu festivals organized for Indians made fall a busy season in New York City. By 1994 every weekend from late September to early November featured multiple cultural activities (Chatterjee and Khandelwal 1995). In that year a new event was added, Dussehra, or Vijaya Dashami, which in the Hindu lunar calendar precedes Diwali by twenty days. In North India, Dussehra is celebrated as the culmination of weeklong enactments of the Hindu deity Ram's victory over the demon king Ravana; to celebrate this mythical event, huge effigies of Ravana and his fellow demons are burnt. Thus, when an Indian charitable organization, AWB Food Bank, decided to stage a large Dussehra fair in the New York area, it invoked the popular theater tradition associated with Dussehra. The fair was held on Columbus Day at Nassau Beach Park on Long Island and featured food stalls, a ferris wheel and other rides for children, and a cultural program on a central stage. "For the first time in the United States," the organizers claimed, fifty-foot effigies of three demon kings appeared and were lighted on fire amidst cheers. Thousands of families of mainly lower-middle- and working-class Indians attended, most of them from Queens and Long Island. No elite American or Indian dignitaries were present, and no speeches made extolling the relationship between the two countries.

In 1994, on the same weekend as Dussehra, the Bengali community of New York celebrated its annual Durga Puja festival in honor of the Hindu goddess Durga. In Queens by the mid-1990s several Bengali groups were holding their own Durga Pujas. The largest was organized by the East Coast Durga Puja Association, which booked three days at the Gujarati Samaj Community Center in Flushing. Attended only by the Bengali community, this was a quieter, less public event than the AIA's Diwali or the beachside Dussehra.

Also in fall 1994, Indians from the state of Gujarat celebrated Navaratri, the nine nights of the Goddess, with *raas-garba* (traditional folkdance) events in which both men and women participated. While the raas-garba in Edison, New Jersey, held over several weekends, was the biggest one in the New York metropolitan area, smaller raas-garbas were organized by Gujarati organizations in Queens as they had been for many years. Although this was originally only a Gujarati activity, other Indians also joined the dancing. In October 1994 a widely publicized raas-garba program was held in a tent in Flushing Meadows–Corona Park in Queens, and deliberately attempted to be more than a Gujarati festival. Its flyer announced: "First time ever in a giant tent—Raas-Garba—in Queens, New York," and included pictures of Indian film stars with an invitation to "play Dandiya-Raas with your favorite movie stars." Raas-garba dancing had by now become popular with young South Asians of various regional and religious backgrounds who gathered to perform at this and other Indian cultural events.

Queens also featured a busy round-the-year calendar of festivals of other religions. Muslims from India joined coreligionists from other national backgrounds in observing Ramadan and the festival of Id. Sikh festivals were usually observed in local gurdwaras. Apart from celebrations of major festivals of each religion, a host of smaller ones were announced on ethnic television programs. None of these celebrations assumed the stature of Diwali, and they remained confined to limited populations of Indians. In many instances, however, non-Hindu Indians joined public observation of large Indian festivals such as Diwali.

Festivals for Punjabi immigrants (of various religions) were advertised in Indian ethnic media in the Punjabi language and featured less-syncretized Punjabi folk cultural activities. In the mid-1990s a daylong Punjabi Khed Mela, or Punjabi Sports Fair, focused on teams from New York and other overseas Punjabi communities, but also featured Punjabi folk singers and dancers, as well as movie and television personalities flown to New York from India.

In the late 1980s Guyanese and Trinidadian immigrants of Indian origin began organizing cultural events in Queens featuring Indo-Caribbean music and dance performers, along with actors and musicians from Bombay's film industry. These were usually not the top stars, but rather performers who had become popular in Guyana and Trinidad as a result of appearances there. In 1988 an East Indian Diaspora Steering Committee, established to commemorate migration to the Caribbean, celebrated "East Indians in the Diaspora, 1838–1988" with a "Film Star Nite" at Colden Center for the Performing Arts at Queens College in Flushing. Programs by Guyanese organizations were also aired regularly on ITV, and the husband-wife team of Dheeraj Guyaram, a Guyanese, and Bindu Kohli, from India, presented cultural performances in various Queens locations which attempted to build a bridge between the two immigrant communities.

Indian diaspora beauty pageants brought young Indian women from all over the United States and other countries to competitions in New York. By the 1980s several states were holding their own contests, and winners then competed for the title of Miss India America (Friedman and Grinsberg 1997). At the 1988 event, held at the Sheraton Hotel in midtown Manhattan, movie stars from Bombay were a major attraction, and a poster read: "Don't Miss The Glitter, Glamour And Top Movie Stars Along With The Most Beautiful Indian Girls From All Across North America." Sponsors of the event were Indian businesses in New York, and tickets were available at Indian stores in New York and New Jersey. In 1990 an India Festival Committee was formed to hold "The First Ever Miss India-Universe Pageant" at the Marriott Marquis hotel in Manhattan. The event's brochure featured pictures of participants from Canada, Fiji, Germany, Guyana, India, Israel, Jamaica, Kenya, Singapore, Surinam, Sweden, Trinidad and Tobago, the United Kingdom, and the United States. Included with a short biography of guest of honor Padmini Kolhapure, a female movie star, was a message from New York's Mayor David Dinkins: "Through tonight's beauty pageant, you enhance the quality of life in the Indian community and contribute greatly to making New York City a 'gorgeous mosaic.'"

Many layers of Indian culture thus flourished in New York City. In Manhattan, a continuation of national Indian culture was maintained from the 1960s through the 1990s by upper-class Indian immigrants. With their resources and contacts within established American circles they presented one image of Indian culture to multicultural New York. Manhattan was also the backdrop to a "new Indo-chic" (Sengupta 1997) characterized by burgeoning Indian classical music concerts, English-language literature by Indian writers (with laudatory *New York Times* reviews), and midtown Indian white-tablecloth restaurants.

In Queens, the explicitly regional and religious cultural activities for Indian audiences were closer to the popular culture of India itself. Here activities were organized by and for Indians, either with pan-Indian appeal or for particular segments. Indian movies, especially those from Bombay, were the major element in this emergent Indian American popular culture, which transcended religious, regional, international, and generational boundaries. The power of this movie culture in the Indian immigrant community may be appreciated by the selection of film star Amitabh Bachchan as the chief guest of honor for New York's 1997 India Day Parade in Manhattan, which celebrated the fiftieth anniversary of India's independence. If Indian New York had made the move from that borough to Queens by the 1970s, some two decades later, it was Queens that now influenced such major events in Manhattan.

[3]

Worship and Community

Religion plays an important role in most immigrant communities (Chen 1992; Park 1997; Ricourt and Danta 2002). While some immigrants adopt new religions or denominations, for others, like Indian immigrants, religious continuity prevails (Fenton 1988, 1995; Williams 1988, 1996).

The religious landscape of India is characterized by a Hindu majority (82.6 percent of the population in 1980) and smaller populations of Muslims (11.3 percent), Christians (2.4 percent), Sikhs (1.9 percent), Jains, Jews, and Parsis (or Zoroastrians) (all less than 1 percent). This religious diversity also includes many denominations, sects, and philosophical schools under these larger faiths (Chopra 1982; Davis 1995). The relationship between these religious communities, both at home and in the United States, must be contextualized within South Asia's sociopolitical history. To most Indians, underlying their own religion's continuing salience is the past and present reality of "communalism," or separatist tendencies and even conflict between religious communities. Acknowledging their religious diversity, few Indians subscribe to the Western or American separation of the religious and secular worlds. Although secularism in India is under intense pressure from rising communal forces that have influenced recent political developments, historically Indian secularism has stood for tolerance and respect for all flourishing religions, rather than a pushing aside of religion from everyday temporal life (Baird 1978; Das 1990; Mohan 1990; India International Centre Quarterly 1995).

In the United States, Indian immigrants have displayed little questioning of their faiths. Unlike in other immigrant groups, conversion to different religions is all but absent (Danta 1989; Park 1989), and energies are focused

[67]

on transplanting their religions to new settings (Fenton 1988; Williams 1988, 1992). The different conditions of daily life, however, produce shifts in practice, with their patterns varying among the different religious communities. Moreover, Hinduism, the majority religion at home in India, faces the challenge of being a minority religion in a predominantly Christian country; and Islam, a minority religion in India, is fortified by the large number of believers from many other nations living in the United States.

The growth of New York's Indian population from the 1960s through the 1990s included representation from the entire diversity of its religious traditions. In Queens there was a greater range of houses of worship than in suburban areas or in most other U.S. cities, where the Indian population was sparser. Even after years of fundraising these other locations had at best one Hindu temple that tried to embrace the maximal number of Hindus in a far-flung area (Narayanan 1992). Most such temple-building in the United States also produced tension among different groups of Hindus over the selection of deities from their pantheons. In suburban areas, visiting a Hindu temple normally required driving, and these houses of worship accordingly experienced most activity on weekends. Since the number of Indians of other religions was even smaller than the number of Hindus, in most suburbs or states beyond New York they were even more isolated. They had first to locate the handful of their nearest coreligionists, then link themselves to nationwide and international religious networks, and, in most instances, worship in smaller, private settings.

The first attempts to establish Hindu houses of worship in Queens featured the same struggles, but later the growth of the immigrant population permitted the building of multiple temples. The religious diversity of India also seemed to find congenial soil in Queens, where Indian Islam, Christianity, Sikhism, Jainism, Judaism, and Zoroastrianism all became established. The socioeconomic diversity of the Indian population of Queens was also reflected in the rise of popular forms of Hindu religious practice complementing more sedate temple activities.

In Queens, Indian Muslims interacted not only with South Asian Muslims from Pakistan, Bangladesh, and Afghanistan but also with Arab, Iranian, Indonesian, Malaysian, and African American followers of Islam. Similarly, Indian Christians and Jews encountered coreligionists of other nationalities. Sikhs, though originating in India, already had sizable overseas groups on the West Coast of North America and in other parts of the world. Hindus of Indian ancestry from Guyana and Trinidad interfaced with those from India in Queens, where both groups existed in substantial numbers; whereas the Indo-Caribbeans had already preserved their religious traditions in a diasporic setting for many generations, this was a new challenge for immigrants from India. The followings of Indian religions in Queens also sometimes included white Americans who had converted to or shown serious interest in Hinduism or Sikhism.

Because New York City enjoyed regular linkages to the home country, the Queens Indian population maintained intimate connections with religious resources and developments in South Asia; such items as religious statues, calendars, books, and ritual paraphernalia were readily available. The baggage of travelers arriving in New York City often included religious articles, not only for their own use but also to oblige requests from friends. Religious leaders and clergy also entered this network of overseas exchange; many arrived frequently at international airports in Queens for temporary or permanent stays in the United States. In these and other ways, South Asian religious life in New York City shared much with that in other overseas communities (Bowen 1987; Knott 1987).

Regular contacts with India also made people conscious of rising religious fundamentalism and communalism in India. Indian immigrants elsewhere in the United States often responded more fervently to these developments, but in Queens communalism as expressed in houses of worship, public meetings, or support for youth camps was more subdued. Such activities did occur in Queens, but without any unified communitywide voice or action. Queens was utilized by some groups to generate funds and political support for developments in the home country, but it did not become a primary battleground in religious politics.

To Indians, the variety of their religions nested easily within the larger multireligious diversity of Queens. Here South Asians of different religions interacted with adherents of virtually every religion in the world. The two square miles of Elmhurst-Corona, for instance, contained scores of houses of worship of many different faiths, and a number of churches had multiethnic congregations and services in different languages, with some Indians represented here as well (Chen 1989; Sanjek 1998). In Flushing, a row of old white American Christian churches, a Jewish synagogue, a Chinese Christian mission, a Korean Presbyterian church, and a Korean Buddhist center shared Bowne Street (named for a sixteenth-century Queens Quaker) with a Sikh gurdwara, a Swaminarayan Hindu temple, and a South Indian Hindu temple.

Muslims

From the 1960s onward Indians formed part of New York City's rapidly growing Muslim population, which included both immigrants and African Americans. Muslim houses of worship represented a range of founding groups, sects, and schools but also stressed the importance of pan-Islamic unity. The small Indian population of the 1960s and early 1970s had included Muslims who participated in pan-Indian activities. Like Indian immigrants of other faiths, most were highly educated persons who shared their compatriots' predominantly professional profile. The tension between national and religious identities faced by Muslims in India was not irrelevant to Muslims here, but it remained enveloped in their Indian national identification (Naim 1989). In those early years Indian secularism marked the entire young and middle-class Indian New York community.

In the following decades some Indian Muslims joined the American Federation of Muslims from India (AFMI), which championed the cause of a secular and diverse home country. AFMI provided humanitarian, economic, and technical aid to needy Muslims in India (Husain 1997). The increase in the New York Indian Muslim population in the 1980s and 1990s, however, did not bring corresponding growth in AFMI's membership. AFMI's trajectory instead paralleled other pan-Indian organizations that drew support from the educated and professional elite of early-wave Indian immigrants throughout the United States rather than from the large local New York community. AFMI's small contingent marched annually in the India Day Parade to celebrate the nation's Independence Day, but in the 1980s and 1990s pan-Indian Muslim organizations such as AFMI were eclipsed by more strictly religious organizing on the part of South Asian Muslims. A Muslim World Day Parade organized by Pakistani Muslims was held in Manhattan each year from 1986 on, but was attuned to the wider pan-Islamic community; Muslims from India, as well as Africa and even Latin America, participated (Slymovics 1995). The more secular Pakistan Independence Day Parade celebrated the nationhood of that Islamic country.

Beyond the private religious practice of *namaz* (daily prayers) and *zikr* (silent sacred chanting), communal worship is integral to Islam. Even before the appearance of Hindu temples in New York, Indian Muslims avowed their faith in existing mosques alongside coreligionists of other nationalities. In the 1970s the most evident signal of the growing South Asian Muslim population in New York was the founding of their own houses of worship. Mosques opened for both Sunnis, the majority of Muslims in South Asia, and Shias, as well as for various religious schools, or *fiqh*. In Queens, Indian Muslims shared mosques with other South Asians, particularly with Pakistanis, with whom many shared regional languages and other cultural commonalities. In the 1980s and 1990s new, predominantly Pakistani mosques evidenced that immigrant nationality's growing demographic concentration in Brooklyn, while new Bangladeshi and Afghan mosques appeared in Queens. Some mosques in the immigrant core areas opened in storefronts and residential housing, while others were new buildings of Islamic architectural design. Mosques were not only sites of worship but included *madrasas* (schools) that offered classes in Islamic learning and performed *nikah* (marriage) and *dawah* (conversion to Islam) ceremonies.

After its founding in the 1970s, the Masjid al-Falah Mosque in Corona, Queens, became a center of worship for South Asian Muslims. Situated in a commercial area peopled mainly by Latinos and diverse Asians, it was distinctive with its Islamic dome and minaret. Although Muslims of different nationalities were visible at its Friday midday service, Pakistani and Indian Sunnis were the largest bloc of worshippers. In the buildings around it were the offices of the Edhi Foundation, a charitable agency founded by a Pakistani family that helped Muslims around the world; and a halal butcher shop whose signboard read: "Islamic Zabiha Meat—The First Halal Meat Shop in America: We slaughter all our animals and chickens strictly according to Islamic sharia [law], one at a time." The owner of this store, an Indian Muslim, came to New York from Bombay in 1953. "In the 1950s we worshipped at the new Agashahi mosque in upper Manhattan, and later many more places opened in Queens. In the late 1960s I used to deliver halal meat from my house, but the demand for business was growing rapidly in the early 1970s. In 1974 I opened my first store on Woodside Avenue in Elmhurst. After working there for twelve years, I moved to a store on 102nd Street and Northern Boulevard [in North Corona] for a few years. In 1990 I moved to the present location adjacent to the mosque. This is an ideal location."

The office of the Islamic Circle of North America (ICNA), situated in Jamaica, Queens, served as the headquarters of a national religious and cultural organization. Housed in a single-family residential building, it included classrooms, a reading room, and a small mosque. Muslims of different nationalities participated in ICNA activities, although South Asian Muslims were predominant. Its director minimized such differences, emphasizing "the common fold of Islamic brotherhood." ICNA organized conferences on Islamic topics and published a national newsletter. It also voiced public concern whenever it felt that Muslims were unfairly stereotyped or scapegoated.

Organizations such as ICNA and the Islamic Center of Long Island, in Westbury, maintained links with other such Muslim groups in the United States and around the world. A recent addition to this Islamic institutional network was the Muslim Center of New York, which opened in 1996 next to the Hindu Center in Flushing and close to the concentration of South Asian businesses on Main Street. This neighborhood already contained a number of established American and immigrant temples, churches, and gurdwaras, but the center's Islamic architecture was a novel addition to the neighborhood. Muslim families from India and Pakistan, and smaller numbers from Bangladesh and Afghanistan, attended services here.

Two other Muslim houses of worship represented older currents of the South Asian global diaspora. An Indo-Guyanese mosque in Richmond Hill was located amidst the Guyanese residential and business concentration. Although the majority of Indo-Guyanese were Hindu, some had brought their Islamic and Christian faiths to New York. Located near the Shri Lakshmi Narain Mandir Hindu temple, the mosque comprised two combined single-family dwellings, and, architecturally, merged into the surrounding residential area. The majority of worshippers were Guyanese Muslims, but they were joined by immigrants from other Caribbean and South Asian countries as well as African Americans. As with other mosques, its proximity attracted followers regardless of the ethnic composition of its founders.

During the 1990s the numbers attending this mosque increased considerably. On a Friday in 1995 hundreds gathered for midday *Juma* prayers. The several halls, each overflowing, were connected to a sound system transmitting the imam's message. The gathering included about fifty women in their own separate space. After prayers the worshippers poured out of the two buildings and gathered in informal groups on the street, where they socialized while waiting for rides or beginning to walk back to homes or work. The predominant language was Guyanese-accented English, with a sprinkling of Urdu or Bangla spoken by Indians, Pakistanis, and Bangladeshis.

Although worshippers were mainly male, the imam explained, his mosque was responding to a growing number of women by providing a space for them to worship. He acknowledged cultural differences between Indians from Guyana and those from India, especially in language, but believed they could unite as fellow Muslims. He maintained contacts with Muslims around the world but also enjoyed cordial relations with local Guyanese of other faiths. As evidence of international ties, he pointed to an Arab scholar visiting New York who had joined in that Friday's service. A few minutes later a young African American man appeared at the office and requested an official conversion to Islam. He explained that he had long been interested in this religion, and because this mosque was so near his home, it was a convenient place finally to declare his new faith.

The Ismaili Nizaris, followers of Imam Aga Shah, are a distinct community within the larger Muslim world. Pointing to their long history of adapting to new situations, Williams writes, "the Nizaris have gone from Arab culture to Persian, to Indian, to East African, and now the descendants of those earlier immigrants are adapting to a new cultural setting in modern western technological societies" (1988, 192). The number of Ismailis in the United States had grown to an estimated 40,000 by the 1990s, with most coming from the Indian subcontinent. Based in traditional business occupations and with a tight-knit religious network, Ismaili immigrants were known as a prosperous group. They had little contact with other Muslims, however, and their primary reference point was the global Ismaili community.

Ismailis around the world are organized into local and national councils under their leader, the Imam Aga Shah, who issues *firmans*, or official edicts, for the worldwide Ismaili community and supervises their spiritual and material well-being. The National Council for USA is located in New York, but activities for the city's own Ismaili population are administered by the Regional Council for Northeastern USA in Rego Park, Queens; this is one of four local councils that include the Midwestern in Chicago, the Southwestern in Houston, and the Western in Los Angeles. Through a system of committees and meetings, these Ismaili councils oversee their members' spiritual practices, education, economic advancement, and health care. The council office in Queens itself contained an Ismaili mosque, or *jamat-i-khana*. The Queens Ismaili Nizari Muslims participated in Indian and South Asian activities and extended their charity to non-Ismaili groups, including the South Asian women's organization Pragati, which first received support from them in the mid-1990s.

Despite religious differences, everyday interaction between Indian Hindus and Indian and Pakistani Muslims was common in Queens neighborhoods. South Asian Muslim identity did become more distinct in the 1990s, with store signs bearing Islamic phrases or symbols and more public celebration of Muslim festivals such as Id and Ramadan, but no Muslim commercial or residential enclaves emerged in Queens. South Asian employers hired employees of different faiths, and South Asian immigrants patronized ethnic businesses owned by proprietors of religions and nationalities other than their own.

Hindu and Muslim immigrants also participated together in cultural activities. Indian movies and their Bombay stars and musicians were immensely popular among Pakistanis, and Pakistani ghazal or qawwali singers such as Ghulam Ali and Nusrat Fateh Ali Khan appealed to Indian music lovers. A Pakistani Muslim cabdriver said of his favorite music: "I recently heard music composed by Jagjit Singh [a contemporary Indian ghazal singer] for the poetry of Mirza Ghalib [a Delhi-based nineteenth-century Urdu and Persian poet]. They are his best so far. Before hearing that, I did not know that good ghazals were composed in India; I knew only of Pakistani singers. I am sure to go to Jagjit Singh's concert whenever he visits New York next!"

The celebrations of the fiftieth anniversary of the independence of both India and Pakistan in 1997 were opportunities to observe peaceful ethnic, religious, and cultural coexistence in New York. While the original events in 1947 had been marred by widespread riots following the partition of British India and the creation of the separate nation of Pakistan, and political tension between the two nations has continued, none of this was evident in New York fifty years later. In fact the organizers of both the Pakistan Day Parade and the India Day Parade, held a few days apart in August 1997, operated out of the same building in Jackson Heights, Queens (*New York Times* 8/15/97).

Christians

Although Christians are found in scattered populations all over India, their largest communities occur in South India, with the state of Kerala containing the biggest concentration. Syrian Christians there trace their origins to St. Thomas's visit to India in the first century. Other Christians along India's west coast converted after the fifteenth-century arrival of the Portuguese in India. A number of Christian Indian professionals arrived in New York City in the 1960s and 1970s, including many female nurses from Kerala who initially lived near hospitals in Queens where they worked. Eventually, when these women married or their husbands immigrated, their professional households moved outward to suburban areas, and by the 1980s sizable clusters lived in Westchester County. Another movement of Indian Christians occurred in the 1980s and 1990s, when large numbers moved from the core areas to Floral Park and Bellerose in eastern Queens.

In some instances, Indian Christians joined established white American, now multiethnic, churches. Hsiang-shui Chen (1989) described one Elmhurst Reformed church where a Tamil service was begun by a group sharing the building with Chinese- and English-language congregations. Also in Elmhurst, the One Shepherd, One Flock congregation, led by Reverend Howard, formerly a pastor in New Delhi, shared a church building with independent Korean and Spanish congregations. This North Indian congregation of fifty conducted its service in a combination of English, Hindi, and Urdu; sermons were translated into the Indian languages, and Jesus referred to by the Indian version of his name, Yeshu. Their service, conducted on Sunday afternoons, used Indian musical instruments to accompany hymns sung in Indian languages.

In eastern Queens, where sizable numbers of Keralite Indian Christians had moved by the 1990s, services were conducted in English or Malayalam, the language of the state of Kerala. A sign on one church on Hillside Avenue announced the Sunday service conducted by Reverend Subhash Cherian; other congregations shared their buildings with diverse immigrant groups, including Indo-Guyanese Christians. The Keralites were well aware of their particular locus in the spectrum of Indian diversity, and documented it in a book titled *Kerala Immigrants in America: A Sociological Study of the St. Thomas Christians* (Thomas and Thomas 1984).

The several hundred Roman Catholics from Goa, the former Portuguese colony that is now part of India, worshipped in the parish churches of Queens, where they interacted in regular social gatherings. By 1986 the Indian Catholic Association of New York had a membership of about 1,000, 400 of whom attended a mass on St. Thomas's Day led by John Cardinal O'Connor at Saint Patrick's Cathedral in Manhattan (Williams 1988). In 1992 Indian Catholics of the Syro-Malabar, Malankara, and Latin rites met for the first time at a convention in Queens to "recognize the difficulties faced by them as immigrants and work for the benefit of the community" (*India Abroad* 12/21/92).

Sikhs

Sikhs were an early, and large, component of the Indian global diaspora, and now have sizable populations in East Africa, England, and North America (Bhachu 1985; Gibson 1988; Leonard 1992). Followers of founder Guru Nanak, a fifteenth-century saint who rejected both Hinduism and Islam, and of the subsequent lineage of ten gurus, in the seventeenth century they formed a political organization, the Khalsa, to resist the Mughal ruler. By the mid-nineteenth century, when their home area of Punjab was annexed by the British, the Sikhs were known as "a martial race" and became an important component of the Anglo-Indian imperial army. As soldiers or in search of jobs they soon began to travel widely, and created migrant communities throughout India and also overseas (Mazumdar 1984).

Although Sikhs are a distinct religious community, the lines between Sikh and Hindu were blurred in Punjab until recently. A single family might have both Sikh and Hindu members, and intermarriages between Sikh and Hindu were common. Many Hindus visited Sikh gurdwaras, and some taught their children about Sikh religious practice. Following the Indian army's attack on the Sikh Golden Temple in Amritsar in 1984, differences between the two religious communities sharpened (Gibson 1988; Williams 1988). These developments affected Sikh–Hindu relations, and separatist tendencies emerged within the Sikh community, as typified in its annual Sikh World Day Parade, held since the late 1980s in New York City as well as other locations worldwide.

After informal meetings for more than a decade, a Sikh Cultural Society of New York was incorporated in 1968 (Williams 1988). In 1972 a gurdwara was established in Richmond Hill in a former Methodist church building, and it became the center of the entire East Coast Sikh community. Other gurdwaras appeared later elsewhere in Queens. Flushing had two, one on Parsons Boulevard and a smaller one on Bowne Street, where nearby Sikh residents could walk to worship at any time. Hundreds of families visited on Sundays, and attendance soared on Sikh festival days, when programs featured recitation of *gurbani*, or verses from the sacred book, the Adi Granth Sahib; devotional songs; and speeches by religious leaders. Religious services at gurdwaras always included distribution of blessed food, *kada*. (White Americans who converted to Sikhism worshipped in the Sikh Brotherhood Dharma.)

The Sikh community in Queens ranged from educated professionals to working-class immigrants. In the late 1980s and the 1990s family reunification produced growing numbers of rural and working-class arrivals, many of whom settled in Richmond Hill near the gurdwara. Unlike most earlier immigrants, this cohort found jobs in small businesses and automobile-related occupations. It included many single men who lived in conditions reminiscent of those in the early twentieth-century West Coast Sikh enclave (Jensen 1988; Leonard 1992).

In 1994 a melee at the Richmond Hill gurdwara made headlines in the ethnic Indian and mainstream newspapers. According to one report, "a dozen people were injured and five arrested after fighting broke out between two political factions at the Sikh Cultural Center and Gurdwara in Richmond Hill." The police reported the cause of the fight to be a dispute over gurdwara elections. One combatant was charged with illegal possession of a weapon, and four men, all from a single residential address in New Jersey, with disorderly conduct (*India Abroad* 7/29/94).

Many ordinary Sikhs remained unaffected by the sectarian struggles. In 1997 a middle-aged Sikh woman accompanied by her two young children inquired in Flushing about directions to several local places of worship. "We arrived from India a few months ago, and live in Elmhurst. I heard about the gurdwaras and [Hindu] temples in Flushing, and want my children to see them. . . . After all, it's the same God everywhere. It's important for these children to go to him in whichever place or form he is worshipped," she said as they embarked on their religious tour.

Jains, Jews, and Parsis

Jainism, an Indian religion tracing its roots to the sixth century B.C.E., shares many cultural similarities with Hinduism, including an emphasis on ahimsa, or nonviolence. Jains had started meeting in Manhattan family gatherings in the 1960s, but in 1981 the Jain Center of North America found permanent space in Elmhurst. Its three-story building housed a hall for worship and the organization offices. In the late 1980s up to 50 people attended weekly on Friday evenings, and about 100 came to monthly events; in all, some 400 families were affiliated with the center. Many Jains, however, also visited North Indian Hindu temples in Queens that included Jain deities in their pantheons.

Besides providing a location for prayers, the Elmhurst Jain center organized social gatherings, youth activities, and conferences in collaboration with Jain centers elsewhere in North America, including the Jain Center of Greater Boston and the Jain Society of Metropolitan Washington. A Federation of Jain Associations in North America (JAINA), founded in 1980, brought together twenty groups from all over the country in biennial conferences. Overseas Jains also maintained contact with organizations in India, particularly the Bharatiya Jain Sangathan (Indian Jain Association) in Pune, in the Indian state of Maharashtra. In response to a call for help from this Jain charitable organization in India in 1995, JAINA donated $33,000 to assist victims of an earthquake in Maharashtra (*India Abroad* 7/29/94).

Visits by Jain monks from India provided a stimulus to U.S.-based Jains. In the 1970s these visitors included Muni Chitrabhanuji, who eventually settled in the United States, and Muni Sushil Kumarji, who established Sidhachalam, an ashram, or retreat center, in the Poconos Mountains in Pennsylvania. More Jain monks continued to travel from India, and in 1994, "Two disciples of Acharya Tulsi recently concluded a 21-day training program in Preksha Dhyana for 15 people in Milwaukee, among them 10 Americans. . . . The Jain Monks, Samans Siddhaprajna and Sthitaprajna, from Ladnun, Rajasthan, are visiting the United States to experience the Western way of teaching. As guests at the Cardinal Stritch College in Milwaukee, their lectures on Preksha, a form of meditation practiced by Jains, attracted some members of the audience who expressed the desire to learn more" (*India Abroad* 10/16/94).

Several Jewish communities have long lived in India, the oldest being the Bene Israelis around Bombay and Konkan, in the Indian states of Maharashtra and Karnataka, and others around Cochin, in Kerala. During British rule, Baghdadi Jews from Iraq also settled in Calcutta and Bombay. By the 1990s some 50,000 Indian Jews had moved to Israel, and only an estimated 8,000 remained in India (*News India* 12/4/92). Indian Jewish immigrants to the United States came from all these diverse communities, and many clustered in New York, including some who remigrated from Israel. In 1987 about thirty Bene Israeli men, women, and children gathered to celebrate Hanukkah at a residence in Kew Gardens, Queens. The evening socializing over dinner was complemented by a recitation of scriptures. The cultural ambiance was Indian—the vegetarian cuisine, women in saris, and conversation in Indian English. In addition to coming together to worship several times a year, these Indian Jews kept in touch through their newsletter, *Kol Bina*. They considered themselves distinct from other Jews in the United States, but occasionally attended American synagogues.

In 1987 a leader of their community, Elijah Jhirad, was invited by an American Jewish group, the Temple B'nai Israel of Elmont, Long Island, to speak about "Jews of India." Addressing an audience of over a hundred, he described the long and peaceful history of Jews amidst the "tolerant and broadminded" conditions in India. He explained that it was important for all Jews to know about the Indian Jewish experience "of how, as a minute minority, we preserved our religious practices for centuries, and how the history of Jews has not been one of exclusion in all cases. . . . It is only after living in Israel for some years that I rediscovered my identity [as a] Jew." Afterward he joined in the Shabbat service.

Zoroastrians, or Parsis, settled in western India around Bombay in the seventh century, and have maintained their traditions of worship to the present. In New York the small Parsi population met in religious centers, or *derbe mehers,* and in social and cultural events organized by the Zoroastrian Association of Greater New York. In 1995, at a school auditorium in Westchester County, it sponsored a Parsi play that had been performed in India and England, and 500 people attended.

Hindus

Hinduism, the majority religion of India, has no single sacred text or clerical order, and many call it a culture or way of life rather than an organized religion (Davis 1995). According to historian Romila Thapar, Hinduism "is not a revealed religion but grew and evolved from a variety of cults and beliefs, of which some had their foundations in Vedic religion, and others were more popular cults which became associated with the more sophisticated religion" (1966, 132). Throughout its history, Hinduism's response to other forms of religion has been to add new layers, and the meaning of Hinduism accordingly often lies in new adherents' perceptions of it (Burghart 1987; Juergensmeyer 1991).

In New York, as elsewhere in the United States, Hindu immigrants had to renegotiate their relationship to their religion. Ardent Hindus strove to re-create their faith in authentic forms, but the impact of the new milieu could not be avoided. In India they had learned and practiced Hinduism almost by osmosis, without formal instruction. In the United States a number of immigrants now made efforts to learn more about Hinduism to answer queries from Americans and from their own children. If Hindu immigrant parents found it a challenge to transmit their religion to their children, the children, in turn, found the vast expanse of Hindu beliefs and knowledge overwhelming. While conversion to other religions was not a worry, parents did fear that their children might lose interest in their religion. The chief responsibility for religious teaching was assigned to temple priests and religious leaders who provided classes in Hindu theology and philosophy, and also Indian languages, dance, and music, all deeply embedded in Hindu tradition.

The younger generation of Indian Americans reared in the United States inevitably viewed religion differently from their parents. Its social significance was slight for them, and few considered how they might pass on Hinduism or Indian culture to their own offspring. A letter to an Indian newspaper by a young Indian American expressed their perspective:

> Building temples will not benefit my generation. The second generation doesn't really know the difference between the various temples and sects. We never grew up in India and we were never aware of the different divisions. All that we know is that we are second-generation Indian Americans and our problems are vastly different from that of our parents. . . . I would really like to know the real purpose in building temples—is it to foster religious education or is the primary reason a need to transmit Indian culture? Or are the two so intertwined that they cannot be separated? (*India Abroad* 6/2/89)

In Queens, the second generation's participation in Hindu worship was certainly less than that of their immigrant parents, but it varied considerably by family, and by adherence to particular sects or philosophies.

Starting in Flushing with the temple inaugurated on July 4, 1977, Hindu houses of worship in Queens multiplied over the next two decades. But beyond temples, visible to Indians and non-Indians alike, Hinduism was practiced in domestic forms of worship, in a variety of private religious gatherings, and in large-scale public festivals. This four-part categorization was not necessarily recognizable to believers, whose worship practices might include a blend of all four. By the late 1990s more than a dozen Hindu temples existed in Queens, but less noticeable religious gatherings, and domestic worship, as well as newly begun Hindu festivals, were also now firmly established.

Domestic Worship

Domestic worship was ordinarily practiced by Hindu immigrants regardless of any other participation in private religious gatherings, worship at temple, or festival attendance. An act of worship, or puja, might occur at a home altar as well as in a temple. The nature and location of home altars varied by family convenience and preference. Some had small sections of a living room or bedroom where deities were worshipped regularly. Altars were also found in kitchens, where they were usually tended by women who might begin their day's work with morning prayers. Regarded as one of the purest and cleanest places in a Hindu home, a kitchen was deemed a suitable place for communion with gods. Reflecting the particular family's faith, a home altar could include one or several favorite deities, as well as images of saints or religious leaders whose teachings were followed by the family. More affluent and devoted families had a separate prayer room that served as a miniature temple.

Home altars were used for both daily prayers and special observances. The prayers featured recitation of scriptures, lighting of incense or ghee (clarified butter) lamps in front of the deity, and sometimes meditation. The duration of prayers varied with individuals. For some immigrants, daily prayers were shortened after settlement in the United States; for others life abroad intensified their spiritual quest and made them more steadfast in religious practices. On religious festivals, family members might pray together. Domestic worship permits Hindus to practice their faith without travel to temples or other public locations, and is perhaps the most powerful medium for maintaining religion and culture within their own families (Williams 1988).

Private Religious Gatherings

A range of private religious gatherings—from events at a devotee's residence, to weekend programs in rented locations—was in evidence throughout Queens by the 1980s. Attendance at these events was more common among North Indians, while for South Indians temples played a more central role in religious life. Four kinds of private religious gatherings could be identified.

First were activities that occurred as the religious component in a social event at a person's house or in a rented restaurant or hall. It was common to include religious rituals in naming ceremonies for newborn children (*namkaran sanskar*), housewarmings (*greh-pravesh*), or birthday parties. These usually occurred in the early part of the event, and were followed by a meal and socializing. If a priest presided, he might recite from the scriptures, perform *havan* (a sacred fire ritual), and end with distribution of *prasad* (blessed food) to those attending. Many guests arrived during or even after the ritual, and came primarily for the social gathering.

Often followers of Hindu sects different from the host's or priest's participated, and non-Hindu Indians might also attend. In 1990, for example, the housewarming party of a Hindu couple was attended by an Indian Muslim family who were close friends, and members of this family sat through the religious ritual performed by a Hindu priest. It was also common to find Jewish or Christian white American families invited, the work colleagues of the host. Such guests were often curious about the ritual and asked questions about Hindu tradition of other guests. In some homes a priest translated Sanskrit verses into English for the benefit of those who might not know their meanings, including U.S.-reared Indian American youth.

These pragmatic expressions of Hinduism in homes might grace a social occasion with auspiciousness but blurred any line between religious practice and secular life. For example, after a religious ritual, a cake might be cut and "Happy Birthday" sung. Most such events occurred on weekends to suit American work schedules. Birthday celebrations are common in contemporary urban India also, but not so exclusively scheduled on weekends. Hindu weddings and funerals in Queens had religious ceremonies of a more familiar nature to adult immigrants. Most priests who presided over these rituals were associated with local temples, although some had their own private followers.

The second type of occasional private gathering was sponsored by a family or individual for an overtly religious purpose. In Queens by the 1980s such gatherings occurred with considerable frequency; one or another relative or member of one's devotional circle might be sponsoring such an activity each week or month. The gathering might be arranged to observe an auspicious day on the Hindu calendar or to express gratitude to God for a new job or the birth of a child. It was common also to vow that if a desired result was fulfilled, the devotee would perform a service or sponsor a religious ceremony either at his or her home or at a temple. Some gatherings were spinoffs from religious sects that met regularly in their own space or at a temple. Programs included performance of rituals, group chanting, and devotional music.

The scheduling of these gatherings depended on the gender of the host and guests. Those on weekends were attended by men and women, but weekday gatherings were mainly for Hindu homemaker women. Several gatherings of this kind took place every day in Queens but were invisible to most because of their private nature. One such weekday gathering in Queens in the early 1990s was attended by about seventy-five women; the only male present was a Hindu priest whose major occupation was to lead such ceremonies. Most women belonged to the sect of the hostess. Nearly all were North Indian, with most from Punjab. The religious ceremony took place between 11:30 A.M. and 1:00 P.M. and was followed by lunch and tea. Most women had left by 2:30 in order to arrive home in time to meet their children returning from school. All attendees were from Queens and lived within a few miles' radius. Sharing information on rides to and from the event was an important part of preparatory communications.

The third type of private gathering consisted of observances of their own religious festivals by Indian regional groups. Individuals from such groups visited existing Hindu temples for regular worship but did not have the resources to build their own temple. Most often they met as a group once or twice a year in rented school auditoriums, churches, or community centers. The celebration of Durga Puja by Bengali immigrants illustrates this type of ritual gathering (Chatterjee and Khandelwal 1995).

Durga Puja is a Hindu festival, but in the state of West Bengal, it is also celebrated by Bengali Muslims and atheist Communist Party adherents. In Queens the East Coast Durga Puja Association was created in 1990 to celebrate it each fall, and by 1994 the event had moved from a Flushing public school to the Gujarati Samaj Community Center. The weekend program combined religious ritual with cultural activities such as Bengali dance and musical performances and screening of Bengali movies. During one celebration a film on Satyajit Ray, the noted Bengali Indian filmmaker, was a popular draw. Space was available to display and sell Bengali newspapers, magazines, audiocassettes and compact discs, and imported traditional saris.

In the religious component, the core of the festival, food, hymns, and rituals were offered to the goddess Durga. This culminated in a *visarjan* ceremony, in which in India the image of the goddess was submerged in flowing water; in the United States alternative arrangements were made to represent that ritual. Bengali immigrants regarded these days as a visit of the mother goddess to Queens, and were sad at her departure. All the activities, including arrangements for goddess images to arrive from Bengal, preparing traditional food, gathering ritual paraphernalia, and outfitting the visarjan ceremony, required considerable mobilization of human and monetary resources. The association's brochure explained that in earlier years a smaller Bengali community was unable to observe the full set of ritual events. In the mid-1990s, however, trained Sanskrit scholars chanted religious texts, elderly experts advised on ritual matters, younger Indian Americans volunteered at food tables and in cultural performances, and immigrant Bengali women artists prepared decorations for the images of the goddess and painted the floor in *alpana* patterns (a form of floor-painting practiced by women in most regions of India, with varying names such as *rangoli* and *kolam*). Other Bengali groups in Queens held their own Durga Puja in other rented locations.

The fourth type of private religious gathering was organized by members of established religious sects whose headquarters were ordinarily not located in Queens. The local Queens membership held its regular activities in homes or rented locations, and such gatherings were referred to either as *satsang,* meaning "company of the truth" or "collective worshipping," or were known by the sect's name. Most satsangs in Queens were associated with larger international sects or religious orders.

In 1988, one satsang met every Sunday morning at a private home in Flushing. The space was rented by a member family who had pledged to sponsor a temple for the satsang on the premises. About fifty people attended weekly to sing religious hymns with other devotees, following the path of *bhakti,* which emphasizes devotion as the primary means of worship. Most members were North Indian, and the hymns were in Hindi. The satsang occasionally sponsored ceremonies at other devotees' homes, and periodically organized larger events in rented spaces. At one Sunday gathering, attendees were invited to a three-day religious program in Toronto, "to be attended by hundreds of devotees."

A second satsang met on Friday evenings to discuss the *Bhagavad Geeta* and other Hindu scriptures. The meetings, averaging fifteen people, rotated among members' homes. During the gathering participants took turns to read and discuss particular verses of the text, following the devotional path of *Jnan,* or knowledge. The entire event was conducted in English because the group comprised members speaking different Indian languages, and the coordinators were an Indian–white American couple.

The range of private Hindu gatherings also included events that were part of tours by preachers from India. Religious leaders such as Dada J. P. Vasvani, especially popular among Sindhis, and Sant Morari Bapu, well known in the Gujarati community, were invited by Indian immigrants to give day- or weeklong programs on Hindu scriptures. These religious leaders and their messages reached even wider Indian audiences through coverage in the ethnic mass media.

Temples

Temples are the most public expression of Hinduism in the United States, and building them has become an activity of Hindu immigrants all over the country. As soon as a sizable number of Indians gathers in an area, their Hindu segment begins to plan a temple. As a result, most Indian concentrations in the United States had at least one Hindu temple by the 1990s. The multiple temples in Queens were a sign not only of the growth and resources of its immigrant population, but also of its internal diversity.

The Flushing Hindu temple, or the Ganesha Temple, so named after its main deity, was founded by the Hindu Temple Society of North America in

1977 (Hanson 1997). Built to resemble Tirupati Devasthanam, a large Hindu temple in the Indian state of Andhra Pradesh, the architecture and interior were South Indian in style and ambiance. Besides Lord Ganesha, the primary deity in the inner sanctuary, statues of other deities adorned the central hall. South Indian tradition marked the performance of rituals and ceremonies. The priests were selected from a pool of Brahmins who had received scriptural training in India. The temple attracted more South than North Indians, but it accommodated a range of devotees of different Indian regional subcultures, including North Indian–style *arati* (waving of lights to gods), devotional songs, and religious festivals. The Ganesha Temple also affirmed the unity of all religions; the logo on the front of its building and on its stationery bore the primordial Hindu symbol *Om* in the center and was surrounded by symbols designating Islam, Christianity, Buddhism, and Judaism.

Over its first two decades, the Ganesha Temple became known all over the United States, and worshippers traveled to it from great distances. Though autonomous in operations, it was a member of the Hindu Temple Society of North America, which included temples in Pittsburgh, Chicago, Houston, and Los Angeles. It considered India's Tirupati Devasthanam its parent temple, and communication with it in India was maintained through visits by religious leaders as well as the arrival of sacred images, books, paraphernalia for the deities, and other ritual articles.

Still, the Ganesha Temple was essentially a neighborhood temple. Its founding secretary, Dr. A. Alagappan, explained that its particular site had been selected in the early 1970s because of Flushing's growing Indian population. "We could have gotten much bigger space than this one in suburban areas, but we wanted to make sure that the temple was within reach of people." This vision of its founders continued to be a reality for Hindu immigrants, from the richest and most highly educated to those of lower social status, and from many Indian regions.

The temple's biggest public event was an annual parade during the Ganesha Chaturthi festival in the fall. Lord Ganesha's statue was carried in a chariot along local streets, and accompanying devotees, many barefoot and dressed in traditional costumes, sang and danced.

The Ganesha Temple was also a cultural center that promoted Indian languages, dance, and music, as well as religious training, particularly for young Indian Americans. In 2000, Citylore, an urban folk art organization, honored the temple for its contribution to multicultural New York City. The temple newsletter, *Ganeshanjali,* announced a busy calendar of programs and carried information about temple officers, committees, and financial matters. Over the years the temple complex had expanded from a single lot to almost an entire block as it acquired single-family homes that it used as offices or accommodations for priests. In 1997 it opened a large auditorium, or *Kalyana Mantapam*, which replaced the temple basement as a location for cultural and social events. The steady stream of worshippers, including women and priests in traditional dress, and the many visitors' cars marked this temple's distinct cultural presence in its neighborhood.

The Geeta Temple, on Corona Avenue in Elmhurst, had a North Indian ambiance. It was founded by a swami, or Hindu monk, who in 1969 opened a small temple a few blocks from its later location, a former A&P supermarket. With funds from an expanding group of followers, the new temple opened in 1983. It contained a large central hall with verses from Hindu scriptures inscribed on the walls and a series of deities popular in North India, including statues of Lord Mahavira, the founder of Jainism, and Sai Baba of Shirdi, a twentieth-century saint with an Indiawide following. A separate shrine to one side was added later for worship of Lord Shiva. Aside from its three *shikhars,* conical structures over the roof of a temple representing the summit, the temple's plain white exterior was not particularly Indian or Hindu in appearance. A sign in the front reading "This is a place of Worship" identified the purpose of the building and possibly deterred graffiti vandals.

Most worshippers at the Geeta Temple were North Indian Gujarati, Hindi, and Punjabi speakers. Aside from the founder-priest, who continued to be a leading figure at the temple, there was no core of priests, and altars were often maintained by volunteer devotees. Visiting religious leaders and devotional singers from the United States and from India were frequent guests at the Geeta Temple. Overnight vigils were held on festivals such as Krishna Janamashtami, the birthdate of Lord Krishna, and large celebrations on Navaratri, a festival popular among Gujaratis. North Indian Hindu immigrants living in the vicinity were frequent visitors, but those living farther away reserved visits for major festivals, including Deepawali. The Geeta Temple cooperated with smaller houses of worship in Queens, including the nearby Jain Center of North America, the Satyanarayan Temple in Corona, and the Flushing Hindu Center, and cosponsored large religious events with them.

In the late 1980s a group of North Indian Hindu immigrants planned a Hindu center on Kissena Boulevard in Flushing, only a few blocks from the South Indian Ganesha Hindu Temple. These enthusiastic Hindu organizers took several years to raise funds to build the center, and construction continued even after its opening in 1987, including the addition of its shikhar in 1997. (The Muslim Center of New York next door opened in 1996.)

The Hindu Center's central prayer hall was adorned by an array of Hindu deities in front and elaborate series of deities on either side; worshippers normally offered prayers in the front, and then stopped at each deity on both sides. This central hall was also used for group singing. The center hosted overnight vigils, recitations of scriptures, and talks by visiting Hindu leaders, and offered space for social activities such as birthday celebrations and wedding ceremonies. The premises included an office and accommodations for its resident priest. The center reached worshippers through flyers and a mailing list, and maintained contact with other Hindu temples.

The Swaminarayan Temple, on Bowne Street in Flushing, was the national headquarters for Bochasanvasi Swaminarayan Sanstha, a flourishing sect of Gujarati Hindus who follow a nineteenth-century religious leader who initiated a new path for the worship of the god Vishnu (Hanson 1999). The sect has many temples in India and in other countries with Gujarati communities, with the largest in England and East Africa (Williams 1984; Barot 1987). The Flushing Swaminarayan Temple comprised a central hall with images of Lord Swaminarayan, a form of the god Vishnu, other deities, and the lineage of the sect's gurus. Space was allocated on one side for visits by the current sect leader. A few hundred people attended on weekends, but several thousand might be present for special events. The sect's stress on traditional family values was evident in the family groups of parents and children who visited the temple and volunteered for its activities.

All visitors to the Swaminarayan Temple were welcomed and introduced to the sect's philosophy by a volunteer. The temple was active in New York civic and cultural events and often represented Indians in local multicultural activities. In 1991 it sponsored a month-long "Festival of India" in New Jersey, with elaborate wooden gateways and huge Hindu statues—some shipped from England, where a similar event had been staged earlier—arts and crafts displays, exhibition halls, and conferences and concerts on the grounds of a school. Thousands of Swaminarayan followers from the United States and beyond visited the festival.

Other Hindu temples of varying sizes existed in Queens: the Vaishnava Temple, in Hollis, attuned to devotional practices of India's Gujarat region; the North Indian Satyanarayan Temple, located first in Elmhurst and later in Corona; the Arya Samaj Mandir, in southern Queens, which was North American headquarters of this North Indian reformist sect; and a temple of the saint Sai Baba of Shirdi, in Flushing. Several Guyanese Hindu temples were located in Richmond Hill, the largest being the Shri Lakshmi Narain Temple. Trinidadian Hindus constructed their own Shiva Temple in North Corona, where they celebrated their annual Immigration Day on May 30, the date of the arrival of the first Indians in Trinidad in the 1830s. The Indo-Caribbean Hindus also organized pilgrimages to India; one Guyanese travel agency in Queens advertised travel packages to Hindu places of worship in the "sacred land of our ancestors."

Indian Religions in the United States

As elsewhere in the United States (Williams 1988), Hindu practice in Queens reflected its American milieu. For example, most religious activities took place on weekends to suit work schedules, social events were intertwined with religious rituals, priests explained sacred texts in English, and some items used in rituals were made in America. However, Hinduism in Queens also enjoyed regular exchange with India, from where many religious paraphernalia, including books for chanting and articles for puja, were imported and readily available in local stores; items that were not available were easily arranged to be sent from India. Moreover, since houses of worship were located in residential neighborhoods, it was possible for people to visit them on weekdays at virtually any time of the day, and female and elderly immigrants who did not drive benefited from this proximity. One devout Hindu visitor from India remarked of Flushing's Ganesha Temple, "I enjoy coming to this temple as frequently as possible. In my hometown of New Delhi I had to travel many miles to visit a South Indian temple. This one is so close to our home in Flushing. Also the ceremonies are carried out in the most authentic ways. I miss this temple when I am back in India." Although Hinduism in Queens was not an exact replica of Hinduism in India, it came closer to it than in many other places in the United States.

Indian Hindus in Queens frequently encountered interested white Americans who visited their temples, some of them quite knowledgeable about Hindu traditions and practices. They also encountered American Hindu converts, a few at their temples or private religious gatherings, but mainly as members of *guru bhakti* groups.

The guru bhakti devotional paths, which follow a spiritual master and his or her disciples, are a longstanding feature of Hinduism (Juergensmeyer 1991). Although in India some gurus are nationally or regionally known, thousands of lesser-known gurus have smaller followings. A few of these groups arrived in the United States in the 1960s and 1970s, and some high-profile Indian "new age" paths developed wide appeal among Americans (Fornaro 1980). A few survived in less visible circumstances in the 1990s, with the majority of their devotees still "American cousins" of Indian Hindus (Williams 1988, 129; Brooks et al. 1997). The popularity of guru bhakti groups in the United States reflected their ability to transcend international cultural lines, but their activities had less appeal to Indians in Queens. Nevertheless, they were a reminder of Hinduism's contemporary complexities.

Among guru bhakti organizations operating in New York City, the Sri Chinmoy Center had its headquarters in Jamaica, Queens. The mainly American devotees of this order participated in the India Day Parade, and presented music and dance concerts choreographed by their Indian spiritual leader, Sri Chinmoy. The followers of the International Society of Krishna Consciousness (ISKCON), known popularly as Hare Krishnas, had their main temple in West Virginia and a local branch in Brooklyn, but they proselytized publicly all over New York City, including Queens. The Brahmakumari order, which has an exclusively female membership, conducted activities from a center in Astoria, Queens. Followers of the Chinmayananda Mission, headquartered in California, also engaged in spiritual outreach in small groups in Queens. In the most visible publicity campaign in Queens, flyers, posters in subways and buses, and newspaper advertisements for guru Nirmala Mata offered the promise of awakening *kundalini*, the dormant spiritual power in human beings.

Each Indian religious community in Queens responded to the new conditions in novel ways. As in Britain (Burghart 1987), members active in their house of worship often became spokespersons for their religious communities in addressing the wider American public. Both Hindus and Muslims took on the role of explaining their traditions to a society with little understanding of them. For Sikhs, reflecting their diasporic history as well as contemporary political developments in India, religion had become their primary group identity. Indian Christians and Jews, on the other hand, had to delineate their identity as distinct from the dominant Western traditions of their faiths.

Houses of worship had to interface with local civic groups that were not always tolerant or accommodating. The chairwoman of the Holly Civic Association, whose Flushing territory included twenty-three houses of worship, among them the Ganesha Temple, stated, "They came gradually, so at first we didn't notice, until now they are all over. It's just too much. They're taking over the neighborhood. We believe in the right to worship as you want; I mean, Flushing is the birthplace of religious freedom. But what about our rights as residents? These churches don't even look like real churches. You know, a Hindu temple just doesn't fit into our architecture here" (*Newsday* 2/23/90). Although Ganesha Temple officers claimed to have faced no serious incidents of hostility, they preferred to overlook minor instances of discrimination by their non-Hindu neighbors and some public agencies. They believed it was wiser not to be provoked, and remained focused on the temple's religious mission and tolerance toward others. Nonetheless, the temple cultivated contacts with local civic bodies and the police precinct, informing them of scheduled activities.

Indian immigrants encountered American stereotypes of Muslims as being fanatics and terrorists. Many South Asians (of all religions) complained of discrimination during both the late 1970s Iran hostage crisis and the early 1990s Gulf War.[1] In 1988 Indian and Pakistani worshippers at the Islamic Center in Woodside, Queens, were the target of a series of rock-throwing incidents. Then one night seven men attacked worshippers with baseball bats and iron rods. Mr. Ali, the imam of the mosque, stated that although a general hostility had long prevailed in the neighborhood, this incident "had the tone of racial and religious intolerance. . . . They shouted racial slurs: 'Pakistanis go home,' 'Moslems go home,' but mostly the word Moslem was used" (*New York Times* 7/7/88). The secretary of the mosque reported that even police officers arriving from the local precinct to quell the attack were abusive toward its victims, and a complaint was filed with the police department's Civilian Complaint Review Board (*New York Times* 6/28/88).

Debate over the role of religion in their identity as Indians became acrimonious for some immigrants with the rise of Hindu fundamentalism and resultant communalist politics in India during the 1980s and 1990s. Political parties espousing Hindu fundamentalism found support in all overseas Indian communities, where among some immigrants religious nationalism exerted a greater appeal than did pan-Indian secularism. Books appeared extolling Hinduism and asserting India's identity as a Hindu nation. In Queens a newspaper called *The Hindu Voice* was published by a group of Hindu nationalists, and the Hindu Swayamsevak Sangh, a right-wing organization promoting an exclusively Hindu identity for India, founded a chapter that was linked to others in the United States. In 1996 some six hundred people joined the Hindu Swayamsevak Sangh's New York celebration of Hindu Unity Day; the chief guest, Dr. Shobhan Lal, lauded his organization's movement for "restoration of Hindu dignity, regeneration of Hindu ethos, and reinvigoration of Hindu identity" (*New York Times* 7/12/96). Visiting Indian politicians who boosted this Hindu nationalist cause received financial support to continue their struggle in India.

Hindu nationalist identity was also espoused by some young Indian Americans who formed Hindu clubs on university campuses across the United States to counter the existing South Asian or Indian student groups. More than four hundred students and other nationalist supporters attended YUVA 94 (Youth 94), a conference at Northeastern University in Boston hosted by the Hindu Students Council. Various chapters of the Vishwa Hindu Parishad of America, Inc., an overseas branch of an India-based Hindu group, the Global Hindu Organization, held summer youth camps teaching Hindu traditions and the history of India from a Hindu nationalist perspective.

Indians in New York who supported their homeland's secular traditions made attempts to oppose the Hindu nationalist position through organizations like Ekta (Unity), but their impact was limited to circles of leftists and intellectuals. In 1993, on the first anniversary of the Hindu fundamentalist attack on the Babri Mosque in Ayodhya, India, an exhibition opened at Columbia University in New York City, sponsored by SAHMAT, a New Delhi organization dedicated to communal harmony. (Meaning "consensus," SAHMAT is an acronym for the Safdar Hashmi Memorial Trust established in memory of the progressive theater personality Safdar Hashmi, who was killed by fundamentalists.) The exhibit, "We All Are Ayodhya," depicted the history of both the Babri Mosque and secularism in India. This message, however, did not reach the wider local Indian population.

Still, New York City did not become a major battleground between these contending parties. Hindu nationalist versus secularist struggles were not waged openly, but rather smoldered in certain organizations. Much more typical of religious stances that swayed Indians in Queens was the news in 1995 that statues of Hindu gods in India were consuming the milk offered to them by devotees in temples. This reached New York by telephone and fax, and within a day thousands of Hindu immigrants rushed to temples in their Queens neighborhoods with milk cartons to participate in what many deemed a living miracle. Long lines formed in front of the Ganesha Temple in Flushing, which remained open the entire night. Local Indian reporters covered the events for ethnic cable television, and the *New York Times* carried a picture of a Hindu god being fed milk in Hong Kong (9/24/95). Queens, obviously, was not to be left out of this transnational miracle-seeking, and the story reverberated for days in conversations among Hindu immigrants and in their telephone calls to relatives in India.

Businesses and apartment buildings on Main Street, Flushing

South Asian businesses on 74th Street, Jackson Heights

South Asian businesses on 74th Street, Jackson Heights

Intersection of Liberty Avenue and Lefferts Boulevard, Richmond Hill

An outdoor celebration of the festival of Dussehra, Nassau Beach Park, Long Island, 1994

Masjid-al-Falah Mosque, Corona

Sikh Gurdwara, Richmond Hill

Ganesha Hindu Temple, Flushing

Geeta Hindu Temple, Elmhurst

South Asian women shopping in Flushing

India Day parade in Manhattan, 2000

India Day parade in Manhattan, 2000

All photos by author.

[4]

Building Careers, Encountering Class

Well-paying jobs were the basic motivation for the post-1965 Indian immigration. At first largely from middle-class, well-educated backgrounds, Indians migrated to the United States to further improve their standard of living. The contrasting economic conditions in India and the United States in the 1960s and 1970s fed those expectations, and the professional careers and business achievements of Indian immigrants during these decades underlay the "successful immigrant" image attached to the entire group (Helweg and Helweg 1990). This "model minority" myth became entrenched as well among these immigrants themselves, affecting their self-perceptions and their definition of community needs and issues (Abraham 2000). By the 1980s, however, the occupational diversity of Indians here was increasing rapidly, and in the 1990s the population included growing numbers of lower-middle- and working-class immigrants, a change most evident in New York City.

Class differences have been important throughout the history of Indian immigration to the United States (Mazumdar 1989), and they affect Indian ideas about race, ethnicity, gender, culture, and Americanization. Indian immigrants in the United States have been studied primarily as a professional population (Saran and Eames 1980; Saran 1985; Helweg and Helweg 1990) or for their distinctive cultural characteristics (Williams 1988); their changing socioeconomic profile has received less attention. Moreover, the studies of economic success do not sufficiently emphasize the impact of class on ideology or pan-Indian activities; with a few exceptions (Lessinger 1989; Bhattacharjee 1992; Khandelwal 1996a; Visweswaran 1997; Abraham 2000), the formation of class divisions among Indians and the creation of an increasingly stratified immigrant community have received no sustained examination. Focusing on economic activities among Indian immigrants in New York City from the 1960s through the 1990s, this chapter outlines the transformation of a predominantly professional population into one encompassing various middle- and working-class occupations. By the 1990s, whereas some Indians' financial successes made American headlines, other immigrants were unemployed, and many others experienced downward mobility.

Skilled Migrants

Through the 1950s and 1960s, Indian universities churned out thousands of graduates who faced serious unemployment or underemployment. The nascent economy of independent India acutely needed trained people, but either sufficient paid employment was not available, or it was available only in areas without urban standards of living. By 1970, 80 percent of India's doctors resided in urban areas, although these contained less than 20 percent of India's population; and at the same time, 15,000 to 20,000 doctors were without jobs (Tinker 1977, 9–10). Beyond the lack of employment, inadequate work facilities and limited career advancement also confronted Indian professionals. These employment conditions dissuaded educated and skilled Indians from staying in India, and many turned to overseas migration. In a single month in 1965, nearly 2,000 Indian doctors took examinations offered by the Educational Council for Foreign Medical Graduates to certify them to work in U.S. hospitals (*New York Times* 2/27/65). Although the movement of Indian professionals to America had already begun in the 1950s, the larger portion of that decade's flow was to Great Britain. By the early 1970s, with rising British antagonism toward immigrants, it was redirected to the United States, where the 1965 Immigration and Nationality Act had opened the door more widely to immigrants from beyond Europe.

With the USSR's launching of Sputnik in 1957, expenditure for research and development in the United States increased from $7 billion that year to $14 billion by 1966, and the number of scientists and engineers employed in American industry grew correspondingly. Many of them came from other countries, including India. The stream of professional immigration from Asian countries, including India, increased along with the growth of Great Society social welfare programs in the United States under President Lyndon Johnson. In 1965 two new government health programs, Medicare for aged and disabled workers, and Medicaid for low-income persons, were passed, and demand for medical personnel rose throughout the United

States. America produced only 7,000 physicians in 1963—too few to staff the country's expanding health care system (*New York Times* 2/27/65). In 1968 the president of the American Medical Association (AMA) called the nation's health the "best ever," but lamented, "The nation needs more physicians, nurses, and technicians and technologists to meet increasing demands for health care" (*New York Times* 1/16/68). The world distribution of medical and scientific professionals, and their training, became issues in international politics. India worried over losing its best personnel and protested against a "brain drain," as one Indian report in 1965 characterized the exodus of 20,000 physicians and scientists to Western nations (*New York Times* 2/27/65). The AMA countered protests from sending countries by asserting that the United States did not "recruit" foreign medical graduates (FMGs), and challenged the accuracy of figures on Indian doctors in the United States. But at the same time, the AMA reported that in 1965 alone some 8,804 medical interns and residents had arrived in the United States from overseas and that 60 percent of house staff physicians in New York City hospitals had received their medical degrees abroad (*New York Times* 2/27/65).

Employment prospects for skilled immigrants in the United States were so inviting that medical doctors even migrated from Britain, and during the 1960s that country also became anxious about physicians leaving for the United States (*New York Times* 2/16/66, 9/17/66). But losses of personnel and the resources invested in their education were more serious for developing countries. Before 1965, 50 percent of all FMGs in the United States came from Europe and the Americas, and only 10 percent from Asia; by 1972, 70 percent came from Asia, with India, the Philippines, and Korea the leading sources of new arrivals (*Immigration and Naturalization Reporter*, spring 1997, 6).

Thousands of Indian doctors also came to the United States for advanced medical training every year. Few returned to India, despite pleading by the Indian government. The situation was so serious that in the late 1960s the Association for Service to Indian Scholars, or ASSIST, was formed to persuade Indian professionals to return home. In its first year it received only sixty applications and placed only nineteen people in jobs (*New York Times* 4/25/67). This brain drain was further highlighted by a study from one of India's leading medical institutions, the Medical College of Baroda, in Gujarat (Bhatt et al. 1976, 290–292). Of 624 graduates from 1949 to 1965, 194 went abroad for further training, and only 28 returned to India; from 1966 to 1972, of 722 graduates, 390 went abroad, and only one returned.

As a result of this skilled labor emigration, a preponderance of professionals characterized the Indian immigrant population in the United States. From 1961 to 1968, 67 percent of Indians employed in the United States

[93]

were in professional categories, and from 1969 to 1971 the figure jumped to 89 percent (Wong and Hirschman 1983, 395–397). Ninety-three percent of Indians admitted in 1975 were "professional/technical workers" and their spouses and children (Fisher 1980, 11). And in 1976 the *New York Times* reported: "At the end of last year, 1,143 Indians held faculty positions in American colleges and universities" (4/25/76).

Although the proportion of highly educated professionals was also large among many other Asian immigrant groups, it was highest among Indians. In the 1980 U.S. Census, 24.9 percent of Koreans, 25.1 percent of Filipinos, 28.5 percent of Japanese, 32.6 percent of Chinese, and 48.5 percent of Asian Indians were in the "managerial, professional" category. If we add the "technical, sales, and administrative support" category, 76.5 percent of employed Asian Indians were contained in these two occupational groupings (the corresponding figures were 52.3 percent of Koreans, 58.4 percent of Filipinos, and 62.7 percent of both Japanese and Chinese) (Wong and Hirschman 1983).

Although Filipinos had a larger absolute number of medical professionals in the United States than did Indians, the proportion of this group and its influence on immigrant community affairs and politics was greater among Indians. Moreover, in this category Indians had a larger percentage of doctors than did Filipinos, among whom nurses predominated. These middle-class Indian immigrants also played a role in perpetuating the model minority image. When Asian Indians were shown in the 1980 census to have the highest "median income of persons 15 years or older with income" of any ethnic group, including white Americans, the news was celebrated in New York's Indian immigrant circles. This celebration continued into the 1980s and 1990s, when Indians mentioned the "high income levels" of their group as its leading characteristic. Similar pronouncements portrayed Indians as new kinds of immigrants, highly educated and sophisticated, who could quite easily integrate into upper- and middle-class America.[1]

While some analysts of Indian migration emphasized U.S. demand and South Asian supply factors in creating this profile (Burkhi and Swamy 1987), popular writer Joel Kotkin ventured a cultural and religious explanation for Indian immigrant success. Kotkin stamped Indians as one of the "most recent to emerge of the modern global tribes," and identified certain Indian communities as "tribes within tribes," concluding that "virtually wherever they have settled, they rank among the most professionally and economically mobile groups" (1993, 204). Similar ideas remained prevalent among some Indian immigrants themselves. The cover letter addressed to two thousand "Businessmen and Professionals" for a 1995 international survey conducted by one Indian community leader in New York stated:

This research is based on the premise that culture does influence economics. The World Bank report makes the assumption that all men are equal and that people all over the world are the same. As a matter of fact they are not. This is very well supported by the regional economic landscape of India. Some regional communities produce better businessmen, some warriors, some *babus* [white-collar workers], and some others literary giants. . . . The purpose of this research is to identify Indian socio-economic acumen which [has] made Indians economically enviable. This research will also help in identifying the most successful community, as perceived by many. Please send your "Success Story." Success stories will be analyzed to identify significant characteristics contributing to economic success. (Unpublished document in author's possession.)

Not celebrated in 1980 was the U.S. Census documentation that incomes were declining among Indian immigrants who had arrived after 1975. This changing economic profile, which continued in later decades, was produced not only by the family reunification process but also by shifts in the American economy. In New York City, where the impact of economic change registered most deeply on the Indian immigrant population, difficult economic conditions followed the city's 1975 fiscal crisis and 1987 stock market crash, including a growing disparity between suburban and city employment conditions and job downsizing (Edel 1989; Sanjek 1998). Roger Sanjek argues that with shrinkage in midlevel jobs in the 1980s, a growing number of immigrants moved into the underground economy of cash transactions, tax avoidance, and subminimum wages. Global economic changes since the late 1980s, particularly the upsurge of Asian economies, moreover, have created shifts in Asian immigration flows to the United States. In the 1990s a few young Indian professionals in the United States even began to relocate to India (Roy 1994).

Oral Histories of Early Migrants

In their narratives, Indians who had arrived in the 1960s and early 1970s described decisions to migrate as based on educational and career opportunities. In some cases this motive was coupled with a desire to break away from family control and to build lives of their own. At first these immigrants paid little conscious attention to the continuation of Indian values and cultural traditions in the new land. Most immigrants were men, either single or newly married, some with young families. In general they were imbued with a "spirit of adventure" and with desire for "making new beginnings," as several put it.

These immigrants found that professional jobs were abundant, and had little difficulty in finding them. One man explained that on his first day in New York in 1969 he visited several offices with his portfolio of educational degrees and certificates. "It was a day of my life that I will never forget. On the very first day—within one day—I had three job offers. In the evening, I returned to my friend's house, with whom I was rooming in Queens, for his advice on which one to select."

Many Indian medical professionals started as residents and interns in New York's inner-city hospitals. They saw the chances of establishing successful professional careers as much brighter in the United States than in India. Many also pursued special courses to advance their skills. At this early stage they were not concerned about unequal wages or glass ceilings, as many would be in later years. New York City, with a large number of job opportunities in universities, hospitals, and business firms, soon became a fast-growing point of concentration among Indian immigrants.

Mr. Rao left India in 1968 and worked as an engineer in London for two years. He had married before leaving India, and his wife and a daughter remained there waiting to join him overseas when he decided to start a new job in New York in 1970. In view of political and economic conditions in Britain, he felt that the United States would be a better place for both his career and his young family. During his first year in New York he lived with a friend in a Flushing apartment, and when his wife and daughter joined him in 1971 they moved into an apartment in the building next door. He continued in the same engineering job for years, receiving promotions and feeling settled in this country. In 1976, with just a few years' savings, he and his family moved to their own single-family house in Bayside, Queens. As his daughter grew up, his wife, who also had a college degree, worked in an office. With a two-earner income, Rao invested successfully in real estate and small businesses. The Raos were active in their regional Indian organization, which they helped found in Queens in the early 1970s. They worshipped at a Hindu temple and maintained their traditional food and dress habits at home.

Rao was ready to retire in the late 1990s. He said he had had a long and good career, but in the last few years he felt as if he had begun to stagnate. Now, after working hard for all these years, he was ready to return to India. He was only waiting for his daughter to marry, leaving his wife and himself free from their family responsibilities. He and his wife had given much freedom to their daughter and would accept her choice of a husband as long as "it is within our basic cultural limits." His innermost wish was that she would marry an Indian professional so that the young couple could have a stable life, both economically and culturally.

Dr. Chandran came to the United States in 1966 soon after graduating from a medical college in India. For a few years he worked in a hospital in

Ohio, during which time he returned to India to marry a bride from his own region and caste. In 1969, accepting a job offer from a prominent hospital, he and his wife moved to New York. "In comparison to other places, New York had so many more Indian immigrants. In Queens, in particular, where we started living, we had many Indian families and friends of our age. It was like finding a community in which every one was enthusiastic about building cultural and social institutions." While Dr. Chandran built his medical practice, his wife devoted herself to raising their two sons "in as much a traditional Indian way as possible." She never worked outside the home, but remained active in Indian community affairs. "We are grateful to God that my husband's income was more than sufficient for our family, and so I did not have to work." In the 1980s and 1990s the Chandrans were known as community leaders who made regular financial contributions to religious and cultural activities.

The American economy, which had previously offered Indian immigrants easy entry into American professions, began to change in the early 1970s. By the mid-1970s U.S. interest groups were protesting against the competition presented by foreign-born professionals, particularly medical doctors. With the demand for foreign skilled labor declining, in 1976 Congress severely curtailed opportunities for foreign-trained medical graduates to enter the United States with occupational visas. As a result, immigration of Indian physicians in the 1980s and 1990s occurred primarily through family reunification visas.

Exacerbating the effects of this policy in New York was the city's 1975 fiscal crisis and its aftermath. Family reunification was producing a wider variety of immigrants, fewer of whom were as highly educated as their predecessors, but the changed economic conditions in New York (see Edel 1989; Sanjek 1998) also limited opportunities for professional jobs even among highly qualified immigrants. Over the next two decades many Indians would turn to jobs in manufacturing, sales, and small business.

The process of economic diversification within New York's Indian population began with professional immigrants who switched careers and opened ethnic businesses. In the late 1960s and early 1970s, ex-professionals opened a few Indian-owned groceries, electronics and appliance shops, and insurance agencies in Queens. In doing so they pioneered a new arena of nonprofessional work in which later Indian immigrants would follow. Soon a core of ethnic Indian businesses was joined by traditional merchants from India and its overseas communities, and by immigrants who found their first employment in these Indian businesses and would eventually open businesses of their own.

One day in 1970 G. L. Soni, a civil engineer living in Elmhurst, spotted a business location for sale in his neighborhood. He consulted with his brother about the need for an Indian grocery store in Queens, and on the auspicious day of Vijaya Dashami, or Dussehra, the Indian festival, opened House of Spices on Broadway in Elmhurst. Sitting in his office at the back of his store, Soni reminisced, "The Indian population was multiplying in Queens and yet there were no Indian stores. This business location was great because it was near the junction of E/F and 7 subways, and many apartments where new immigrants lived. Sam & Raj opened here in 1973 before they moved to their present location on 74th Street, and we started another store in Flushing, the other large area of Indian concentration. I did not know anything about business and had to start from scratch. At that time, we were all professionals who turned businessmen."

Over the next twenty-five years Soni expanded his store into a chain of retail grocery businesses, and later into one of the largest Indian wholesale grocery business in North America, distributing his House of Spices and Laxmi brand items to grocery stores in every town with an Indian population. In response to increasing Indian retail competition, Soni moved completely out of the retail business. "I have survived and expanded only because of constantly changing and repositioning. Otherwise, at this time when the conditions have completely altered, most of the pioneer businessmen are facing difficult time."

A. Sahani came to the United States in 1971 as a mechanical engineer but soon, as an agent of an American insurance company, started his own insurance firm, serving the growing Indian population in New York. First his younger brother, and later his own wife, who joined him in New York after their marriage in India in 1978, helped in his expanding business. Sahani's clients were primarily North Indians engaged in particular business lines and from certain castes. Over the years Sahani maintained social ties with his clients and became a part of their social networks; he and his family regularly attended many social events and other community activities. He had survived the competition from new Indian insurance agents by maintaining his base of long-settled Indian immigrant families.

Two Indian engineer friends decided to make a career move in 1973 by opening an electronics and appliance store, which they called Sam & Raj. They remained at their Broadway location in Elmhurst until 1976, when their lease expired and then moved to a nearby space on 74th Street in Jackson Heights. Subhash Kapadia ("Sam") remained in this business for twenty-five years, keeping the name Sam & Raj after his original partner left. In the 1970s Sam & Raj became a household name for the middle-class Indian customers of its electronic goods and appliances, stocked both for local voltage and for use in India. Not only Queens residents but Indians visiting New York from other states or from India soon became familiar with 74th Street and Sam & Raj. Kapadia became active both in his Gujarati community and in the Jackson Heights Merchants Association. He noted, however, that his local patronage declined in the late 1980s and the 1990s. "Many more Indian stores have opened in this area, and it is difficult to compete for every cent. At the same time, the purchase power of Indian customers has gone down. Now a major portion of our business comes from mail orders rather than retail sales to visiting customers."

The Indian professionals-turned-businessmen differed from the professionals of the 1960s and 1970s, who maintained upper-class Indian networks in either Manhattan or the suburbs. Queens-based businessmen were active in almost every new regional and religious community organization in the borough, and often served as leaders in cultural activities. Still, some of these businessmen also maintained their alliances with Indian professionals, and together formed an elite layer of pan-Indian community leadership consisting of highly educated upper-class Indians. As the Indian immigrant population expanded to include lower-middle-class and poorer Indian immigrants, the gap between elite leaders and ordinary residents in Queens also widened.

New Occupations

In the 1980s and 1990s, the overwhelming majority of Indian immigrant households in New York City consisted of married couples, plus, in most cases, children, and, occasionally, other relatives as well. Overall, Indian immigrant women had lower educational attainments than men, but in contrast to the trend in India, half of them were employed outside the home. Several husband–wife employment scenarios existed. Some highly educated women worked as professionals, like their husbands, either in the same or a different field. There were many Indian husband-and-wife teams of physicians, some even operating a joint practice. Among early immigrant couples, the wives of professional men were often self-employed, running a travel agency or operating a small business from home. Most Indian businesspersons were male; wives of businessmen nonetheless often played supportive roles, sometimes as active partners or as managers of a portion of the business. In other married-couple households, the husband was professionally employed, and the wife worked in a nonprofessional job earning an additional, though lower, income (see also Leonard and Tibrewal 1993).

Many immigrant women, in spite of their education, assigned priority to childrearing rather than to their own careers, and thus took part-time work or lower-paying jobs that allowed them time for their family responsibilities. Such women, then, formed part of the Indian working-class labor force, which also included later nonprofessional Indian immigrants and elderly family members arriving to join middle-class adult children.

Indian professionals made mutually beneficial use of ethnic networks both for creating employment contacts and for securing a clientele of patients or customers. The dynamics of ethnic networks, however, were significantly different for entrepreneurs who employed other Indian immigrants. By the 1980s new immigrants were seeking employment in Indian ethnic businesses, but such work situations seemed to be creating more intraethnic tension than ethnic solidarity.

Immigrant employees often hoped that ethnic commonality with an employer would assist them in succeeding in this country. Indian employees in Queens, however, expressed frustration over working for an Indian employer; their commonly repeated maxim was "Never work for a fellow Indian." As one immigrant said, "They exploit you, use you to the maximum, and then claim all that in the name of brotherhood. My employer never let me forget that he gave me a job when I arrived in this country. It was as if that onetime help had made me a slave for a lifetime. I slaved not only for him at work but many times for his wife and entire family. I worked there only as long as I waited for my green card. Once I had a sound legal status in this country, I broke off and started my own employment."

In turn, employers often complained that Indian employees were not trustworthy. Some talked about their hope of building ethnic bonds with new employees. "One wants to help them settle in the new country. I gave him a job and even sponsored him, but he was all the time thinking of breaking away. It seems we cannot trust even our own people." Behind these interpersonal tensions lay diverging employer–employee expectations that were only exacerbated by the presumptions of ethnic commonality.

Although the family reunification immigration preference system, one not based on skills or levels of education, had increasingly broadened the pool of less-educated and nonprofessional Indian immigrants, emerging class differences among Indians were not due solely to such premigration differences in background. Unlike earlier immigrants, many later immigrants, regardless of education or skills, could not find suitable employment in New York's economy. By the late 1980s and 1990s family reunification plus the changing New York economy meant downward occupational mobility for many Indian immigrants. Some experienced long years of economic instability in which they moved between salaried employment and running a small business, or between unemployment and a paid job. Several who immigrated to New York in the 1980s expressed frustration: "In this country, you have to struggle till your last breath"; "This is endless struggle, a pit which has no bottom"; "My children do not understand our problem and keep wondering why we are always in financial difficulties." One immigrant, trained as a physician, married an Indian woman with a permanent resident visa and a working-class job in Queens. Unable to find a job in his field, he lamented, "The hope of getting established in my profession can be realized only in a hospital in a suburban area or in a distant state where such jobs are still available. Maybe instead of languishing in New York City, we should move to North or South Dakota, where I can get a job and my green card in shorter time."

Family reunification immigrants sponsored by relatives already in America included young persons, either single or recently married, as well as a growing number who had raised families in India before immigration and, as a result of long waiting periods for their green cards, were middle-aged with grown children. Often coming from well-off situations in India, and with settled careers and families, they dreamt of improving their living standards as their sponsoring relatives had done. Major considerations in their decision to immigrate were their children's education and careers, and in some cases it was these children who persuaded their parents to leave India.

Adjustment to the New York economy of the late 1980s and the 1990s was especially hard for such immigrants, who found it demeaning even to consider a working-class job in the new country. And once employed, several spoke of the constant threat of being "fired" or "laid off," concepts unfamiliar to them in India. Moreover, although their incomes in India seemed small by comparison to American earnings, the social and family support there gave them a sense of security now missing. Their teenage children also noted their own lowered living standards after migration; many who had gone to top schools in India now attended public high schools and colleges. "In India," one said, "I would never have to work to pay for my higher education. Since we came here, I cannot go to a private out-of-town school, not only because we cannot afford it, but because I cannot leave my parents by themselves in their miserable financial difficulties. So I work full-time to pay my college education and support my parents as much as I can."

In her late forties, Ratna arrived in New York City in 1984 with her husband and two young children. Her husband's older sister, living in Queens with her own family since the 1970s, sponsored their immigration. Before migrating, Ratna had lived in Delhi, where her husband had worked in a government office and she had taught sewing and embroidery in a girls' school. At the time they immigrated, her daughter was twelve years old and her son seven. Ratna and her family initially lived with her sister-in-law's family in Jamaica, Queens.

I knew that arrangement was temporary because those shared situations create lots of tensions between families. So while my husband looked for a job, we also searched for a place to move in. One day, when we were visiting a friend in Flushing, we saw the neighborhood and liked it. It had many more Indians than Jamaica, and we could even have a small apartment at a reasonable rent. In 1985 we moved into this apartment. This building is owned by Indians and has many Indian tenants. But we could not pay even this rent with my husband's salary alone. He is not very ambitious and is contented working part-time as a sales clerk in an Indian store. So I had to work.

Ratna was employed in the warehouse of an Indian wholesale garment importer, where she made alterations on garments before they were shipped to stores. Since she did not have a car, she relied on public transportation, and had to change buses to and from her workplace. "It becomes difficult to wait for buses in winter. I want my children to grow up soon, so that I do not have to do this job. Besides, I do not like the business owners. You know, if your employer is good, you do not mind being paid a little less or undergoing a difficult commute. There is no humanity left in these people. They are so proud of their money and their business that they do not talk to fellow Indians normally. To them we are just employees and nothing else."

Ratna longed for socializing with friends, but most of this occurred during visits to India, for which she saved carefully. Eventually she left her job and began doing piecework sewing jobs for different garment firms at home. She felt she had more flexibility in this kind of work, since she could accept or reject consignments according to her own convenience. Working from home also brought relief that "it is the business owner who travels to drop and pick up the work, not me."

Kumar was in his late twenties when he came to New York in 1988. Before he migrated his family had arranged his marriage within their caste, and his wife joined him about two years later in Queens. Both were college educated, with master's degrees from urban Indian universities. His older brother, an established Queens resident, had sponsored him for immigration and promised him a job. Within a few months of his arrival, this brother leased a corner store for Kumar to run. The couple, now with a young child, lived in a one-bedroom apartment in Flushing.

> I work six days a week, from 5:30 in the morning to 9:30 in the night. I have to open the store in the early morning, set up coffee, etc., take care of the inventory, orders, and all that stuff the whole day. By the time I close my store in the night, I am dead, and just want to sleep. There is no time for my wife and child. You were asking me about friends. What friends can I have with this crazy work schedule? On weekends, we have to do weekly shopping, etc., and we visit our brother sometimes, that is all.

His wife added:

When we got married and I was waiting to join him in New York, I had so many dreams about our married life in America. But here, I am in a worse situation than even in India. He is away to work all the time, and we hardly spend any time together. He is so depressed by the kind of work he does and the kind of people he has to deal with. I asked him many times if I could help him at the store. But every time, he says, "No, that neighborhood is not a good place for women to work." The other day a storekeeper was robbed at gunpoint and then killed. I tried to find a part-time job of teacher or babysitter for myself in this area. No, not for the money, but just to know that I am alive, that I can work too. But once we had our child, I had to give up that idea. I could go through the delivery only because my mother came from India to assist me, otherwise these things are so difficult here. My sister-in-law is very nice, and she is my only friend, but I cannot share everything with her. After all, she has her own family, and my brother-in-law will not like it if we complain about my husband's job all the time.

Suresh was in his late thirties when he arrived in California in the late 1980s. At the time of his immigration he worked as a college professor in an Indian city and was near completion of his Ph.D. degree from a prestigious university. His wife had received a green card through family sponsorship, and the couple traveled to the United States to assess the prospects of moving here. His wife found a job immediately, and Suresh, with neither a green card nor a job, stayed on in hopes of continuing his academic career here, preferably at an American university that would support him while he finished his Ph.D., after which he would be eligible for a faculty position. Through contacts from his small network of Indian and American academics, Suresh was able to teach only occasionally as an adjunct professor. He could not return to India, since without a green card he might not be allowed to reenter the United States.

The couple depended mainly on his wife's income and moved to New York when she was offered a job there. Suresh's job search continued without success. As a temporary measure, he accepted a position with an American life insurance company trying to penetrate the growing Indian market.

Initially I felt very uncomfortable. The business language and profit-oriented goals were alien to my career philosophy. For years, the scholar in me had developed critiques of capitalism and its damaging impact on human lives. But I had to be real. I had responsibility as a husband and father for my young child. At least the insurance job gave me livelihood and means to support my family. And very important, it sponsored me for a green card, which would take much longer if my wife had sponsored me as her spouse. There is no job satisfaction here. I feel particularly miserable when I think of how my Ph.D. in India was a mere inches away from my reach. But would a Ph.D. degree in social science help me in getting employment in this country? I cannot change my job till I am through with my green card process. My immigration status has messed up my professional career. Living an insecure life of an immigrant, you realize how racist this country is. I had little chance of competing with white Americans for a university position—that is clear racial and anti-immigrant discrimination. My insurance company is more subtle in this respect; they stereotype and exploit me. They have no value for my academic training and intellect; they only want to use my ethnic resources to get insurance business from my community. I see representation problems for Indians every day in this country. I have to struggle furiously against cultural misunderstandings in my son's school education. I am trying to channelize my activism in community organizations, but there I am encountering affluent Indian professionals and businessmen who are politically quite conservative.

As the process of occupational diversification continued into the 1990s, Indian immigrants could be found working in virtually every level of New York's economy, ranging from prestigious, well-paying occupations to working-class and minimum-wage jobs. However, "the ethnic success" of Indian immigrants still made the headlines in the American press. In 1987 the *Wall Street Journal* extolled the Indian "immigrant saga" with more success stories (Sterba 1987). But it also reported that "for every rising entrepreneur, there are poor Indians scrubbing restaurant kitchens." According to the 1980 census, 9.9 percent of Asian Indians were below the poverty line, a figure approaching the 12.4 percent poverty rate for all Americans.

The 1990 occupational distribution of the Indian labor force over age sixteen in New York indicated a far different picture from the professional success sagas (see table 4). In Manhattan, Indians age sixteen and over in professional occupations (including health services) amounted to 40 percent of the total; the figure was identical in suburban Nassau County and slightly higher (46 percent) in Westchester County. In the Bronx, professionals accounted for only 30 percent of Indian immigrants, and in Brooklyn for 24 percent. In Queens, professionals made up only about 9 percent of the total working Indian population, and were outnumbered by manufacturing employees and retail sales owners and workers. Significant numbers of construction workers, larger than in any other borough, also worked in Queens. Professionals employed in health services were only 4 percent of the Indian workforce in Queens, whereas in Nassau and Westchester Counties they accounted for 31 and 32 percent.

Ethnic Niches

From the 1970s through the 1990s, Indians penetrated a number of business niches in New York City's economy, including the diamond trade, the

Table 4. Indian Employees (16 years and over) by Occupation in New York City, 1990

Industry	Borough/County					
	Brooklyn	Bronx	Manhattan	Queens	Nassau	Westchester
Construction	446	316	14	1,042	65	72
Manufacturing	1,064	534	284	3,342	561	461
Retail	1,604	961	444	8,845	1,105	404
Professional[a]	552	604	744	1,553	528	526
Health Services	1,177	960	571	1,082	1,877	1,205
Other	2,311	1,778	1,262	12,605	1,891	1,132
TOTAL	7,154	5,153	3,319	28,469	6,027	3,800

Source: Social and Economic Characteristics, 1990 U.S. Census for New York State.
[a]Excluding health services.

garment business, newsstands, taxicab driving, and retail discount stores. Although each niche had its own unique economic characteristics, an employment hierarchy among Indians was apparent in all five. Both established and newly arrived Indian immigrants worked at various levels in the same niche, creating a stratified ethnic workplace population. The American dream of upward economic mobility, moreover, pervaded all these employment sectors.

In the 1970s representatives of Jain and Marwari merchant families from Rajasthan in western India began to examine opportunities in New York's diamond trade, based on 47th Street in midtown Manhattan and dominated by Jews. They quickly realized the potential of the market in small low-priced diamonds ignored by established traders; by the mid-1980s the Palanpur Jains formed the second largest ethnic concentration in the diamond district. "Today the Palanpur Jains are a powerhouse in the $2.6 billion-a-year uncut diamond trade. . . . Their timing was exquisite and their perseverance was inspiring. Their product now sparkles in bracelets and earrings, nearly all priced under $1,000, in the showcases of Zale's, Gordon's, Kay and the rest of this country's mass market jewelry retailers" (Gupte 1987). As a result of these American-based Indian diamond merchants' enterprise in New York, India became the world's biggest exporter of small polished diamonds, with the United States its most important market.

These affluent Indian diamond merchant families formed a tight social group. They lived in spacious Manhattan apartments, formed their own professional organizations, and, in some instances, were active in pan-Indian community organizations. Socially, they preserved traditional values and kept American influences at a remove from their families. Business was handled exclusively by men, and women remained homemakers. Most marriages in this community were endogamous, arranged with children of sim-

[105]

ilar business families in India. These families were in regular contact with India and traveled there frequently (*New York Times* 7/20/98).

Competition among Indian and other immigrant entrepreneurs was also evident in New York's garment trade. Here, too, Jews were the established group, but the number of Chinese, Korean, Latin American, and Indian immigrant entrepreneurs had been increasing. This change in apparel shop ownership accompanied an outflow since the 1960s of standard production work from New York to other states and overseas. In 1959 only 6 percent of all U.S. garment sales were imports, but by 1984 half the garments sold were imported from overseas contractors using cheaper labor (Waldinger 1986). In New York's changing garment industry some immigrant entrepreneurs provided links to these overseas contractors. Beginning in the 1970s, many Indian entrepreneurs established themselves in this overseas business, and by the 1990s a few hundred Indian import companies operated from showroom-offices in Manhattan's garment district. Instead of receiving supplies from local sweatshops (often in Queens) like other Asian or Latino contractors, Indian garment contractors sent orders to India or other countries where garments were sewn at cheaper rates.

A multitiered workforce marked this Indian ethnic niche. At the top were the firm owners, who dealt with financiers, airline carriers, transportation companies, designers, salespersons, and their own employees. In the 1980s other Indian immigrants, some of them highly educated immigrants who sought their employer's sponsorship for an immigration visa, began working for these Indian-owned companies as warehouse supervisors, shipping clerks, and messengers. Businessmen from India frequently traveled to New York to maintain links with the Indian owners of these businesses; the New York–based owners also traveled to India to supervise production and facilitate overseas shipment. (Unconnected to these firms, some Indian women in Queens also worked as operators in sewing factories or did contract piecework at home.)

At the same time, an ever-growing number of Indian immigrants, primarily men, found low-wage jobs in small Indian-owned businesses such as travel agencies, restaurants, and stores. In the 1980s a large number also moved into the newsstand business in New York City subway stations. A few Indians had entered this business in the late 1970s, running one or several newsstands on an individual basis. The turning point in expanding this new ethnic niche came in 1983, when Bhawnesh and Suresh Kapoor, brothers from New Delhi, bid for and won a Metropolitan Transit Authority contract to operate 143 subway newsstands. This move by the entrepreneurial Kapoor brothers, who were already operating several newsstands, depended upon loans from the Small Business Administration and from Indian immigrant friends. The MTA decision was challenged in court by the

Subway News Dealers Association, a group of ninety-six individual owners who had also bid for the contract. (For a while this association was led by another Indian, Kirtisingh Chudasma; *New York Times* 9/30/84.) However, after a favorable decision from the New York State Court of Appeals, the Kapoor brothers controlled every newsstand in the subways and Long Island Rail Road stations. All these newsstands were staffed by immigrants from India, Pakistan, and Bangladesh. A *New York Times* article placed the Kapoors "at the vanguard of an enormous ethnic transformation that has changed the nature of two endangered species of city folklore and life: the corner candy store and the neighborhood newsstand" (1/3/86).

The Kapoor brothers were only the topmost layer of this new South Asian business niche. They kept some newsstands under their own management but subleased others to Indian immigrant investors, hardly any of whom had the time or inclination to spend long hours underground at the newsstands. But with a continuous supply of newly arrived immigrants, many of them relatives, they had a ready source of employable labor. These newest immigrants, unable to find other jobs, accepted this low-paying work readily.

In 1988 the MTA terminated its contract with the Kapoor brothers because of a default on the lease payments. After the Internal Revenue Service also prosecuted them for failing to pay taxes in full, the Kapoor brothers were convicted and sentenced to jail. Many Indian newsstand operators, however, remained in this or related businesses, and newly arrived immigrants continued to fill open positions.

In an attempt to deflate the myth of the family-firm route to ethnic group success, Johanna Lessinger challenged the popular notion that newsstands were small businesses run by entrepreneurs with family labor. "Instead, many involve a complex grouping of investors, owners/operators and workers within which actual economic relationships are often exploitative, working conditions harsh and social mobility illusory. Thus while investment in a newsstand may be profitable, those involved in daily operation find themselves poorly paid, subtly stigmatized within the Indian community and marginalized within U.S. society. Such work is not necessarily the route to social mobility or a vast improvement over manual labor" (1989, 3).

Many newsstand workers I interviewed were young, college-educated immigrants who had accepted these jobs in the hope of moving on to better occupations; others were older immigrants who had left middle-class jobs in India and now experienced downward mobility and loss of social prestige in this occupation. Besides being tedious work at near-minimum wages, these jobs provided no benefits or vacation. Some immigrants who worked a few hours every day at newsstands claimed they were helping a friend or family member; in reality they were waiting for a job with a better income.

Beginning in the late 1980s, a sizable number of South Asians became New York City cabdrivers; during the 1990s an estimated 43 percent of New York Yellow Cab drivers were immigrants from India, Pakistan, and Bangladesh (Advani 1997). With employment opportunities scarce in other areas, cabdriving provided immigrants an opening that required minimum investment and few skills. My interviews with South Asian cabdrivers revealed that like newsstand workers, they viewed this job as temporary work and hoped to move to better-paying work in the future.

Kumar, a graduate of an Indian university, was in his late twenties when he immigrated to join his brother in California. He could not get a "decent" job there and did not want to "live as a burden" on his brother's family. A friend who worked as a cabdriver in New York invited him to move there. "I just told my brother that I am going to New York to see my friend. I have not contacted them in the last two years, and they don't know my whereabouts. I know if my brother knew I was a cabdriver he would be so embarrassed in the community."

Singh left India in the early 1990s and worked in the Middle East and London for a few years. He came to New York because he heard it was easy to get a job here. He learned about cabdriving through his circle of friends and obtained a driver's license and passed the required tests. "That was not difficult for me, since I know English very well and have always been good in adapting to new situations," he said. "Now I share an apartment in Queens with two other Indian men. That is the only way we can pay that rent. These friends are my family and my relatives in this foreign country. I miss my family in India a lot, but I don't think I will ever go back to India." Singh had also filed "papers for immigration" to legalize his status. He said he would leave cabdriving if he found a stable job or saved enough money to start a small business. He also said he could not marry until then. "Right now I can barely survive on this income. One cannot support a family with this occupation."

Sharma, in his mid-fifties, had been driving a Yellow Cab in New York City for more than four years. He was married, but his wife and children lived in Delhi while he shared an apartment in Queens with another Indian man. "I go to India once or twice a year, and since I have a green card it is not difficult for me to travel back and forth. I once brought my son to New York so that he [could] see America. I take lots of gifts for them every time I go back. This is the best arrangement, and I will never move them to America. This is not a country to bring up a family, especially young girls. When I am tired, I will retire back in India."

Mahesh was in his thirties and had tried several jobs in New York. "I like cabdriving because in this job I do not work for anybody else. I am my own master. I have to drive the cab till I make my day's rent. After that it is up to me. Sometimes, if I am lucky and get a good passenger, I can cover that amount real soon. That day, I stop driving before my shift ends, go for a good dinner in a restaurant, and return the cab to my partner, who does the night shift."

Mahesh's account of flexible hours and freedom to work is misleading. Most drivers drove cabs owned by garages that rented out their fleet to drivers for a flat payment. Most paired with another driver, usually a friend, to make maximum use of the twenty-four-hour rental period. Some South Asian immigrants had purchased existing taxi medallions and rented their cabs to immigrant drivers, but most of these owners drove their own cab for one twelve-hour shift and rented it to another driver for the next. Such arrangements point to both ethnic networks and ongoing economic stratification among South Asian immigrants. Owning a medallion was the dream of many immigrant drivers. In the mid-1990s, when New York's Taxi and Limousine Commission announced the sale of new medallions, many South Asians bid for them, often with loans from garages or moneylenders. Their plan was to pay off the loans by renting the cab to other drivers.

One South Asian immigrant who owned a medallion had been driving cabs in New York City for eight years. "For a new driver who has to rent a cab on everyday shift, being a medallion-owner is an enviable position. But once I had a medallion, I soon realized that I was locked into the system. I could not be free till I had paid back my loans. For that I had to be on the road continuously, and the rest of the time I had to rent out the cab to another driver. Luckily there is no shortage of people looking for jobs, but when I see them, I think of how I started in this work. And I wonder if I and they will ever be able to get out of this circle."

Whether they liked the work or not, nearly all cabdrivers felt that they could not do this job for very long. Some related how grueling it was to sit at the wheel for up to fourteen hours. One said, "It is not good for your health. Soon your back begins to give way. I am sure many of us will have serious health problems later on." Others pointed to the high risk of violence while driving. In the 1990s several cabdrivers were murdered, and taxi-driving ranked second in mortality rates among New York occupations, after small convenience businesses such as gas stations, minimarts, and corner stores (Advani 1997).

One driver voiced the pain and embarrassment of many of his colleagues: "Many people treat me as if I am nothing else but a cabdriver—I have no feelings, no dreams, no social life. I want to scream and say that I was not born as a cabdriver, and hopefully, I will not remain one all my life. The whole city is against us; the cops fill their [summons] quotas by coming down on us. If we do not take a passenger because of safety concerns, or just because I am too tired to drive any more, it is considered a racial thing.

The truth is, this country is racist. We never thought of these things before we came to this country."

Cabdriving reveals the viability and expansion of South Asian ethnic networks in finding employment. On the job, cabdrivers shared traffic information and kept in touch with one another through citizens'-band radios, using a combination of Hindi, Punjabi, and Urdu. As a driver explained, "If one of us is in trouble, we know about it through the radio and can come to his rescue. In this lonely job this radio is our companion and community." A regular companion was South Asian music, played continuously in their cabs. But "we have to be careful with Americans. They don't understand this music." Although it seems these drivers had little interaction with upper-class Indians, almost all had such a relative "who came here long time ago." They visited these relatives on special occasions, but friendships and social contacts were with people also engaged in cabdriving or other auto-related businesses, like trucking or gas stations.

The reality of an Indian immigrant working class in New York City was also evident among the growing number of Indian workers in retail businesses, including such American-owned store chains as Woolworth and Duane Reade, or the less prominent National Wholesale Liquidators (NWL), a Jewish-owned chain selling low-priced household goods in fifteen stores in Queens, Manhattan, Long Island, and New Jersey. In 1995 the entire staff of the NWL branch on Kissena Boulevard in Flushing, known as "Store No. 3," was South Asian. Most workers at this store, male and female, were from the Punjab region extending across India and Pakistan, and included Hindus, Muslims, and Sikhs. The dominance of Punjabi culture was evident in the use of Punjabi names and accent in store announcements and interstaff communication. Male workers did aisle stocking, unloading, and managerial and security tasks, while female employees staffed the cash registers. Only recently had the manager, a Pakistani immigrant, hired a few non–South Asians. "Our customers have been complaining about language and ethnic exclusiveness of our staff. So I hired some blacks. They are immigrants, too—everyone is an immigrant here—but they don't look as different as our people do."

Most NWL workers lived in the vicinity of Store No. 3 in ethnically diverse Queens neighborhoods, and had been recruited from the continuous flow of newly arrived immigrants. Originally the owner of the chain had hired a Sikh as a manager, a man described by one immigrant employee as "a Sikh born in the U.S., and therefore an American compared to us immigrants." Eventually this Sikh American manager brought in immigrant workers from his own Punjabi ethnic group, and the pattern continued. According to Store No. 3's manager, "On an average, four to five people come by looking for work every day. This is much less than earlier. There were many more in 1988–89. At that time people did not know where to go—wandered here and there—went to petrol pumps [gas stations] or painting jobs, or stores like ours. At that time [ethnic] job lines were not established. Now there [are] information, links, and set areas of employment."

Tensions among Punjabi employees based on Hindu-Muslim religious or Indian-Pakistani national differences were minimal. "There is some of it, which is natural in our people . . . but nothing serious." The manager explained that during the 1996 World Cup Cricket Series, played in South Asia and broadcast live to many countries around the world, male NWL workers, both Indian and Pakistani, attended midnight-to-five-A.M. telecasts of the matches in a movie theater in Jackson Heights. (Thousands of South Asian cricket fans, primarily men but some women as well, watched these matches in three movie theaters, in Queens, Manhattan, and Long Island.) "We teased each other according to which side was winning or losing, but next morning we all came to work in the store normally."

Sukhwinder, an NWL worker in her late forties, arrived in New York from India two years ago, and worked as a cashier.

We came to New York because my husband's sister who lives here sponsored us for a green card. My husband's family—parents, brothers, sisters—all live in America. It took us many years to get green cards, but we were not sure if we should make the move. My husband had a good job in India, and we were well settled there. But our relatives persisted that we should join them here. We could make a good life here, make good money, and give good education to our children. What is the use of missing India now or regretting the decision? The die is cast now. . . .

First only my husband came to New York, to see if he [could] get a job. He was lucky to find one in this store where I work now, and soon the children and I joined him. We admitted our children in schools—they say you cannot keep children out of school here, even for a short time, unlike India, where you wait for the school year to start—and I looked for a job. I had never worked in India, but we couldn't survive here with only one income. First I worked in a garment factory about which another Indian woman had told me. In the meanwhile, my husband had told his manager that I would like to have a job in this store. So when a vacancy came up, I was given this cashier's job. This is not difficult work, but it is very tiring. I have to stand for hours without a break, and by the end of the day I am exhausted. Then I have to go home and do housework.

My husband left for California six months ago. His brothers who live there kept telling us that they can find him a better job there. After a few months of trying, he has got a factory job with benefits. I am told that is what's important in this country—benefits. So now, I and the children are going to join him there. I think I will have to do a job there also; we cannot survive on one salary in this country. And even then, it is barely a hand-to-mouth situation. But at least then we will be together again.

In the late 1980s Indians in Queens began to appear as street vendors selling newspapers at busy traffic intersections and distributing flyers on streets for Indian or other businesses. These "cash jobs" paid subminimum wages, offered no benefits, and depended on the good graces of the employers, often Indian businessmen. Every day for almost two years, Mr. Singh, in his early fifties, spent the early-morning hours in front of a Queens subway station with an elderly relative selling newspapers to Manhattan-bound commuters. "It is better than seeing the sad and worried faces of my wife and children at home. We have been living with a relative for a year now, but for how long? I was a post office worker in India, but my education and skills are meaningless here." I also met a few Indian women who, unable to find employment, made samosas to sell to stores or for private parties. Other women worked for cash, assembling belts or mechanical parts for a factory at home, doing household cleaning work, or babysitting. One explained, "This is easier than going away from home for the whole day to work outside. My children are young, and I like to be at home when they come back from school. At the same time, I get some cash, which is handy in running the household. It is not much, but better than depending solely on my husband's small salary."

An anonymous letter printed in *India Monitor* (7/22/1992), a local Indian newspaper, expressed shock at the situation of poor Indian and South Asian immigrants in the New York.

> A few weeks ago I visited a friend in an upper Manhattan hotel for transients. The hotel used to be a second home for immigrants from Eastern Europe at the end of World War II. . . . Today, Indians, Pakistanis, and Bangladeshis constitute about 50 percent of this hotel's population. Others come from Haiti and Dominican Republic. . . . I believe that there are at least eight other similar transient hotels in the neighborhood . . . and there are over 500 people from the Indian subcontinent living in them. . . . Some of them have lived there as long as three years and they seem to be unable to move to a cleaner and more wholesome atmosphere. Some say they are going to be there for "a few more weeks," but you take a hard look at them, look into their sunken eyes, watch their parched lips, and see their sinking cheeks, and wonder if they can really do so. . . . Many of the Indians in these hotels work in grocery shops, drive livery cabs, sell newspapers. . . . A substantial number of them stay put because they are undergoing strong psychological and emotional problems. They do not know where to go for help; some of them are even beyond help.

In the 1990s poor Indian immigrants were to be seen all over the city, in pockets in every borough. In Queens they were more obvious because of the larger size of its Indian population.

Organizing Class Interests

By the 1990s the Indian population in New York City ranged from affluent professionals who lived in large homes to a growing number of low-income immigrants who struggled for survival. The interests of upper-class
immigrants dominated pan-Indian community activities and its politics of
representation both within and beyond the South Asian community. Ethnic
directories and handbooks featured lists of successful professionals, affluent
businessmen, and high-achieving college whiz kids. An American corpora-
tion's handbook for Indian immigrants (AT&T 1990) included short articles
on "Tax Information," "Buying a Home—Closing Costs," "How to Be Your
Own Investment Manager," and "Franchise Business." A page on "Helpful
Organizations" listed agencies promoting trade, investment, and business
with India; it did not include any government offices or social service agencies that working-class Indian immigrants might need.

The celebration of elite Indian success was also evident in an article in
American Demographics (Mogelonsky 1995) that presented a sociocultural
and economic profile of Indian immigrants for corporations and businesses
to know better their prospective customers. "The Asian-Indian population
of the U.S. is affluent and growing. Asian Indians often work as professionals and entrepreneurs. Marketers divide the group into three segments, but
all Indians are keenly interested in financial security, good value, and shopping around. Although Asian Indians assimilate easily into U.S. culture, the
best way to reach them is to support their communities and traditions."

Indians in established careers and successful businesses emphasized an
individual work ethic and dissociated themselves from, or refused to ac-
knowledge, problems facing any disadvantaged group. One Indian professional presented the following views at a panel on minorities in various occupations:

> There is no single group that is a disadvantaged minority. We are all minorities
> in our own ways, and we are all competing with each other as individuals and
> not so much as individuals against a whole group of advantaged people. . . .
> The other day I was listening to a highly successful industrialist who was being
> asked by the interviewer what his success formula was. He quickly responded,
> saying there was no substitute for hard work. The truly successful do not talk
> about being a minority, being underprivileged, being this or that. They are
> simply too busy perfecting their art, their chosen pursuit. This must be one's
> goal—minority or majority.

The social circles of upper-class Indian immigrants in New York City ra-
diated outward to Indians of similar class and occupational background in
other parts of the country (Gordon 2000). These class-based networks oper-

ated in social and cultural spheres as well, but they were most evident in oc-cupational organizations. According to various estimates, by the 1990s there were about 30,000 Indian medical doctors in the United States. Founded in 1982, their professional organization, the Association of American Physi-cians from India (AAPI), grew rapidly into the largest Indian organization in the United States. In 1989 it had fifty chapters and 5,000 members span-ning the entire country, and chapters and membership continued to grow in subsequent years. In 1995 a separate AAPI Queens/Long Island chapter was inaugurated to represent this area's roughly 1,500 medical doctors (*News India* 1/19/96).

Over the years, AAPI had become the leading vehicle for Indian profes-sional influence on mainstream American politics. Its annual convention, which rotated among large American cities, attracted not only thousands of Indian doctors but also major American political figures. The 1994, 1995, and 1996 conventions in Atlanta, Chicago, and Boston presented keynote addresses from Speaker of the House of Representatives Newt Gingrich, President Bill Clinton, and House Minority Leader Richard Gephardt. The 1994 convention also featured a forum on the Clinton administration health care proposal and its effect on foreign-born doctors. The influence of AAPI was also expressed in fundraising for American political parties, and several Indian doctors were large donors to presidential election campaigns. In the 1990s, AAPI was one of a handful of Indian organizations to have a perma-nent office in Washington, D.C.

Indian immigrant doctors also maintained close contact with state and national governments in India. Their financial investment was welcomed in India, and personal bonds between overseas Indian doctors and Indian politicians were common; AAPI conventions were thus often attended by senior Indian diplomats and government representatives. An AAPI chari-table foundation was even created for projects in India.

During the 1980s Indian immigrants in other professions also formed na-tional occupational organizations. The American Association of Psychia-trists from India, founded in 1980, grew into many chapters all over the country. In 1988 the Society of Indian Travel Agents was formed, and held its first meeting in New York. In 1996 officers of the Indo-American Phar-maceutical Society, established in 1988, formed ties with AAPI and the In-dian Dentists Association "to present a strong force in the community" (*News India* 1/19/96).

The agendas of all these organizations included advocacy for Indians and fighting discriminatory practices in their occupational arenas. Several were subgroups of mainstream organizations, including the American Medical Association and the American Psychiatric Association. While certain Indian regional or religious backgrounds were more prominent than others among these professional organizations' members and officers, they were all pan-Indian in purpose and spirit, and officers of Indian religious minorities were elected from time to time.

Financial seminars and conferences for Indian professional immigrants occurred regularly around the country. In the 1980s a number of Indian-owned banks were formed—the State Bank of Texas, the National Republic Bank of Chicago, the First National Bank and Trust Company in Junction City, Kansas; most of their investors were Indian businessmen and professionals, especially physicians, who attended forums on investment opportunities in New York City and elsewhere (*India Abroad* 11/20/87). In 1995 The Indus Entrepreneurs (TIE), a group of Silicon Valley professionals, brought hundreds of South Asian immigrants to San Jose for a conference on product marketing and public relations, with selected South Asian entrepreneurs and American industrial leaders as speakers (*India Abroad* 5/19/95).

By the 1990s thousands of young Indians in mainstream organizations and professions, largely in their twenties and ranging from the U.S.-born to recent skilled immigrants, became members of the Network of Indian Professionals (NET-IP), a nationwide organization. Founded in the early 1990s by young Indians in New York and Chicago, NET-IP rapidly sprouted chapters all across North America. According to Mahesh Ram, a cofounder, the genesis of the New York chapter was the recognition that although young Indian Americans met, and even surpassed, the educational requirements that constituted "merit," they lacked access to traditional white American occupational networks. Focused on creating new networks within mainstream professions, NET-IP members included software designers, engineers, physicians, and teachers who attended its lunches, seminars, and fundraising drives.

Among working-class Indian immigrants, little organizing was attempted before 1992, when a small group of progressive South Asian activists formed the Leased Drivers Coalition (LDC) to represent cabdrivers, with help from the activist pan-Asian Committee Against Anti-Asian Violence (Advani 1997). During its 1992–93 Operation Safe Cab campaign, which pressured the city Taxi and Limousine Commission for new taxi safety requirements benefiting drivers, the LDC discovered other mobilization efforts already under way. "Trying to build support . . . we turned to communities, rather than to established unions, and circulated petitions at fairs, Indian/Pakistani restaurants, and mosques. . . . In October 1993, after three Pakistani drivers were murdered in a twenty-four-hour period, seven thousand drivers demonstrated in midtown Manhattan about the need for better safety measures. This speedy and well-planned mass demonstration was called by other small drivers' organizations, many of them ethnic-specific groups, unknown to us, which had active networks organized around particular CB radio channels" (Advani 1997, 218). The LDC worked with a few South Asian cabdriver leaders, such as Salim Osman, an attorney in his home country of Pakistan; but young U.S.-educated South Asians supplied the main leadership. Aside from a few progressive South Asian organizations, the larger Indian community of New York City had remained oblivious of cabdriver struggles and LDC activities.

[5]

Family and Gender

The imagery of family is widely tied to the success of Asian immigrants in the United States. And like other Asians, Indian immigrants themselves consider traditional family values to be a cornerstone of their culture, and a key distinguishing feature between themselves and Americans (Chen 1992; Kibria 1993; Bacon 1996; Park 1997). Indian immigrants in New York therefore assigned high priority to preserving their family traditions in the United States. From the 1960s through the 1990s that task became more possible as New York's typical Indian families changed from nuclear husband–wife units to extended family networks of related households, a result of relatives immigrating primarily via family-sponsored visas.[1] This family reunification process fostered such traditional practices as arranged marriage, more salient caste identification, and patriarchal religious activities, all boosted by more pervasive contact with the home country. These trends, however, also met challenges from within the New York community, mainly along gender and generational lines. By the 1990s progressive women and U.S.-reared youth were often perceived as opposed to the traditional Indian family and as threats to its patriarchal values. Conservative elements in the community even branded individuals who did not conform to established roles as more "American" than Indian.

Social and Family Roles

Despite centuries of change in Indian society, the degree of continuity remains striking. Although other religions and also regional variations exist,

[117]

the ideal Sanskritized Hindu social system sets norms for social life to which many Indians aspire, and may practice almost religiously (Embree 1989). According to this view, the individual and family life cycles are divided into four *ashrams,* or stages. First is *brahmacharya,* the student stage, when one's chief pursuit is education under the guidance of parents and teachers. *Grahastha,* the householder stage, follows, marked by attainment of an independent livelihood, marriage, and raising children. The third stage, *vanprastha,* begins when one's children become adults raising their own families, and parental responsibilities have been completed. The final stage, *sanyasa,* is the search for spiritual truth, which may involve actively renouncing society. Originating in ancient scriptures, these concepts underlie patriarchal social values.

In contemporary urban India the education of young women in the first stage, and their employment in the second, are accepted, yet otherwise the four-ashram "map of living" remains intact. Indians expect to complete their education, obtain a job, and get married in their twenties. Deviations, such as marrying late, not establishing a stable career, or, for women, not bearing children within a few years of marriage, are considered socially abnormal.

The ashram framework, or *dharma,* sets out separate gender roles for men and women: women are in charge of the home, including food preparation and everyday family needs, while men provide household income by working outside. Ideally, men have the final say in major decisions, especially in career and property matters, but women influence these decisions through informal channels. This separation of gender roles also results in considerable social segregation between men and women. These gender roles are integral to children's socialization in India, where they are affirmed in mythology, high culture, and popular media (Das Dasgupta 1986; Kakar 1988).

Marriage plays a pivotal role in maintaining this social framework, and is important not only to the married couple but also for their network of relatives. Starting with their involvement in arranging a marriage, Indians' social behavior toward many others is determined by whether they are on the "girl's side" or the "boy's side" of each new related couple. The new couple also orients its social relationships between the two sets of parents and their relatives. It is taken for granted that an Indian bride leaves her own parents' home and joins her husband's family, symbolized by changing her family name to that of her new in-laws. The Hindi terms *maika,* or "mother's home," and *sasural,* or "in-laws' home," or their equivalents in other Indian languages, now divide a person's social universe.

Increasingly, educated individuals in contemporary India, particularly in its urban sector, have more say in arranging their own marriages, but gender-role expectations display much continuity. Marriages are considered permanent and should not be altered by either partner's free choice. Other social rules also apply to both sexes, but more leeway is allowed to men. Historically, a woman's social world had centered on her marriage, while men acted in the world outside the home. Men's deviations from expectations seldom brought penalties and were easily forgiven, whereas women who strayed from prescribed gender behavior risked ruining the reputations of their natal and marital families.

Over the course of the twentieth century, the traditional Indian joint family household frequently gave way to nuclear family residence, particularly as people moved to urban areas. However, as scholars of Indian society have pointed out, extended family ties survived. Sylvia Vatuk (1975, 1980, 1989), for example, argues that although not all members of an Indian family may live under one roof, notions associated with joint family living have not been abandoned. Her research in urban India demonstrates that joint family links are maintained through shared fiscal responsibilities, care for the elderly, and visits to ancestral homes located in small towns or villages. Thus "the family as an idea and as an ongoing social entity endures in its essentials, though distance separates some of its members" (Vatuk 1989, 193). Among Indian family members themselves, "the outside observer gains the distinct impression of widespread confidence that the fundamental cultural basis of Indian family is strong enough . . . to withstand the dramatic social transitions that are occurring" (Vatuk 1989, 189).

Each Indian family, whether joint or nuclear, exists within a "community" (the Indian English word) that is distinguished by religion, caste, cultural practices, and endogamous or intracommunity marriages. Members of an Indian community do not necessarily live in the same geographic area but do maintain links through visits, family gatherings, and communal religious observances. In North India this community is called *jat-biradari*, which connotes both common caste membership and brotherhood. (A caste, or jati, which shares a name, traditions, and typical occupational specialization, is composed of several communities, or biradaris.) In the multicultural United States, Indian immigrants at first considered all other Indians as their new American ethnic community, but their traditional notion of community began to reassert its importance as the number of relatives in New York or elsewhere in the United States steadily increased.

A distinct perception of self and society is contained in Indian notions of family and community (Roland 1986; Bacon 1996). Whereas the "self" in American society is an individualized unit that creates a new relationship when two such persons contract a marriage, in India persons are embedded in social relationships and communal identities that exist both before and after marriage. As people behave according to their community affiliation, religion, caste, class, and gender, it is more difficult to assign neat boundaries between self and others. As Sudhir Kakar has pointed out, even lead or heroic characters in Indian films, novels, and folk tales "are symbolic revealers of a much larger universe" (1988, 4), and as Alan Roland has noted, "[Indian] subjects emphasized again and again . . . a constant indulgence of each other, and a sense of we-ness and partial merger" (1986, 44).

In keeping with these orientations, Indian immigrants in New York continued to view each other more in terms of social roles than in terms of individual identities. Often when they wanted to cement a relationship with a nonrelative or convey closeness, they ascribed a quasi-family relationship to the person, using such expressions as "He is like my son" for a younger man or "I treat that woman like my mother" for an older woman. Given the strict gender differentiation, men and women of similar ages could be close friends only if they had "a brother–sister relationship," Indian code words for a nonsexual relationship. Indians expected all persons to behave according to their cultural notions of proper ashram and family role behavior, making judgments about whether behavior was appropriate for "an older man of a father's age" or whether "she behaves like a daughter or not." In nonwork contexts with other Indians, a professional woman was expected to play her traditional role in a social gathering, behaving like a wife and homemaker, and a young person was expected to display respect when interacting with any elder. Failure to behave according to such expectations was undesirable and was often labeled "Americanized." Correspondingly, Indians found this desired role behavior frequently missing among Americans, and considered them lacking in social sensitivity. Puzzlement or disgust at American social behavior led to stereotyping. Some viewed American notions of family, marriage, and community as so different from their own that they regarded American society as devoid of social institutions. Some Indian immigrants even wondered if Americans had any family system at all, if American marriages were based on anything real, or if Americans were serious about any relationships.

Early Immigrant Families

Indian immigrants of the 1960s and 1970s were primarily young white-collar professionals who were starting new families in the United States. In those years, students who stayed on and adults immigrating for job reasons were viewed as two separate categories, with different experiences and social networks. In later years these two groups in effect merged and saw themselves as an earlier wave of immigrants, distinct from later arrivals (Nandan and Eames 1980).

The Indian foreign students had often developed relations with white Americans interested in India, some of which resulted in marriage. These biracial households remained on the margin of New York's emerging Indian community; in later decades a handful of non-Indian spouses, male and female, were visible at Indian events, but their participation was peripheral. Unless the host of an event was especially open-minded or the few non-Indian spouses made concerted efforts to belong, the Indian community did not embrace them. Their presence would become ever more conspicuous with the mounting flow of new immigrants from India.

Ahmad, an Indian student who settled in New York in the 1960s, recalled his compatriots who married American women.

> When you saw your friends getting married like this, and when you may have your own [such] relationships, it was difficult to have an arranged marriage with an Indian. I myself spent several years being divided by the two different directions. It was hard not to commit to a relationship [with an American] here, and to dodge my parents, who constantly nagged me from India. Eventually I did decide to marry someone from my own religion and regional culture in India, whom my parents had recommended. I did so because I did not want to engage in a lifelong struggle to preserve my culture and to constantly explain to my wife what Indian culture was.

Like Ahmad, many other foreign students decided to enter what some Indians called "a modern arranged marriage," with a partner, usually of their own community, selected from a set of persons recommended by their own family.

Indians who came directly from India to New York for career reasons were even more likely to enter arranged marriages. In fact many had already married in India and reunited with their spouse in the United States after they had secured adequate employment to support a family. Others returned to India to marry. In either case these immigrants began rearing families in households governed by Indian expectations and social norms. Although they entered mainstream American professions and spoke English at work, at home their diet, dress, gender roles, worship, and language were Indian. Change here was minimal. At a conference on the family organized by Indian immigrants in New York City in 1984, adjustment in marital relations was illustrated by the cover page of the proceedings, which featured pictures of two households: one in which a traditional husband neglected to help his wife in the kitchen, portending a problematic result, and one in which both spouses shared chores, spelling harmony. But even though more women worked outside the home than in India, and even though men shared some domestic tasks, little fundamental change oc-

[121]

curred in their "maps for living" or in lived patriarchal relationships (Saran 1985, 40–41).

This early wave of pioneer middle-class Indian families had choices in facing the disruption of family and marital life that immigration to the United States presented them, but they remained confident that they could meet the challenge via "modern" Indian family norms. When sociologists in the 1970s did observe change in Indian immigrant family organization, it was primarily structural. "One of the most significant consequences of the Indian migration to the United States has been the shift away from the joint family to the conjugal family . . . In the United States those mechanisms that link together urban families in India are frequently impossible. Kin-ship-linked families residing in New York, Chicago, Boston, and Houston cannot recapitulate the patterns of cooperation and close contact character-istic of urban Indian families in India. The geographic distance is a major barrier" (Nandan and Eames 1980, 199, 203). From the 1960s through the 1990s, however, Indian immigrants made consistent efforts to re-create such links by using immigration law to bring relatives in India to the United States. They also used modern communications technology to shrink the distance between households, thus strengthening extended family net-works. As a result, Indian joint families and communities were steadily re-constituted in the United States. As the decades passed, virtually every In-dian nuclear family had relatives living nearer at hand and in closer touch.

Family Reunification

Like other post-1965 immigrant groups, Indians utilized the preference system of the Immigration Act of 1965 to sponsor their relatives for immi-gration (Chen 1992; Park 1997; see table 1). They continued to use the two occupational visa categories, but growing numbers already here also made use of the four family reunification categories to sponsor relatives. Since a naturalized citizen could sequentially apply for multiple sponsorships, it was possible for one family to bring several more to the United States. Each new immigrant could sponsor a spouse and nonadult children while still a resident alien, and the range of sponsorable kin expanded with naturaliza-tion, possible after five years. As the number of established families grew, family reunification came to dominate Indian immigration. Thus from the early 1980s to the early 1990s, about three-fourths of total Indian immigra-tion to New York City was derived from family-preference visas used by U.S. citizens and permanent resident aliens (first, second, fourth, and fifth preferences in table 1) to sponsor their families for immigration (New York City Department of City Planning 1996, tables 3–4 and 3–5).

Typically, family A, once established in this country, would sponsor immigration of family B, usually that of a sibling in India. On arrival, initially family B would reside with family A while the male head of family B looked for employment. With shrinking opportunities in professional markets, and a widening socioeconomic spectrum among sponsored immigrants, this period of "joint family" settlement became increasingly lengthy by the 1980s and 1990s. In many cases immigrant women, often not highly educated and never before employed, sought jobs to contribute income to their households. Once on its own, family B could repeat the process with family C, and so on.

New York City had a far greater number of initial sponsors of such family migration chains than did other American cities. This trend accelerated not only the growth and size of the new Indian immigrant population but also its widening socioeconomic composition. Later immigrants had fewer choices in jobs available to them, and many turned to blue-collar work or the underground cash economy. Ironically, the established immigrant sponsors often played a role in solidifying the wider economic spectrum. In a number of cases, the professional family A established or invested in a small business that supported the newly arrived relatives, thus creating further socioeconomic hierarchy or paternalistic relationships within the Indian community.

By the 1990s the Indian American community was characterized by these extended family networks of households in the larger metropolitan areas such as New York City, Chicago, and Houston, all of which had substantial Indian concentrations. Other related households or networks might exist throughout the rest of the country. The distribution of each extended family network was ultimately determined by the location of jobs, but families sought to bring relatives to live as close by as possible. They constantly looked for job opportunities for one another, and a major share of family communication at gatherings was devoted to exchanging such information. Family networks also crossed national boundaries, and in Queens contact through communication and travel extended to India, Britain, Canada, Kenya, and other countries.

Identity and Gender Roles

In the 1960s and 1970s, except for some nurses and other professionals who immigrated on their own, Indian women in New York were dependents of male immigrants. Soon, however, their roles and activities could not easily be categorized as "traditional." By the 1980s significant numbers of women were visible in the workforce, and some even founded new community organizations. This emergence of Indian women in public spheres led to debate about gender roles, empowerment, and community leadership. In the 1990s gender became a pivotal issue in Indian American politics.

The lives of these Indian immigrant women in New York were not monochromatic stories of bewildered traditional women adrift in the United States. Neither were their experiences simple linear transitions from Indian to modern Western society. Indian women's experiences and viewpoints varied widely, running along class and generational lines. Significantly, few women were inclined to reject wholesale their cultural traditions for American social patterns and values. Instead, the sense prevailed that they faced the challenge of redefining their traditions and roles in the migration context.

From the 1960s through the 1990s, Indian women in New York City redefined family and community roles. Change was evident but also complex, particularly for college-educated women raised in urban families that placed a high value on a woman's education.

Meera and her husband came to the United States as foreign students in the late 1960s. They met at an American university where both were enrolled in Ph.D. programs. After completing their degrees, they married and decided to settle in the United States. They moved to New York City when the husband found a job there, and began married life and careers together. Meera, however, gave up work when they had their first child, her priority being to raise her child at home. Admittedly she was not aggressive about pursuing her career, and did not consider the option of day care. Three years later they had a second child.

> I have not worked outside for more than fifteen years now, and I am completely tied up with house chores. I cook, clean, pick up and drop kids at school, and wait for my husband to come back home. I have no time to pursue any of my talents, let alone a full-time career. My husband comes back home tired and does not help in any housework. His ambition is to achieve success in his profession. He says he wants to rise like a star, illuminating the world around him. And I think every day that my life is passing in routines, without any sense of achievement or satisfaction. At times I wish I was an uneducated woman who could not think or reason. Life [might] have been more satisfying then.

Meera lived in a middle-class section of Queens, not far from Flushing and Jackson Heights, to which she often drove. She had built a circle of Indian women friends, most of them also mothers, and immersed herself in Indian cultural activities.

Farida was a college-educated woman in her mid-forties. Her sister sponsored Farida and her husband for visas, and they arrived in the city in 1978.

Farida worked in a managerial position, and her husband was an engineer. By 1990 their two children were teenagers.

> My husband was okay before we came to the U.S. Then this drive to excel took over him. He has no time for home, for me, or the children. His work, his computer, and his books are his only world. In the beginning [of our problems], it was very difficult. I used to write to my sister-in-law [husband's sister] in India, with whom I was close. She was very patient and supportive—would explain her brother's temperament and the need for me to be patient. She sometimes even mediated in our fights on my behalf. But how long could this overseas counseling last? Usually, by the time my sister-in-law responded from India, the immediate issue was over for us.
>
> After spending so many years on sorting this mess, I have given up the fight and reconciled to this state of affairs. I have my own life, my job, and other activities that keep me occupied. There is always something to do or to participate in. I can live within the marriage with all these supports. My husband does not accompany me for such activities, but I do find friends who are willing to go with me. But we try to attend our [home region] community events together, since we both know families there.

Farida was satisfied that her two children had done well in school, but she did not consider them Indian. "They are very smart and do not need any guidance from parents in planning their future. . . . They constantly tell us that we do not know how things go on in this country. I am carrying out my share of responsibility in supporting them, but soon they are going to be fully independent. I know my daughter will marry someone of her own choice—without even consulting us—so why bother?"

Most Indian women who arrived in the 1960s and 1970s, despite their education, assigned primacy to their roles as wife and mother and adjusted career demands to family needs. They considered women's empowerment an ongoing struggle to be waged within the marital relationship. Rearing families in a new social and cultural milieu was a challenge. Both husbands and wives felt like pioneers charting unknown territory. For some, raising families was coupled with building cultural and religious institutions, resources they hoped would help their children learn about their Indian backgrounds. The children participated in these community activities, but they also observed the segregated gender roles played out at home and in such settings, and constructed their notions of Indian culture accordingly.

Most Indian marriages in the early wave of immigration survived, but a few, fraught with difficulties, were short-lived. Early in her thirties, Nirmala faced a crisis. Her husband, also an Indian immigrant, left her and their young children. Nirmala spent several years vacillating over whether to live in India or New York. First she returned to her home in India and tried to raise her children with the help of family members there. Soon, however, she returned to New York and found a modestly paid job to support herself and her children. "At that time this entire Indian [immigrant] community—our previous friends and well-wishers—avoided me. I was made to feel that if my husband had left me, I had committed a sin. Those days required tremendous courage and perseverance on my part. Only a couple of local families were supportive. Every time I felt like quitting, I would look at my children. That gave me strength. I never considered remarrying. I could not put my own happiness above that of my children. In our tradition, we do not go for that."

Vijaya had experienced only a few years of married life in New York when her husband suddenly died. At that time the couple and their two young children lived in their own home, attached to that of Vijaya's parents-in-law. Vijaya now faced a sea change in her life. "I realized that in addition to the serious personal loss in my life, my social life had also suffered. I was not invited to social gatherings any more, and when I saw family friends, strange questions were asked of me. It was clear that I had no place in the core Indian community, which was bound by marriage and embedded in traditional family and gender roles. Gradually my social circle changed completely and included more women friends and a handful of families who were broadminded [enough] to treat me as an individual in my own right."

Vijaya considered herself fortunate that she had a professional job at the time and could continue in her own career. She also credited her in-laws, who helped her cope with the tragedy. "Even though they had lost their son and brother, they stood by me and treated me like their own daughter. Since then, that has been my immediate family." Vijaya never remarried; her goal was to raise her two children. By the late 1980s she was active in several community organizations and had an established group of female friends.

Such women's experiences were rarely discussed by the larger Indian community, which continued its idealized notions of Indian marriage and family. Except for the handful of individuals who offered acceptance and support, these women were ignored. The existing community organizations did not consider situations like these serious enough to deserve attention.

Despite immigrant efforts to maintain gender-role continuity, change became clear to women—and, even more so, to their children—when they were visited by relatives from India or visited India themselves. Through the 1970s most Indian immigrant families were still young, and nuclear in form, with the choices in relation to American conditions that economic stability and higher education permitted early-wave women. By the 1980s the changing composition of now mature immigrant families began to have an impact on family and gender relations.

Family reunification united many immigrants with their siblings and parents. Elderly parents, either visiting the United States for extended periods or settling here, joined the households of middle-aged sons. Wives now shared their nuclear family with younger or older relatives. Indian immigrant women could not openly criticize these family reunifications, but many were silently unhappy about the outcomes. One woman voiced a common sentiment: "You call this America? It is like living amidst all my in-laws in India. Sometimes one feels good at having social gatherings, and my children now have their cousins as companions. But it also means a lot of responsibility toward our relatives."

Gender roles became inextricably involved in relations between sponsoring and sponsored families in New York City's Indian immigrant community, and intrafamilial tensions grew. While some reunifications did occur on the wife's side of the family, testifying to the power of American law over Indian traditions, most sponsorship of relatives strengthened the patriarchal nature of Indian households. Having reared their children in relative freedom, women now found that newly arrived relatives brought traditional joint family gender-role expectations with them from India. These relatives, to make matters worse, viewed them as "very Americanized."

The later-arriving immigrant women in the 1980s and 1990s had fewer options and less personal freedom in their households. Like their predecessors, a significant number were well educated and entered professional employment, but growing numbers had lower levels of education and did not secure independent incomes. They looked for support to older female relatives already in the United States, but found that these women's lives were distinctly different from their own—either reflecting lives lived largely in the United States, or experiences in India that confirmed traditional role expectations. Virtually no outside organized, professional counseling for Indian women existed until the mid-1980s.

Gender and Work

Immigration created a new context for Indian women's employment. In contemporary India, particularly in urban areas, growing numbers of women receive education and work for pay, but homemaking remains their primary responsibility. In the United States, however, women's employment was perceived to be a necessity.

On arrival in the United States, an Indian woman's capacity for employment was reevaluated. The range of Indian female employment in New York City—from professional careerist to household worker—was shaped by education level, financial resources, and the particular nature of each family's encounter with American conditions. Many women with careers in India became homemakers in the United States; other women with no work experience or training joined the American workforce. According to the 1980 and 1990 U.S. censuses, 45 and 49 percent, respectively, of Indian women sixteen years and older in New York City were employed. However, among immigrants entering New York from 1990 through 1994, only 1,171 Indian women reported holding an occupation at the time of their departure. This figure was strikingly lower than for Chinese immigrant women (11,275) or Filipino immigrant women (6,499). Among Indian women who did report a previous occupation, 69 percent were professionals, including 31 percent who were registered nurses (New York City Department of City Planning, 1996, 19, table 2-14).

Employment brought opportunities for women to earn incomes that thus made their husbands less central as sole household providers. But at the same time, employment took time away from their homemaker role, and many women in New York lamented the absence of support from female relatives or household employees that was commonly available to them in India. In contemporary India, organized day care is not widespread, but young children are frequently left with elderly relatives. In the United States, sending one's children to day care was a difficult choice for Indian parents, as it symbolized a substantial change in a woman's role in her family. To raise children in the United States meant additional effort and responsibility for women, with the burden of performing this duty single-handedly. When comparing life in India with life in the United States, immigrants often pointed to the domestic help there for chores such as housecleaning and laundering performed by the large workforce of poorer Indians, many of them migrants from rural areas. Many Indian women in New York City considered performing these chores themselves as a loss of social status (Khandelwal 1997b).

In the 1980s and 1990s, newly immigrating women of more advanced ages and lower educational levels found the transition to work even more difficult. A number of these women had never worked outside the home in India, or had received only limited income from teaching or part-time jobs. There they had unquestioningly adjusted their work to their primary child-drearing role. In the United States, however, work was necessary for survival, since their husbands could not obtain well-paying jobs.

Frustration was clearly evident among the women immigrants arriving during these decades, including those who were university educated. As one said, "We are not used to leaving our kids in day care and focusing on building our careers. In India there is so much help in running a household; first there are elderly relatives or neighbors, or some other kind of paid help [maids, live-in servants] is easily available. There are so many situations in America when you face the entire world by yourself—there is sickness in the family, your child has a problem in school, or there are relatives visiting from India. And nobody understands you, neither your Indian family nor your American colleagues." Some expressed a painful sense of extreme isolation if they did not work. "I thought my college education was for my own development and for me to raise my children in an educated environment. But in this materialistic country you have no worth if you do not earn money."

For many middle-class Indian women, working outside the home signaled a lowering of social status. In the 1990s growing numbers of them worked in low-wage jobs where their college or high school educations were of little use. Many had difficulty finding work in mainstream settings, and turned to immigrant-run ethnic niches and underground employment.

Sunita, an Indian woman in her fifties, arrived in New York in 1986 with her husband and three children. In India she was a college-educated homemaker "with a settled life-style, a large social network, and real estate property." When Sunita's husband received a green card, and the entire family could accompany him to the United States,

We were thrilled, especially our children, who dreamt about having a wonderful life in the U.S. . . . It was like a lotto to them. My husband retired from his excellent job, the children left their private schools. We sold our property to arrange for our air tickets to the U.S.A., and arrived in Flushing, where we rented this small apartment.

In the beginning it was very difficult for my husband to find any job. It took him almost a year to get a low-paying one of running a night shift at a corner store. Soon we realized that we couldn't depend on his one income. For the past few years, we have all tried to find work. My children—of whom the younger one is completing his high school and the older one trying to finish her college—have had better luck. At their age, they have to juggle between school and work to make ends meet. I feel so bad that we as parents cannot even provide them a decent education in this country. My own attempts to find a job have ended in endless frustration or humiliating job situations.

One winter morning, when I had been without a job for many months, I was called by a local store to fill in a temporary job for the day. I was so desperate for any job that I made my way in the snow to the store. On reaching there, I found that they did not need me, that the call was a mistake. I pleaded with them to let me work at least for a few hours, but nobody paid attention to me. I was so hurt that I stopped even shopping at that store. The employers don't care for older people like me compared to young smart women. I cannot accept their attitude. We are from decent educated families and have self-esteem. We are not homeless refugees.

In 1989 Vimala worked as a street newspaper vendor at the Flushing subway station from 5:30 A.M. to 10:30 A.M. She got this job from an Indian
man who worked as an agent for a newspaper company. She had come to
the United States a few years earlier to flee a failed marriage in India. "I
came here on a tourist visa and stayed on. I have many more choices here.
In my few years' stay here, I have worked in different kinds of jobs—whatever I get—in factories, in stores, and restaurants with Indian owners. This
job is okay, but I get very tired. It is especially difficult to leave home in the
early morning in winters and stay outdoors for so long. After this shift, I will
go to my second job of dishwashing in an Indian restaurant in Jackson
Heights. Right now it's part-time, but when it becomes full-time, I will leave
this newspaper job." Vimala shared her spot with two other immigrants, an
elderly man from Pakistan and a middle-aged man from India. While selling
newspapers to morning commuters, she often conversed with the other two
vendors, advising them to be happy with what they were able to earn in this
country.

By the 1990s only a thin line separated some Indian homemakers from
their working counterparts. Many Indian women in Queens assembled ma-
chine parts or sewed garments at home; a few supplied cooked snacks to
Indian food stores. Most of these women did not drive and depended on a
female relative—a sister-in-law, daughter, or daughter-in-law—for shopping or other outings. Some used local buses and subways. I spoke with
some Indian women who, after sending their children to school and men to
work, gathered each day at one Queens residence to assemble belts for a
garment firm. A company agent brought the supplies and assigned the
work, and picked up finished goods in return for cash payments. The pay
was lower than the official minimum wage and included no benefits, but
these women preferred it to regular employment. "This kind of work is not
demanding. We can carry out our responsibilities at home and also earn
some money. After putting in some hours of work every day, I am home to
receive my children when they return from school. This is much better
than being away from nine to five. Even if I worked a regular job, its meager salary would vanish in day-care costs. And who would drop and pick up
my kids from day care every day? In this job, the women workers are
friends. While working, we chat about our lives and share our home-cooked
meals."

Most of these working-class-cum-homemaker women remained invisible. However, there were also Indian homemakers who were financially
comfortable and chose not to work. Such women were married to successful professionals or businessmen. Although most remained content with
rearing their families, a noticeable segment were active in public life, as-
suming leadership roles in Indian community organizations.

Professional working women were present in New York's Indian population as early as the late 1960s, and their limited numbers grew in subsequent years. These women had sufficient education and training to enter employment in health care, the computer industry, or university teaching. A small number built private medical practices as half of a husband–wife team. Others migrated from India as nurses. These women often retooled for American work settings in special training courses or by acquiring new diplomas; as one put it, they "learned the ropes thoroughly."

Professional women typically believed that working in the United States made them stronger persons and more independent. Having their own income freed them from depending on a husband for every expense and gave them more decisionmaking power in the household. Most of them drove, and so had mobility. However, many empathized with Indian men and felt that all immigrants had to work extremely hard to build careers in this country. They also shared concerns with Indian men about discrimination and glass ceilings at work.

Rama had a medical practice in Queens since the early 1970s. When she started, some of her American patients refused to believe that a woman from an Asian country could be a doctor. "Sometimes, even after I introduced myself, the patient would consider me the nurse. Contrary to this, being brought up in an Indian city, I had many women role models. More than anyone else, my mother was an educated woman who taught in a school. Many Americans still cannot believe that non-Western women can be educated and professionals!"

Another successful physician maintained that she saw no contradiction between Indian tradition and being a successful working woman. "I am a very traditional woman—I pray every day, prepare dinner for my family; but when I am at work, I am completely professional. Some Americans may not take me seriously in the beginning, but they accept me when they see I am good at what I do. I think Indian women have tremendous self-esteem that enables them to take up any challenge."

By the 1990s a number of Indian women worked as bank tellers, managers, and administrators. Their jobs required skills and education, and their knowledge of English helped them in communicating with colleagues and customers. One worker in an American bank in Queens enjoyed working with a diverse clientele, although it was the native-born Americans who were most demanding.

> Most of our clients are immigrants from different countries. Many do not know English very well, but it is not difficult to deal with them. Sometimes you even make friends. The few [white] Americans who come here are elderly. They are the ones who give you a hard time. Even before I say anything, they

[131]

have decided that they will not understand what I say. One of them once asked me why I had long hair and told me to go to her hairdresser. Once a man had a problem with his bank account and started saying that this neighborhood, including this bank, was taken over by immigrants. As if immigrants caused his bank problem! There is this implication that because I look different and I speak English with an accent, I am ignorant and cannot be efficient.

Impact on Gender Relations

Indian immigrants saw women's full-time employment not only as a novel gender task but also as their key point of interaction with the new American society beyond the domestic sphere. For some men this view was mixed with fear of losing patriarchal power over their wives. An interplay between traditional Indian gender roles and modern work realities was thus apparent in many employment sites in Queens.

In 1995 an American-owned office hired an Indian woman. A few days later the woman brought her husband to the office to talk with the manager about her salary and work hours. The female manager and other women colleagues were shocked that this new employee's husband had intruded into these workplace matters. The Indian employee explained: "I don't know English very well. And more than the language, I don't know the system in this country. I have heard from my friends how immigrant women workers are exploited for their ignorance and innocence. When I told my husband about the salary and working hours at my new job, he said, 'Why did you agree to that? Let me go and talk to your boss.' I knew I couldn't talk to my American boss, even if she is a woman. So I let my husband do this on my behalf. He is more experienced to handle this situation."

A less trusting relationship was evident in the case of a woman who had worked for more than a decade. She explained how immigration to the United States had produced irreparable damage in her marriage.

> I was employed in India also, and there my husband was fine with it. But here we are having so many problems. First of all, he couldn't get a job of his liking here. And when I got a job, his attitude changed toward me. I cook, clean, and do all the house chores, besides working full-time, but he is always unhappy. He tells me that I am stupid, lazy, and don't know how to do things right. Once I told him, "How can I be stupid when I run an office and supervise many people?" That made him even more mad. He continues to blame me for becoming American, and also spoiling our children.

The impact of women's employment in Indian immigrant families varied with educational levels and individual commitments to traditional gender roles. In most households, sharing in the provision of household income did not produce an equivalent sharing of the house workload, and women continued to hold primary responsibility. In some households in which both spouses were employed, men supported a reallocation of labor in the home. They helped with washing dishes or chopping vegetables, and occasionally even demonstrated their culinary talents, particularly for guests. But overall Indian men balked at the idea of full gender equality in housework, and kitchen-related work remained women's traditional task. Most believed that a system in which the first spouse arriving home starts dinner preparations was too radical a transformation for an Indian household. One man said, "I want to help my wife in whichever way I can. Sometimes we eat out, and at other times we do with a simple meal. But she is ultimately responsible for preparing food. That is the basis of Indian culture."

In the 1990s debate over changing gender roles surfaced publicly in New York's Indian community. An *India Abroad* article titled "Superwoman Balances Career and Family" (2/19/88) called for redefinition of the duties traditionally assigned to men and women in the Indian household. It evoked strong reader responses in the newspaper's Opinion/Letters section. One angry husband wrote:

> I would very much like to know of the [female] physician who runs home to cook. I do not know of any woman who took cooking that seriously. As a matter of fact, I admire the man who can manage to make her do that. I am personally sick of eating pizza, Chinese food, spaghetti and meat balls. . . . Of all the people I know, no man, repeat, no man sits down and watches the tube while the wife is breaking her back over the stove. . . . In spite of all the M.B.A.s, work experience and decision-making, I have not met any [woman] who will take the responsibility of making and tracking investments. . . . [Wives] just want the freedom to have the credit cards to go shopping with and not worry where the money is coming from.

Another letter argued that marital problems usually started when women began to work outside. Instead, this letter-writer believed, they should be "content with play[ing] the roles of wife and mother just like their mothers did back in India. . . . The Indian women are following in American women's footsteps. . . . This is perfect groundwork for broken marriages. . . . Let men do their duties of providing financial support and let women do rearing of family. This is our tradition and it has worked for thousands of years" (*India Abroad* 2/19/88). In an interview, Mr. Singh, an educated Indian man, presented his analysis of male fears:

> No matter how educated we are, in India we lived in a society where the entire family, and particularly its women, revolved around us. We were the center of

their universe. My mother lived for me—all her activities had one origin and one end. Our wives are so different from my mother's generation, and our daughters are going to be even more different. We men are so used to our centrality that when women in America deviate from that orbit, we can neither take it nor understand it. We are so confused. How can she have any other interests in life besides me? How come her job can give her security and confidence? For Indian men this is devastating, because they have never seen anything like this in their own parents' generation. Because this happened in America, therefore this must be attributed to Indian women becoming American.

Struggles and Stereotypes

My interviews uncovered several women's versions of the roots of marital problems. After growing up in India and receiving a university education there, Meena married an Indian man already living in the United States.

In India, we had known my husband and his family for a long time, so I was happy my family arranged this marriage. Everyone in our community also thought it was a perfect match. We got married in India, and while he returned to America almost immediately after the wedding, it took me a couple of years to join him here because of my immigration process. . . . Only when I arrived here did I realize that my husband did not have a stable job. He was changing between small jobs and toyed with the idea of starting his own business with loans from family and friends. He talked about his business dreams all the time as if that was his only goal in life. Meanwhile, I took computer courses and almost on my own landed a low-paying but stable job doing computer data entry for a private company.

My marital problems started early on. My husband needed the income I brought to the house but did not appreciate my working outside. He would oppose all my decisions. I will not forget his resistance to arranging a babysitter for our child. Yet he was nonplussed when I asked him that if he did not like my style of handling baby care, he could come up with his own resolution. He kept saying that he didn't like throwing money to an outside babysitter and that this kind of child care was not good for children's upbringing.

I think he developed a complex about me. He knew I was smarter than him. I was liked [more] even in our social circle. So he started avoiding going to parties with me. He would make some excuse, generally that he was busy at work. When he did go, we would almost always fight on returning home. Around the same time, he had started drinking. Once during a fight he became mad with rage, pulled out some papers from his closet, and threw them at me. He said they were divorce papers and that if I did not behave he would force me to sign them. I was scared of the prospect, particularly for our little son's future, and kept quiet. Since then, something has died inside of me. I don't know how these problems will get resolved.

Rukhsana was a high-school-educated homemaker whose husband worked in a clerical job. They lived in an apartment in Queens, and her husband's extended family was scattered all over the New York area.

He leaves for work everyday at 8:30 A.M. and returns late in the evening. Except for housework, I have nothing to do the entire day. But the biggest problem is that my husband doesn't share any decisions with me. He doesn't discuss his work experiences with me, and when I ask him he says I won't understand the situation. Apart from giving me a small amount of money as pocket expenses every week, he doesn't share the household budget with me. If I ask for any more money to run the household, he says that I don't need it, as he buys all the groceries on the weekend. He keeps his money in a bank account which is only in his name, and he deposits his salary there. So I don't have access to that also.

My husband is very suspicious of anyone I talk to. Once he heard me talking to a girlfriend on the phone and wanted to know everything about her. When he learned that she was an older single woman who lived by herself and was not married, he prohibited me to talk to her. He says whenever I want company, I can talk to women in his extended family. Some time ago, I would occasionally call my family in India. He was very angry when he saw the telephone bill and said that I had no right to waste his hard-earned money by making expensive international calls. He said that if my family wants to talk to me so much, they should spend money and call from India. He then put restrictions on our home telephone line so that I could not make long-distance calls.

Lately he fights with me a lot and has turned violent a few times. He comes home and expects everything clean and ready. If he cannot find anything that he has misplaced, he blames me. He curses me if he doesn't like my cooking. What is worse is that I don't know anymore what makes him mad. I do know that he is going through some problems at work, but he won't share anything with me. Sometimes he blurts out that we women don't know how one has to struggle in this country. We just have an easy life here. I try my best to avoid fighting with him by doing all the housework and keeping everything clean, but we hardly communicate anymore. He doesn't seem to understand my viewpoints and feelings anyway. The only way out for me seems to be to obtain a job, but I have no idea where and how to look for one. With my education, who will give me a job? And I don't think my husband will allow me to work for income. No woman in his family has ever worked. I know he cannot even accept the idea.

In the 1980s cases of domestic violence began to surface publicly, shattering the "model minority" image celebrated by so many Indian immigrants (Abraham 2000). Domestic violence in itself was the tip of an iceberg of gender-related problems that had until then remained within the private sphere of household and marriage. These problems included serious resistance to seeking help from outside the family; such moves evoked deep-seated notions of honor and shame in the community. When faced with problems, women habitually turned privately to female friends, the traditional sources of help. In the immigrant situation, however, these sources did not always exist, and some women were left emotionally adrift.

One woman going through a crisis in her marital relationship said she had tried to seek help from her parents and in-laws in India. Every time her husband found out, however, the situation here would worsen.

> It was as if no one could talk to him on my behalf. I know he felt isolated like me, but he became so defensive. It felt like he wanted to make himself aloof so that he was not accountable to anyone. What is worse is that our families in India had no understanding of my conditions here. They would offer solutions that were good for India, not America—like they would ask us to go to an older relative living here who could substitute for them and give us good advice. Who has time in America to do this for a distant relative? When I told my in-laws that the only way to save the marriage may be to seek professional help, they became very angry and said that that would bring shame to their family's good name. I do not think they realized that, short of being beaten to death by their son, I had no other alternative.

Serious cultural barriers existed for Indians seeking outside assistance. Mental health counseling was an alien concept to most Indian immigrants, something that one knew existed in the United States but could not apply to Indians living here. It required some daring for women even to share their problems with friends or a relative. Professional service providers acknowledged that Indian cases were brought to them only in their clinical stages.

When the few Indians who surmounted social and cultural barriers sought help, they invariably found the existing system culturally insensitive. In the 1980s cases came to light in which Indian women, distraught with crisis in their domestic life, sought help in an American-run women's shelter. In one instance shelter workers were unable to help an Indian woman who knew only a few words of English and after arriving would not eat and for two days turned away all food. After a considerable search, they located a female Indian service provider who was able to communicate with the woman. She discovered that besides loss of appetite because of fleeing her home, the woman was a vegetarian and would not consume any food containing meat, something the shelter workers had not considered. In addition, someone at the shelter, trying to be helpful, mentioned that services included assistance in obtaining a divorce. This *was* understood by the Indian woman, but it only heightened her anxiety. She had left home because her husband was violent toward her, and she was worried about the welfare of her children. What she wanted was someone who could persuade her husband to stop his behavior so that they could resume married life; she did not even contemplate divorce.

While conservatives in the immigrant community chastised Indian women for becoming Americanized, some outsiders portrayed them as hopelessly traditional. The first judgment focused on their alleged deviation from accepted Indian gender roles; the second, on their traditional dress and appearance and their firm commitment to family and marriage. Activities in Queens in the 1990s defied both stereotypes. Indian women did maintain Indian traditions, in many instances more so than men. Continuity was particularly apparent in food. Being in charge of home activities, women were responsible for food preparation, and Hindu women were usually more ardent vegetarians than men or their U.S.-raised children. A number of women were adamant that husbands and children could eat "anything," but no meat would enter their kitchens. On any given day in Queens, Indian women could be seen shopping with their family or women friends and relatives. Special energy was added around Indian festivals, including some geared to women, such as Karva Chauth, a North Indian Hindu festival during which married Hindu women observe a day-long fast for their husband's long life, and women gather for group rituals.

Change in their lives was evident as well. Besides employment at various jobs, they used city subways and buses, drove cars, shopped, visited libraries and post offices, and dropped off and picked up children at local schools. Such activities belie portrayals of Indian women living in ethnic ghettos, as these typical Queens neighborhood routines immersed them in multicultural diversity. Amidst this new American scene, Indian women became aware of their own traditions in new ways. An Indian sales clerk commented on how Indians were similar to or different from other Asians such as Chinese and Koreans: it is interesting that although they, too, are immigrants, their women do not wear traditional dress. But she found more affinity between Indians and Latinos, "who look like us, and for them also family and relatives are very important. Besides, they are warm people." One mother cooked Indian food at an International Food Day at her child's school. Another taught her child about their religion so he could report to his class. "It is very difficult for us to tell everyone about our heritage in a few words," she said. "But if we do not simplify, neither my child nor his classmates will understand it."

However subtle and complex the changes in Indian women's lives, immigrant community boundaries were still clearly drawn. Marriage continued to be the central fact of a woman's life, though not always without strain. Divorce was taboo, and considered a sure sign of Americanization. Indians' widespread belief that sexual freedom was a hallmark of American society placed them on guard with Americans, as it did with their own U.S.-reared children, particularly their daughters. Their fear and disapproval of sexual openness extended to progressive Indians who supported equality between men and women or the right to proclaim a gay or lesbian sexual identity. For most Indian immigrants this was not an issue of an individual's democratic rights but an essential departure from "Indian" values. Even the moderate elements in the Indian community, who considered domestic violence a valid issue, found homosexuality unacceptable. They even took issue with making this debate public, and considered that idea in itself a deviation from the Indian way of living.

[6]

Elders and Youth

Before 1990 the center of gravity in New York City's Indian population was the cohort of first-generation adult immigrants from India. The 1990s, however, witnessed a shift away from this generation's social dominance. On the one hand, the older members of this generation who were aging in the United States now faced retirement and the third and four ashrams, or stages of life. Moreover, the Indian American elderly population was also being augmented through family reunification as many younger adults brought their parents here from India. On the other hand, the numbers of second-generation children who were growing up in this country were also burgeoning. During the 1990s this younger generation of Indian Americans rapidly emerged as a vocal group in many spheres of Indian life in New York City, from cultural activities to community politics. These two demographic developments transformed the working adult immigrant cohort into an in-between generation with direct responsibilities to the other two, but also standing apart from them.

The Elderly

The two subgroups of Indian elderly in New York, immigrants aging in this country and parents joining immigrant adult children, came from the same age groups and cultural background, but their life experiences varied with their immigration trajectories. Indians aging in the United States were far more exposed to American society and had given years of attention to planning their own retirement. The immigrant parents depended much more on their adult children, and frequently traveled between their old and new homes in India and the United States. Like other Asian immigrants (Sanjek et al. 1989; Guo 2000), both groups encountered new situations in which immigration had transformed the traditional system of family care for the elderly.

Indian immigrants overall viewed American society as poorly suited to aged persons. This view was based less on state-supported health care or social security than on its perceived divergence from Indian society, in which children as a matter of course were responsible for their parents. There the elderly remained integral to their families and performed useful functions such as child care. Some changes were evident in contemporary urban India, where migration for work had frequently split joint family households into nuclear units. Still, senior citizen centers were absent in India; the mere consideration of sending parents to retirement or nursing homes was socially taboo, and in fact was an image evoked by Indians to convey disapproval of American individualization.

Plans for Aging

For immigrants who had spent the better part of their adult lives in the United States, retirement planning was an important part of becoming American. After building careers and raising families, they faced the third stage of life in a different culture, and without cultural signposts. In the process of gathering information on health care, social security benefits, or senior citizen centers, they became exposed to a sector of American life they had never encountered before. Most agreed that the resources available for the aged in this country did not allay their anxieties about being taken care of by their own children, in India still the preferred choice. So, relying on their own ingenuity and learning from other elderly Indians' experiences, each aging immigrant or couple formulated an individual plan to be put to the test amidst unknown conditions.

The first issue was where to settle, India or the United States. Many immigrants had long nursed hopes of returning to India for their retirement. They viewed America as a land for work and career, but with those years behind, they looked to India as home for vanprastha and sanyasa. In fact, for this very reason a sizable number had decided against becoming U.S. citizens. As part of their plans, they made real estate investments in India and cultivated relations with relatives and friends there. Moreover, the pull of cultural familiarity became stronger for many as old age drew closer. About to retire from professional employment in New York, Prabhakar had built a big house for his retirement in an Indian city. The floor plan included space for his hobbies, which he had had little time for during his working years in the United States. "I would like to pursue my lifelong ambition of studying Indian scriptures there. Now, since I have the time, I will start a discussion group with my old friends on analyzing these scriptures. Also, I will take regular pilgrimages to holy places which are not far from my hometown in India."

Indian women immigrants on the whole were more willing than men to stay on in the United States. The chief reason was their reluctance to reenter the patriarchal marital family networks in India, where they would have to cater to their husband's parents, relatives, and friends. Women also adjusted better to everyday conditions in America, where they had more freedom to allocate time to their individual needs and learned more from colleagues and friends of diverse backgrounds. They often emphasized practical reasons for their choice of the United States. Prabhakar's wife, Sudha, for instance, forcefully opposed her husband's plan to retire in India: "He thinks that in the last three decades, while he was in America, India has not changed. He thinks that he will go there and organically settle back in Indian conditions. Not only has India changed, but we have also got used to the American way of life. This is not evident during vacations to India. At that time everyone comes to see you because you are there only for a few weeks. But once we live there the stark reality will emerge."

Returning elderly immigrants found that their lives had diverged from those of friends and relatives who had remained in India. Poor electricity, telephone, and sanitary service in India were additional inconveniences that soon exhausted their initial enthusiasm about returning to their homeland. Many elderly felt divided between the two countries, feeling marginalized in both. Stories of these retirees' dissatisfaction circulated in the U.S. immigrant community, and some middle-aged Indians revised plans for repatriated retirements. A few Indian elderly had made unsuccessful attempts to retire in their land of birth. Their children had remained in the United States and wanted their parents to remain as well, so that they could maintain regular contact, albeit in separate households. Living in India entailed great expense and the inconvenience of frequent travel for visits. Missing contact with their offspring, they eventually returned to the United States.

Krishna considered his retirement plan ideal for Indian families. He had worked as a professional in New York for more than twenty-five years and was about to retire. His two sons had grown up in the United States, had professional careers, and had made arranged marriages with Indian women. They all lived together in one joint family household, where Krishna intended to remain after his working years. "We did not want American daughters-in-law who would break our family. In one's old age all you have is your children. Where else will we go in this age? At the most, our sons may live in different cities, which hopefully will not be very far apart. In that situation, [my wife and I] will divide our time between the two houses." Krishna eagerly anticipated the satisfaction of achieving vanprastha in the United States.

Krishna's dream was impossible for the many Indians who could not practicably reside with their children upon retirement. Instead of returning to India, they began to think about living in warmer American states where they could still maintain access to their U.S.-resident children in New York or elsewhere. One described his plan with evident excitement: "However much it may be my dream, settling back in India is not practical. By now many of my siblings live in the United States, and I have very few relatives left in India. With all my life savings I have decided to maintain two homes in the United States—one in California and another in New York. My wife and I will travel between these two places according to the climate. Sometimes we will visit our children, and other times India. I know we cannot live at either home forever."

Some aging Indians also planned to share their retirement years with other Indian age-peers in Florida. A few of their friends had already moved there, and they looked forward to joining the emerging Indian elderly network there. For still others, plans to return to India were not completely abandoned, having revived with the expansion of the Indian economy in the 1990s. New business ventures to build housing developments in Indian cities wooed elderly Indian Americans to invest and return to India. These investments, however, did not require making a decision to retire in India or the United States. For the successful professionals and businesspersons who could afford them, they were part of a transnational strategy in which a house in India would be used for a portion of the year along with another one in California or Florida.

Uniting with Adult Children

Respecting their cultural traditions, Indian immigrants in the United States usually invited their elderly parents in India to join them once their economic circumstances permitted. Such links mitigated the rupture in filial responsibilities caused by immigration, and parents of most Indian immigrants eventually circulated for longer or shorter periods among the households of their children living in the two (or more) countries. Repeated international travel marked the retirement years of such elderly Indians. Since long airplane trips were uncomfortable for them, their children chose airlines that were sensitive to the needs of their parents in terms of language and food, and tried to find someone to accompany them. By the 1990s every international flight between India and the United States carried a noticeable complement of Indian elderly. Immigrant families living in other parts of the United States often traveled to New York to meet their parents upon arrival or asked trusted contacts living in New York to do so. Such requests were an accepted burden for Indians in New York City, where the topic of elderly travel arrangements reverberated in countless conversations.

Social isolation was a critical problem for these elderly parents of immigrants once they arrived in the United States. In India they had occupied themselves with chores, their grandchildren, and visiting with age-peers in their immediate neighborhood. In the United States they often had little interaction beyond their children's family and household. Most Indian elderly were not fluent in English and did not drive, so their range of activity was limited. Problems were worse in winter, when, fearing sickness, they hesitated to leave the house on their own. With their children at work during the week, they had little adult company. Many Indian elders felt trapped in their children's houses and longed for the weekend, when they could be driven to outdoor locations. Most complained that they had little to do in this country.

Being homebound and isolated, many experienced a decline in self-worth. One elderly Indian man contrasted his life in the United States and in India, where he had been a lawyer before retirement.

> I used to see scores of people every day. My office was full of visitors. Many people waited for my advice, and I was a much-respected person in my town. When I decided to retire, my children in America insisted I should join them here. They questioned our (my wife's and my) rationale for living there alone, and pleaded that we should come to America. We also missed them; sometimes we won't see them for three or four years. So both of us decided to come here. But apart from this emotional bond, I have nothing worthwhile to do here. I feel suffocated in this house. My wife keeps telling me that we should adjust with our children. That may be okay for her; she can keep herself occupied in cooking and other house chores. But what should I do the entire day?

Another elderly retired man had been a professor in India. He carried a bag containing his degrees with him to the United States, but lamented, "They have no value here. My life has no value here. This country is only for young and able-bodied people. Even my pension is reduced to a few dollars here. I try to pass my time by reading books which I order from India. But it is very difficult to live like this. Nobody is interested in my work here. If we live in India, we miss our children. They have left us there alone in old age. If we come here, we miss our society and our own people."

A recurrent topic of conversation among the Indian elderly was the contrast between life in India and in the United States. They frequently mentioned how a day in India was full of social activity. One elderly woman explained: "There you see people the whole day. Someone or other keeps coming to your house—either housemaids or street vendors or friends of your grandchildren. Here even your closest friend cannot visit you without an appointment. Even Indians have become so formal here. In India you can talk to anybody about their families, jobs, children. In America, everyone is so private . . . and they are always on the run. Talking to them seems like you are stealing their time."

Although most elderly Indian immigrants felt isolated in the United States, they noted the difference between living in the suburbs and in the Indian core areas in Queens. In suburban areas with a sparse Indian population, the elderly might not see another Indian person for long periods. One elderly Indian revealed that the nearest Indian family in his town lived two miles away and did not belong to his language group, so socializing was difficult. The two families saw each other at parties, but elderly persons did not participate in every such gathering. The isolation of the elderly was so acute in suburban Long Island that in the early 1990s one Indian organization planned to bus elders to Queens neighborhoods to visit houses of worship and other cultural resources.

The Indian elderly living in Queens core areas had a relatively more active life. In warm weather they walked to houses of worship or parks. They often took young grandchildren in strollers to local parks or playgrounds. Elderly couples were seen together, even more than in India, an indication that in the United States they were more compelled to rely on each other's company.

Rama and her husband joined their son, who was single, in New York. Their other children—three sons and two daughters—were married and lived in Europe. They divided the year between visits among their children and residence in their original home in India. In New York, Rama and her husband lived with their son in a Queens neighborhood with a large Indian population and many Indian stores and houses of worship. Here they were able to form a small circle of elderly South Asian friends. Rama observed:

Everyone has children here. So every day, after finishing our daily chores, we meet in the neighborhood park. Some people bring their toddler grandchildren; others take walks. We know each other very well and keep a tab on who is sick and who is traveling. We often share information about food, shopping, home remedies, diseases, etc. A few months ago, a man started giving physical exercise classes, which are very good. The rest of the time, we watch Indian television. On weekends our son drives us to faraway temples or shopping malls. There are so many Indians in Queens that it is like living in India.

To combat isolation and diminished self-worth, some elderly Indians found employment. One elderly cabdriver said that he did not want to be a burden to his children. "What is the harm in earning some money from your own labor? I drive whenever I want to. Initially, my children were against it, but now they have accepted my decision." An elderly woman worked as a housekeeper for another Indian family. Her own children worked and provided well for her, but she found it hard to spend the entire day alone. She met an Indian couple, both physicians, who needed someone to do housekeeping for them. "Fortunately, they are decent people and consider me part of their family. I would not work for just anybody." She did not disclose her employment in the Indian community. "You know how we Indians are. They will think right away that I have to work because my children cannot support me."

More than a few Indian elders felt that they themselves were treated like servants by their own children. One said that her son brought her to the United States because he wanted a babysitter. "Both [he and his wife] are so busy in their careers that they have no time for their family. They hardly talk to me as a family member, and I have no say in family decisions. Every morning they leave their young child with me and give me directions about how to take care of her. I spend the entire day with this child and take care of all the house chores. My son and his wife are so selfish; they do not seem to be Indian children."

Complaints from the Indian elderly thus ranged from social isolation to exploitative conditions. One elderly Indian reflected on their plight:

> I do not want to blame our children only. Like us, they, too, are unwilling players in this scenario caused by migration between cultures. They are young and so busy in their careers that they cannot understand our problems. I wish there was some solution to this kind of disruption in families. But I have decided that the only way to lead the rest of my life with self-esteem is to continue to live in India, where I have my friends and social circle. From there I can visit my children occasionally. This country is not for old people, and the least for old people like me from another culture. They cannot expect us to become Americans at this late age.

The Younger Generation

In the 1990s a second generation, consisting of immigrants' children, emerged to proclaim new ways of being an Indian in the United States. This generation had been brought up in the United States, and their experience departed significantly from that of their adult immigrant parents. Indeed, many in the younger generation sought not only to make sense of their individual identities but also to redefine the Indian American community in the United States. The 1990s, then, marked the beginning of a reshaping of Indian American ethnic identity.

Indian youth in New York City were diverse in their own ways. Reflecting continuous immigration from the 1960s through the 1990s, some arrived as teenagers, others at younger ages, and still others were born in the United States. The older immigrant youth were more akin to adult Indian immigrants in outlook than to Indians of their own age reared in the United States. Another group, also closer in outlook to the first generation, were the international students who stayed on in this country.

First-generation Indian community leaders, mainly the professional elite, focused primarily on immigrant issues and expected their children to recapitulate their cherished success stories. They devoted considerable energy to creating resources aimed to make their children culturally Indian, and to finding marital partners among other Indians. Indian organizations had youth wings offering activities and socializing for the children of active members. The emergence of the younger generation as adults and leaders in their own right therefore puzzled the older generation, particularly when they began to question an unproblematic transfer of Indian traditions to the United States.

When in the early 1990s the new, U.S.-reared Indian youth generation seemed to emerge rapidly on the scene in New York City, debate about their Indian and/or American identity took center stage (India Sari Palace 1993). First, as increasing numbers of Indian youth explored established Indian activities and conferences, their presence at such events grew quite palpably. Not satisfied by first-generation-led organizations, in the mid-1990s many began to form their own groups and plan their own events, with agendas ranging from cultural issues to middle-class or leftist politics.

Growing Up in Queens

The experiences of New York City–reared Indian American youth were in many ways distinct from those of Indian Americans reared in suburbs or in other parts of the United States. In Queens, they grew up at the same time as the establishment of the local Indian community. Those who had lived in Queens since infancy recalled the years of a far smaller Indian presence. They associated their childhood years with the appearance of local Indian businesses and the changing demography of their neighborhoods. These young Indians received their education in local public schools and identified their friends by the particular school they attended. "P.S. 9," or Flushing or John Bowne High Schools, featured in conversations as indicators of meaningful identities. They also noted how some "made it" to the more prestigious public high schools such as Bronx Science, Hunter, or Stuyvesant, in other boroughs. These shared experiences provided the base of their emerging second-generation networks and were often evoked at social gatherings and ethnic festivals.

The shared experiences that bonded them also demarcated them from their parents' generation. As a sign of respect, the younger generation had been taught not to use first names for persons older than themselves, and generically called their parents' friends "uncle" and "auntie." Informally, New York City's Indian youth called the entire first generation the "uncle and auntie" generation, in which they included their own parents. This immigrant cohort of their elders was considered sharply different from their own; it constantly evoked Indian cultural standards and expectations that remained largely beyond their comprehension. Although parents, uncles, and aunties knew some degree of English, their Indian accents and lexicon were matters of amusement for the younger generation, who often joined other Americans in mimicking them.

Despite familial bonds and affection, the interests of the two generations often conflicted. The image of the uncle and auntie generation was one of constant efforts to keep children under surveillance, discipline them, and impose Indian social expectations on them. Young Indian Americans felt that their parents all gossiped about them, and that the adult Indian community was rife with rumors about their behavior and activities. To combat this, the youth had created their own spaces free from control of their parents and the vigilant uncle and auntie community. Going away to out-of-town colleges was a cherished opportunity to escape this first generation's social control.

These youth growing up in New York City nevertheless cultivated a distinct sense of their Indian ethnic identity. Living within a relatively dense Indian population, they were comfortable navigating the frequent cultural activities around them. In addition, their knowledge of Indian languages, at least conversationally, was much greater than that of youth from suburban areas or states with only a scattered Indian population. They took for granted the diverse languages and religious practices of South Asians from India, Pakistan, Bangladesh, Sri Lanka, or Nepal, and experienced cultural commonalities with fellow South Asian youth. For them, "South Asian" identity was a palpable reality. They had also become aware of Guyanese and Trinidadians of Indian ancestry and the global migrations of South Asians. Some of the young generation had developed an interest in the earlier history of Indians in North America, which few among their elders shared. For these youth, this historical migration of exploited agricultural workers gave them a commonality with other American minority groups.

Growing up in multicultural Queens also brought an ease in negotiating ethnic and racial boundaries. Many young Indian New Yorkers had friendships with other Asians, Latinos, blacks, and whites, many of whom were also children of immigrants. This experience, too, set them apart from most uncles and aunties.

Although some multicultural sensibilities and knowledge of South Asian cultural traditions and diasporic roots might be expected among Indian American youth nationwide, New York City–reared Indian youth grew up amidst these as experiential realities, not with the abstract versions of them that most suburban Indian youth confronted. Living in Queens meant that they did not have to search for the Indian community or its cultural expressions; rather, they lived inside them. This difference was starkly evident when Queens youth encountered those from the suburbs. Many New York City–reared youth appreciated that growing up in proximity to their own culture gave them a clearer sense of being Indian (Sinha 1998).

One New York–reared young person who attended a university elsewhere said, "It was hard for me to socialize with [other Indian American] folks who are always starved for Indian food. They have to go to an Indian restaurant to experience Indian culture! New York City is so different that sometimes I feel I have grown up in a space between India and the United States." Another stated,

> When you travel and meet Indians living elsewhere, you realize the significance of the context in which one grows up. Growing up in California must be quite different from a New York City upbringing. I know we have many things in common—we have the same dishes in Indian restaurants, same languages and religions—but then how come their shopping areas feel so different from Jackson Heights? Their Indian community is so scattered that it is virtually a weekend community; it becomes alive on weekends and dies during the week. In fact for many kids growing up in such places, being Indian means participating in an Indian show or celebrating a single festival like Diwali once a year.

These distinctions became more visible in New York itself when sizable numbers of South Asian youth who had grown up elsewhere arrived in the city in the 1990s for higher education and new careers. They had already heard of Queens' Indian concentrations, and now were eager to access their cultural resources. The activists among them even aspired to engage with the New York community and to influence its shape and political identity. Their commonality with New York–raised youth in terms of their bicultural Indian American identity, though different, was nevertheless strong, and their generational experience bound them together.

Bicultural Identities

For the second generation of Indian Americans, who grew up in the United States, India slipped from being their home country to being their parents' and ancestors' homeland. They could not fully identify with those, including their parents, who grew up in India. The U.S.-reared Indians did maintain links with India through cousins of their own age and other relatives whom they met in the United States or on visits to India, often for a family vacation or a wedding. Nevertheless, they could not identify with contemporary life in India, and regarded it only as a source of their ethnic heritage in the United States. Although both immigrants and their children were Indian, Indian ethnicity had different meanings for each generation (Ganesan 1994).

Most U.S.-reared Indians considered themselves Americans of Indian ancestry. Many enjoyed their visits to India but were certain that they could not live there. Their education, lifestyles, and careers fixed them in the United States. At several public intergenerational dialogues in New York in the 1990s, participants sought to differentiate Indian from American traits. One Indian immigrant asked, "Can you explain what is the American part in your Indian American identity?" The question was answered by a young Indian American. "We will, if you—our Indian parents—first tell us in a sentence what it means to be an Indian!" In another forum, when asked whether those growing up in the United States felt they were Indian or American, a person in his twenties replied, "I know I am an American. I was born and raised here, and I consider this my home. But my roots are in India. I don't know why it is so difficult for [immigrant] Indians to understand people with these two cultural streams. If you only look around, you will find lots of such Americans here. We are not very different from them. Their ancestry is from other cultures; ours is from India."

In the late 1980s a new term, ABCD, for "American-Born Confused Desis," was popularized to describe the emerging generation of U.S.-reared Indians (Basu 1989). Few Indians were aware that this term was a play upon ABC, used by Chinese Americans for "American-Born Chinese." As ABCD was increasingly used to stereotype them, U.S.-reared Indian Americans retorted by calling those reared in India FOBs, for "Fresh Off the Boat," an established American epithet for immigrants who know little about American life.

National distinctions among the South Asian countries such as India, Bangladesh, Pakistan, Sri Lanka, and Nepal had much less meaning for U.S.-reared Indians. Unlike Indian and other South Asian adult immigrants, whose perspectives were imbued with the recent, sometimes belligerent, history of these national formations, such associations were remote to young Indian Americans. Their experience of cultural commonality among these groups here was more compelling than historical facts related in books or by their parents. Moreover, South Asians in multicultural America, regardless of national origin, tended to be treated by others in similar fashion. This young Indian American generational perspective, overriding South Asian national divisions, also often coincided with a progressive political stance. In the late 1980s, "South Asian" gained increasing currency as an identifying label among young Indian Americans, and was particularly noticeable on university campuses and in new progressive alliances. Foremost among those who rejected this new label were adult immigrants engaged with homeland political struggles, for whom their national identities could not be easily dislodged. Developments in South Asia, including Indian-Pakistani disputes over Kashmir and the development of nuclear weapons, which had brought these two nations to the brink of war, kept these national identities alive for some.

Race, long an ambivalent issue for Indians in the United States (Mazumdar 1989), was evaded by the parental generation, who identified instead with the nation of India or their religion. For the younger generation, however, a heightened consciousness of race was integral to growing up American (Sethi 1994). Some Indians compared themselves primarily to white Americans and struggled with the dominant majority's color-determined exclusion of them. Others openly challenged the American racial division as incomplete in regard to South Asians, or as globally and scientifically meaningless. And under pressure to fit into one of the official racial categories (Sanjek 1994b), few U.S.-reared Indians felt comfortable with the "Asian Pacific Islander" census label, one more readily acceptable to East Asians, with whom the popular American ethnonym "Asian" is most usually associated.

On university campuses in New York and around the country, "South Asian/Indian American" students formed their own organizations, with tenuous relations to pan-Asian student groups. Few Indian American or South Asian American students registered in Asian American studies courses. In debates on diversity among Asian Americans, South Asian/Indian Americans frequently mused whether they shared greater cultural commonality with Arabs or Middle Easterners than with East Asians (Khandelwal 1998). Some Indian Americans found affinity with Filipino or Latino students, and others identified with African American political struggles. And many who identified with no single other racial group, particularly those who grew up in culturally diverse areas such as Queens, befriended young people from several other races.

Still other young Indians turned to culture as the defining factor of their identity, an arena free from bounded racial categories but also distinctly Indian/South Asian. Culture was perceived to overarch the complex South Asian particularities of religion, region, and nation. In its emergent South Asian American youth forms, it was also a liberating force that accorded them more power of expression than did their parents' religious and social conventions, which most younger South Asians did not fully understand.

The emergent Indian/South Asian youth culture did not simply maintain and preserve old Indian traditions; it created new cultural modes that responded directly to these youths' generational needs. In New York City, their participation in new and reinterpreted raas-garba and bhangra traditions of music and dance at social events in homes and restaurants, and at parties on university campuses and in Manhattan clubs (Sengupta 1996), became topics of sociological and cultural analysis by second-generation scholars and writers themselves (Gopinath 1995; Maira and Srikanth 1996). Younger South Asian Americans in the 1990s also rapidly moved into creative writing, journalism, and filmmaking (Bald 1996; Khurana and Gill-Murgai 1997; DasGupta 1999; Lahiri 1999). Many among them derided appropriation of South Asian culture by white Americans and offered severe critiques of American racial and ethnic stereotyping (Sengupta 1997). As these developments moved away from India-focused to U.S.-based concerns, New York City became their center. Young South Asian Americans from all over the country began to visit New York, and South Asian New Yorkers traveled elsewhere as bhangra disc jockeys and ethnic cultural figures. At the same time, contacts arose with South Asian artists and cultural activists in London, Toronto, and other parts of the global South Asian diaspora.

Dating and Marriage

In India, the advantages of marriage—continuity of tradition, social stability, maintaining the joint family—seem best attainable through an arranged marriage, which aims to maximize compatibility between spouses and their kin groups. In contemporary India, marriage bureaus and matrimonial advertisements in the press are commonly used to secure the best match. Marriage continued to be pivotal for Indian immigrants in the United States. Indeed, in an alien culture and society, arranged marriage for the first generation was an efficacious way to maintain continuity and stability. For most Queens immigrants, "choice" in marriage meant marrying an Indian from a different caste or region, but even in these cases elements of "arrangement" and familial approval might play a role, in contrast to a purely "love" marriage between two individuals.

In the 1990s the issue of marriage entered new territory. Now, as Indian immigrants prepared to select marital partners for their children, two different generations applied their own expectations and standards, formed in different contexts. Parents regarded marriage by choice or love as unreliable and probably short-lived. An arranged marriage within one's caste and community was still considered the most desirable.

Indian parents looked for maximal social compatibility in arranging marriages, but some realized that in the United States they might have to broaden the search beyond their own community and caste identities. Most, however, adhered to the preferences of Indian society and insisted that even if their child chose his or her own marriage partner, that partner should be from their own caste or at least their own regional group. Even in cases of compromise on caste or regional choices, religious difference continued to be all but insurmountable. Marriage of Hindu and Muslim was the absolute taboo, for most even worse than marriage to a white American or Hispanic.

Typically, one immigrant affirmed that his son in his twenties, who had completed his education and held a professional job, could maintain family tradition only by marrying a woman from their own caste. Another railed that he did not want an American (meaning Americanized Indian) daughter-in-law who would throw aging parents-in-law out of her new household. And another disapproved of her daughter's marriage to a white. "Don't get me wrong. He is a very nice man. But he is not one of us—we cannot communicate with him about our religion, social activities, and in our own language."

The views of younger Indian Americans reflected the modern outlook of contemporary India as well as the impact of American values. For them, marriage concerned first their own individual existence (as distinct from social existence), and they wanted it to be their decision. They found themselves caught between American values, which stereotyped and derided arranged marriage as a restrictive social practice, and the values of their own parents, for whom arranged marriage, including in most cases their own, was the central mechanism for maintaining stable family life.

The U.S.-reared Indian Americans also noted unfavorably the yawning gap in Indian traditions in the treatment of women and men. These differing expectations started at birth, affected both day-to-day matters and major decisions, and were unmistakably present in parental decisions about dating and marriage. Sons were allowed more leeway in dating and "out of the house" activities, while daughters' activities were carefully guarded. Whereas U.S.-raised Indian American women regarded this gap as a "double standard," their parents considered it simply the reflection of distinct gender roles. Often parents made the seemingly circular argument that bringing up daughters more strictly than sons socialized them most appropriately for later roles as wife and mother. Indian parents feared and lamented their daughters' premarital relationships with males because such behavior "will jeopardize their marriage prospects" or "ruin the marriage prospects of the younger sisters, and thus the name of the family."

Indian immigrant families did not apply the same behavioral standards to their sons, and many young men—more than their female counterparts—still considered arranged marriage a serious option. A number of them considered marital candidates among U.S.-reared Indian women, but in the 1990s there was a growing trend of returning to choose a bride in India, where their relatives assisted in the selection process. The purpose of an arranged marriage—to find someone to fulfill the traditional role of wife—seemed more promising with women reared in India than with those raised in the United States.

The options and process were different for U.S.-reared Indian women. Their upbringing was considered a disadvantage in a traditional marriage, because they were assumed to be "Americanized." Many young women rejected efforts to make them appear more traditional for formal encounters with prospective marriage partners. Young Indian American women felt humiliated at being shorn of their individuality and, as one young woman put it, "displayed" as "a show-piece in the market of marriage." Although few men in India wanted to marry a U.S.-reared woman, parents desperate over the marriage prospects of a daughter could usually find a young man who wanted to immigrate to the United States via a marriage visa.

Disputes between immigrant parents and their children over social behavior set traditional expectations against accusations of interference and undue control. An exasperated mother of an eighteen-year-old U.S.-reared daughter said,

> I no longer know what to tell her to do, or not to. I am completely confused. She wants to come back home in the night at two or even three A.M. and doesn't want us to say anything about it. I think she goes to college every day, but I don't know even that. I only know that she leaves home every day some time in the morning. She keeps her room locked so that I cannot find out anything about her. The other day we had a big fight. She was in her room with a boy, and when I asked her about that, she barred us from entering her room. She blamed us for not letting her go to an out-of-town university where she could be free. It is like she is not part of the family; she wants to do whatever she wants to do. We would like her to marry a good Indian man who is mature and settled in life, but we cannot talk to her on that subject.

The younger generation stressed the importance of choice and love in marriage. One young recently married woman explained:

For years I did not tell my parents about my relationship with this man of another religion. We were both serious about each other, so I had to tell my parents when we decided to get married. On knowing, they were first very angry. They tried to dissuade me from making what they called "the mistake of my life." Eventually, after years of my persistence, they had to give up. But I felt bad because they were very hurt, as if I had deceived them! They told me, "You have dashed all our hopes in one stroke. You do not know what all we had dreamt for you." And I said, "You shouldn't have dreamt all those things. After all, it's my life and I have to live it."

Another woman recalled that her parents had been dead set against her marrying a white Catholic man. Although she could approach her mother on the subject, her father stopped talking to her and prohibited her from leaving the house. One day, through the help of friends, she escaped and married the man in court. Even after several years her father still refused to talk to her; he told her mother that his daughter was dead as far as he was concerned. In only a few cases did parents happily consent to their children's marital choices.

Other dilemmas arose for younger-generation men. A number of them revealed bad experiences dating American women. One said, "I did not find a sense of commitment in those relationships. They did not seem to be suitable for life partnerships. So, even if it seemed strange at the first instance, I was persuaded by my parents to marry someone from India." Another man, a successful executive in a New York firm, had pondered his marriage options for several years. He admitted that before entering an arranged marriage in India with someone of his caste, regional, and religious background, he had had a serious relationship with a U.S.-raised Indian woman. "However, this woman seemed to have no interest in my family or family culture. She was a careerist, very aggressive and individualistic. Besides, she was from another caste and regional background. I had no problem with her as my girlfriend, but I couldn't imagine her as my wife, as mother of my children. Frankly, I wasn't sure if I could raise a family with her. It took me quite long to agree to an arranged marriage. I could not take such a big decision of my life based on a few meetings with somebody. But once accepting it, I don't have any regrets now."

With growing numbers of second-generation Indian Americans reaching their twenties during the 1990s, marriages also became more frequent. The persistence of arranged marriage was evident in matrimonial advertisement sections in North American ethnic Indian newspapers. As in contemporary India, these advertisements described the appearance and educational and occupational background of a prospective bride or groom, and were used to reach a wider pool of eligible persons than traditional social networks might be able to cover. Some Indian immigrants in New York also placed advertisements in newspapers in India, potentially to be followed by personal visits there.

The number of such advertisements in selected single issues of *India Abroad* increased from a handful in the early 1970s, to 145 in 1988, to 182 in 1995. In relation to Maxine Fisher's analysis of matrimonial advertisements in a 1975 issue of *India Abroad,* my analysis of one from 1988 showed an increasing emphasis on religion and caste (Fisher 1980; Khandelwal 1992). In 1975 the advertiser's caste was mentioned in 23 percent of advertisements, and religion in 31 percent. By 1988, 33 percent mentioned caste, and 45 percent religion. In 1975, 23 percent listed caste as "irrelevant" to marriage; by 1988 that percentage had declined to 13. In addition, in 1988 advertisers included persons living in Canada, Britain, Saudi Arabia, Hong Kong, the Caribbean, and India, indicating a much larger transnational marriage pool.

In the early 1990s several "marriage conventions" were held in New York City where Indian individuals and their families seeking marriage partners could meet prospective candidates and exchange necessary information in person. In a less formal medium, many regional association conventions brought thousands of Indian families, including prospective spouses, to a common location to meet people in person or pursue ongoing negotiations over weekend organizational gatherings. Throughout the 1990s the Internet increasingly became a clearinghouse for information necessary to arrange marriages.

During the 1990s numerous Indian weddings took place each year in New York. Ordinarily, arranged weddings were harmonious, and tensions over negotiations between the two families rarely surfaced at the ceremonies. With parents who gave only grudging consent to a marriage of choice, however, displeasure was sometimes obvious. At a 1992 wedding of an Indian Hindu man and a Puerto Rican woman, the groom's parents wore long faces and did not hide their disappointment. The father told a guest, "We are mere onlookers. This cannot be our son's wedding. How can we be happy at a Christian wedding ceremony?" At a wedding between Indians of different religions, the parents had reconciled themselves to their children's decision. The siblings and friends of the bride and groom had made most of the arrangements, including selecting the entertainment at the wedding party. As a compromise, the parents had asked for two different religious ceremonies, and as a result the wedding was conducted twice on the same day.

At most weddings, the religious rituals, the bride's costume, and the food were Indian. Indian Christian weddings, of course, were held in churches, but for Indians of other religions the wedding ceremony and reception

[155]

were held in houses of worship, hotels, or restaurants with wedding halls. In contrast to the 1950s and 1960s, when there had been no Hindu priests in New York to conduct weddings, in the 1980s and 1990s temple and freelance priests abounded and offered a choice of suitable religious and regional styles of ceremonies. Some willingly translated the ritual into English for non-Indian guests or U.S.-reared youth. One priest who did so insisted that the younger generation of Indians growing up in America needed to understand the full meaning of the Sanskrit verses and be fully instructed that marriage was a sacred lifelong vow.

During the celebration, brides as well as female guests dressed in traditional saris of bright colors and wore elaborate jewelry, a wide selection of which was available in stores on 74th Street in Jackson Heights. Some families even traveled to India to shop for wedding accessories. One proud mother described how relatives in India had helped her shop for her daughter's wedding outfit at the best stores in India. "Everything was available in America, [but] the range of goods in India is incomparable. This was the first wedding in our family, and I wanted to do our best—best dresses, best food, and perfect ceremony." The most lavish weddings in New York were now fully reminiscent of those in India, where families spend huge amounts.

Segmented Social Gatherings

By the 1990s the isolated family households of the earlier Indian immigrants had developed into multigenerational households linked to extended family networks. These networks were evident in the high frequency of gatherings of friends and family in the New York area, and were now a hallmark of Indian social life. The size of these get-togethers varied from small and intimate parties at the host's home to large-scale events held in rented spaces. The occasions included birthdays, graduations, sweet-sixteens, engagements, and weddings. The rented locations were booked for months in advance, and guests might have more than one event to attend on any given weekend.

At parties in homes the number of guests ranged from a dozen to more than fifty. Food was essential. Although some involved outside catering or potlucks, generally the hostess prepared the elaborate meal for the guests. Married couples attended together, but teenage children were given the decision to come only if they wished.

The mix of guests reflected the social class of the host. At parties given by upper-class and professional Indians, generally in suburban areas, guests were from the same social stratum. At some parties, doctors or business families predominated. The presence of relatives among the guests was also noticeable—brothers and sisters, close or distant cousins, and their families.

[156]

Whereas social gatherings in the 1960s and 1970s had consisted primarily of Indian friends and their families, by the 1990s, after two or more decades of family reunification, relatives frequently outnumbered friends.

Almost instantly after initial greetings, adult guests at these parties separated into male and female groups, and the younger generation of both sexes gathered in their own area. This segregation by gender and generation continued for the entire party, with three separate arenas of conversation and socializing. Women's conversations were dominated by stories of friends and relatives and discussion of clothes and shopping; even career women hardly ever spoke about work matters. In contrast, men's conversations centered on work, sports, or investment strategies. Such gatherings were also occasions to narrate, over and over again from the second generation's viewpoint, accounts of how, years ago, the hosts and a guest couple had become best friends. It was common to hear such statements as "In those years the Indian community was very small, and there were only a handful of Indians" or "In that time—this is before all these Indians arrived in New York—there were so few Indians that we formed one family; everyone knew each other very well."

The mix of relatives and friends was more balanced, and the diversity of class greater, at the larger parties that included the host's entire social network of friends, work colleagues, and extended family. Relatives, in particular, traveled from near and far to attend such parties. The largest parties were in favorite American restaurants or banquet halls in Queens and Long Island that had become familiar places to Indian immigrants. They served Indian food to their special Indian clientele and met needs that included furniture arrangements for ceremonies or even catering by Indian restaurants. Most Indian immigrants, however, preferred the Indian restaurants, of which there was an ever greater range in the New York area. These restaurants had smaller banquet halls for such parties, and it was not uncommon to find a single restaurant holding more than one party an evening. These restaurants could also provide sound equipment and accessories for rituals and ceremonies, or permit the host to hire them from outside suppliers. The most lavish wedding parties strove to replicate proceedings in contemporary urban India, with a separate Ladies *Sangeet*, or women's musical gathering, and other wedding-eve ceremonies.

Guests at these larger parties ranged from a hundred to over five hundred, with weddings usually the largest gatherings. Whereas Hindu weddings included traditional ceremonies such as *saptapadi*, with bride and groom reciting marriage vows while circling a sacred fire, birthdays or graduations featured American-style cakes with customized frosting messages for the occasion. Dancing was an integral part of these parties, and in the 1990s a growing number of Indian DJs in the New York area supplied the music, mainly from Indian films, bhangra, and their own mixes, with a sprinkling of Western music. Dancing combined Indian and Western styles, with younger people taking the lead and older ones joining them.

Tradition, class differentiation, and family ties were simultaneously apparent when relatives of different occupations and backgrounds gathered. At a 1996 party in an Indian restaurant in Queens, a young couple invited several hundred Indian friends and relatives to celebrate their child's birthday. The husband operated a delicatessen, and the wife was taking computer courses in addition to caring for her young child. In a front corner, one of the dozen tables was occupied by several professional families; a man in his late fifties at this table was introduced as the elder brother "who brought the entire family here." Both he and his wife were physicians with their own private practices. They lived in Westchester County and had been sponsors for the younger siblings and their families who now lived in Queens. The physician couple was treated with considerable respect by the entire family; the host couple felt honored by their presence and introduced their professional guests to them. To other guests, they only pointed out the "professional" table.

While weddings or other parties served the purpose of family reunions, some Indian immigrants organized gatherings of extended family members only, smaller versions of the "community" conventions discussed in chapter 7. These gatherings of extended family members permitted the exchange of news of relatives in India and the United States, the circulation of information on eligible marriage partners, and activation of the group's hierarchical generational and gender-role structure. Affirming the social ties of arranged marriages, caste, regional culture, and common religion, these events also reinforced efforts to create directories of Indian jatis, or regional associations.

These family reunions ordinarily were held on long weekends at one member's home. The extended family members went out to dinners together, organized picnics, and arranged group sightseeing tours. One participant explained of such gatherings, which some Indians called "family conventions": "Almost all my relatives are in the United States and Canada now. So even if I visit India, I do not see them there. Besides, the best is if we can organize annual get-togethers where all the relatives could come together. I know that that requires considerable coordinating and organizing, but since I am now retired, I can devote my time toward that. I commit to hosting the first few such conventions at my home; once the tradition is established, then other people can continue it."

In another extended family, such conventions had been held for many years. With the members in India, Britain, Kenya, Tanzania, Australia, Canada, and the United States, in the 1980s they organized winter conventions on a biennial schedule, with the next convention's location and date set before adjourning. This arrangement had worked for more than a decade. Family members took vacations from their jobs at the same time, and planned side trips around the convention date. One wedding was even arranged to coincide with a convention so that all relatives could attend. The main activities were eating and dancing together. Each convention was videotaped, with copies sent to member households. One woman considered these conventions the most fulfilling experiences of her immigrant life. "We older persons get to see our siblings and their families, and our children come to know who their cousins are, and what an Indian family is all about. After living as Americans all the time, working hard in our jobs and raising a family by ourselves, these conventions are our time to be Indian, to feel [we are] our own selves."

These Indian parties and gatherings crossed generational lines, but to one young Indian American woman they revealed negative as well as positive aspects of extended family ties. "I had never known my mom could be so petty and mean about small things. It was like I was seeing a new person. My aunt was also pretty bad. She blamed my parents for bringing them to this country and sealing their happy lives in India. And all the nonsense that started coming out then—family histories of how badly one was treated in India; whose relative had been nasty to whom twenty-five years ago. And all these rules about food, cooking, and kitchen! Even if I tried to know them, one life will not be enough."

Generational and gender perspectives frequently coincided. The U.S.-reared daughters generally considered their mothers subservient to their fathers, forever compromising for them. Some wondered why "she always had to agree with my father." Some younger Indian Americans were unable to accept the social conventions of traditional Indian marriage; they found their mothers submissive, but also "calculating" and "manipulating," and "expecting us to do the same."

Many younger Indians complained that their parents' justification for disciplining them and regulating their activities was fear of gossip among the very guests they socialized with at the Indian parties and family gatherings. One said:

> Our parents do things because they want to show off their children to this community. We are always told to behave in a certain way because of this community pressure. There is so much concern as to what "people" will say. It seems that these people have not left India at all. These uncles and aunties just talk about whose girl is going out with whom, and what she did at a party. They want us to be Indian, but if they could only see the kind of things our cousins can get away with in India! We would never even dream of doing things that they do there. Our parents are just paranoid that we will become Americans.

[7]

The Evolution of South Asian Organizations

By the 1990s Indian organizations in New York City had proliferated. If the hallmark activity of Taiwanese immigrants was starting businesses (Chen 1992, 104–107), and that of Koreans founding churches (Park 1997, 183), the leading activity of Indian immigrants was forming organizations. From the 1960s onward, Indians founded a myriad of organizations serving a myriad of interests. New organizations were frequently additions to and not replacements of existing ones, so that by the 1990s multiple layers of Indian communitywide and more-specialized and focused organizations existed in New York City. Yet while these many associations and interests coexisted, they remained in general distant from one another, with no grand overarching structure. Still, they reflected well the matured diversity of the city's Indian community after four decades, and revealed the cleavages of class, culture, gender, generation, and politics.

The pan-Indian organizations formed in the 1960s and the 1970s represented principally the Indian professional immigrants and their nationalist Indian culture and elite politics. They perceived themselves as informal ambassadors of India in the United States, with the task of bestowing prestige on its national image in their new country. Contemporaneous with the establishment of the new immigrant community in Queens from the 1970s onward was the emergence of organizations representing the cultural diversity of India. Beginning with religious groupings and regional associations, in later years more-parochial organizations formed around even narrower regional identities, religious sects, and jatis. All these organizations were created by the immigrant generation to serve their own social and cultural needs (Khandelwal 1997a).

Though living in the United States, both the elite pan-Indian and the cultural association leaders looked to India as the source of their primary purpose and activities. They largely ignored the situation of nonprofessional Indians (let alone other South Asians) and did not systematically reach out to other American minority, social service, or political groups. This pattern was challenged in the 1980s and 1990s by new organizations of Indian women, second-generation youth, and political progressives. The mid-1990s saw the first clashes between the elite pan-Indian organizations and younger and progressive leaders (compare Eade 1990).

Pan-Indian Organizations

The Association of Indians in America (AIA), the Federation of Indians in America (FIA), and the National Federation of Indians in America (NFIA) were the major pan-Indian associations. Founded between 1967 and 1980, they continued to exist in the 1990s as vehicles for the established leadership of the Indian immigrant community. They filled the top layer in the roster of Indian organizations in New York City and represented Indians in public multicultural and multiethnic American activities. The AIA and NFIA had established chapters all over the country, with their founding New York groups becoming local chapters, and the FIA model of an umbrella Indian organization was replicated elsewhere nationwide. The leaders and members of these organizations were primarily upper-middle-class and affluent Indian professionals who had arrived in the early wave of post-1965 immigration. Buffered by their own economic and professional success in the United States, these leaders were unable to respond to new issues affecting the city's larger and more diverse Indian immigrants of later decades. In addition, their style of hierarchical male leadership and their politics were rooted in a traditional Indian consciousness that appeared increasingly conservative in comparison to emerging female and younger progressive voices.

The AIA was founded in 1967 by a group of professionals with the objective of addressing "the social welfare of the Asian Indians in the United States, and to help them become a part of the mainstream of American life" (AIA 1991). During the decades since then, the AIA undertook several projects (Fisher 1980). In the 1970s it lobbied the Commerce Department for an "Asian Indian" choice in the U.S. Census under the "Asian and Pacific Islander" category. In the same decade the AIA sought and won the extension of "Minority Status to the immigrants of South Asian Americans for civil rights purposes" (AIA 1991). In subsequent years the AIA represented the interests of foreign medical graduates within the American Medical Association, participated in U.S. bicentennial celebrations in 1976, conducted voter registration drives and youth projects, and ran "Project India," which through 1991 had channeled "more than Fifteen Million dollars worth of funds and equipment to projects and relief works in India" (AIA 1991). By the early 1990s, however, the AIA's New York chapter was known in the local Indian community mainly as the sponsor of the annual Diwali festival at the South Street Seaport in lower Manhattan. Instead of serving as spokespersons for issues affecting Indians' place in the American political scene, its leaders focused on representations of Indian culture.

The Joint Committee of Indian Organizations, founded in 1970, reorganized in 1977 under the new name of the Federation of Indian Associations, and aimed to be the principal umbrella group for the growing number of Indian organizations in New York. By 1987–88 the list of seventy member organizations included the American Society of Anesthesiologists from India, Asian Indian Women in America, the International Punjabi Society, the Tagore Society of N.A. [North America], the Kerala Samajam of Greater New York, and the Vishwa Hindu Parishad of America. Like its predecessor, the FIA has concentrated on celebrating such holidays as Indian Independence Day, Republic Day, Gandhi Jayanti (Gandhi's Birthday), and U.S. Independence Day.

Every August since 1980 the FIA has organized an annual India Day Parade in midtown Manhattan to mark Indian Independence Day. Like other ethnic parades, it consists of floats, bands, and contingents of marchers representing various Indian sponsor groups. The Indian ambassador to the United States, the consul general, and other senior dignitaries are always present, and the grand marshal is always a popular star from the Bombay film industry. Ethnic pride is enhanced by the attendance of American public officials such as New York City's mayor and New York State's governor, and the parade's souvenir journal is replete with congratulatory messages from American and Indian officials. Still, the FIA was not recognized by most of New York's Indian population as their leading organization. The election of FIA officers by member organizations was relevant to only a small number of Indians, and apart from the India Day Parade, the FIA had few public activities and little impact on local Indians.

Around 1980 some Indian leaders felt the need for a new national Indian umbrella organization. Many were members of New York's FIA, and they envisioned an organization like it to bring together Indian immigrants from different parts of the United States. In response to this perceived need, the National Federation of Indians in America was formed at the first national convention of Asian Indian leaders in New York City in 1980.

With chapters all over the United States, the NFIA held conventions in different parts of the country. Since many New York NFIA leaders were also active in the FIA, the two groups had overlapping leadership. The NFIA's agenda reflected the perspective of the settled and established middle- and upper-class immigrant cohorts. Only a handful of the successful Indian businessmen or professionals arriving in the 1980s or 1990s joined the NFIA.

In 1989 NFIA leaders organized the First Global Convention of People of Indian Origin in New York City. This ambitious effort, held at the Sheraton Center in midtown Manhattan, included plenaries and panel discussions, a business exposition, banquets, cultural events, and an exhibition of the "Art, History, and Culture" of India. Besides the U.S. NFIA organizers, the convention was attended by international coordinators from Guyana, Barbados, Malaysia, the United Kingdom, the Netherlands, Japan, the Philippines, and India. Although its global ambitions were historic, the limited agenda of its organizers was disappointing to many. Participants discussed issues of ethnic images and representation, but the convention failed to address any concrete issues affecting overseas Indians. At the concluding session, a representative from Britain commented that Indian leadership in the United States was "decades behind" that of the United Kingdom. A second Global Convention, held in 1992 in New Delhi, was reportedly even less impressive.

The elite pan-Indian organizations of New York City had tried to establish links with similar-minded Indian leaders in other parts of the United States and worldwide. They sought recognition from Indian governmental agencies such as the Indian consulate and embassy, and from officials and politicians in India itself. The leaders of these organizations, with few exceptions, were men who resided in New York suburbs and had little regular contact with the Indian immigrants of diverse socioeconomic backgrounds who lived in Queens. Some leaders were aware of their estrangement from the masses of Indians, but were unable to cross class lines and identify with the needs of the growing Indian urban population. Their values of first-generation and male-gender hegemony were, even to some leaders with moderate political outlooks, fixed and conservative, and were out of tune with the new wave of women, younger-generation, and progressive activists.

Cultural Organizations

Organizational expression of the diverse regional identities of Indian immigrants first appeared in the early 1970s. In 1980 Maxine Fisher described ten of those based on an Indian state and language: the Maharashtra Mandal of New York (founded in 1970), the Tamil Sangam (1970), the Cultural

Association of Bengal (1971), the Kerala Samajam of New York (1971), the Telugu Literary and Cultural Society (1971), the Gujarat Samaj of New York (1973), the Kannada Koota of New York (1973), the Sindhi Association of America (1974), the Bihar Association of North America (1975), and the Rajasthan Parishad of America (1975). Their memberships that year ranged from 75 to 1,500 families (Fisher 1980).

Indian immigrants had always been a culturally composite group, but until then these identities had remained submerged in the pan-Indian fold. Indians from each regional culture also acknowledged their Indian national identity, but as they began to rear families, these cultural identities started to surface organizationally. Additionally, the Indian population was now becoming large enough to form separate regional associations, which the continuous arrival of new immigrants would only reinforce.

These organizations celebrated the language, foodways, literature, and history of an Indian state—each with a population outnumbering that of many of the world's independent nations. Their calendars featured their own regional festivals and other cultural events. The Kannada Koota, an organization for immigrants from the state of Karnataka, for example, celebrated the Kannada new year by honoring the region's cultural talent with a program titled "Ugadi and Composer's Day." In 1988 this weekend event was held in a Queens public school auditorium and offered workshops for youth and women conducted by professional counselors and psychologists, a dance concert, music, and dinner. Girish Karnad, a well-known Indian playwright, film actor, director, and producer from Karnataka, was the guest of honor.

The main purpose of these organizations was to reinforce cultural commonality among members; family participation and attendance by second-generation Indian Americans was a high priority. The events accommodated U.S.-reared youth by providing "American food" such as pizza, but otherwise they were showcases for the parental generation's distinctive regional language, performance arts, and food. A number of these organizations also sponsored classes for children in their regional language.

Though not ostensibly religious in nature, most regional organizations emphasized the Hindu cultural ethos of their dominant religious majority, and several openly took on significant roles in Hindu temples. Certain regional associations, however, reflected the religious complexity of their home states. Thus, Bengali association celebrations of the essentially Hindu Durga Puja festival were attended by non-Hindu Bengalis, and Kerala associations included both Christians and Hindus.

These regional organizations displayed no interest in American civic affairs and rarely invited elected officials to their events. Their leaders did not act as spokespersons for the larger Indian community and did not compete with the pan-Indian organizations in any way, even though memberships might overlap.

As continuing immigration augmented each regional population in New York, in several cases multiple organizations emerged. In some instances geography played a role, and a new organization formed when numbers in an urban or suburban area reached a critical mass. In other situations, the reason was strife within an organization: a faction split away, formed a new group under new leadership, and incorporated under a name that distinguished it from the parent one. As a result, the number of Indian cultural Indian organizations multiplied in the 1980s and 1990s. The 1987–88 FIA member organization list included, for example, five Kerala associations.[1]

In addition to the regional associations, smaller groupings began to create informal networks, and sometimes formal organizations. Many of these identities were based on geographic subareas in India with their own distinct dialects or religious practices. Social gatherings and festivals celebrated by Konkanis, from an area in the northern part of the state of Karnataka, or by Goans, from the former Portuguese enclave, occurred in Queens. Even within the inclusive regional associations, smaller networks formed. Thus among Gujarati immigrants, groups of residents from a particular village might meet informally. In the early 1990s a small circle of Indian immigrants who had been posted by their government to Kabul, Afghanistan, reconnected in New York in informal private gatherings and called themselves the Kabul Indians.

By the 1980s, biradari and jati organizations had begun to appear in Queens, with announcements of their community get-togethers published in Indian newspapers. One item, for instance, reported that "the Brahmin Society of New York . . . successfully organized its first meeting and picnic on August 4. . . . About 200 Brahmins gathered in Cunningham Park [in Queens] for the event. The main focus was the introduction of a working committee as well as introduction to all members. The society is comprised of vegetarian Brahmin Gujaratis residing in New York" (*India Abroad* 8/16/91). In Richmond Hill, a temple named after a fourteenth-century saint, Guru Ravi Das, was organized in the early 1990s by a congregation of about one hundred families belonging to one Punjabi caste. The members were mainly recent immigrants, and largely homemaker women and men employed in small businesses.

By the 1990s geographic networks of organizations based on region or caste, as well as religion or sect, had become much more important for Indian immigrants throughout the United States, including Queens and New York City. These networks extended from local regions to areas where Indians might be sparse, and large and small organizations alike fostered contact among their members living in scattered parts of the United States.

Many created nationwide or even transnational directories; the ethnic press was also used to reach to the widest Indian audience. One newspaper announcement appealed to members of one jati: "Open invitation to all our Agrawal/Aggarwal/Gupta families and individuals in U.S.A. to participate in organizing the Agrawal community, to continue our culture, traditions, and rich heritage for the benefit of our children" (*India Abroad* 5/19/89).

Modern telecommunications, databases, and websites made it easier to transcend physical barriers. It was possible for one officer of a regional association network to be from Queens, and another to live in a distant part of the United States. The newsletter of the Association of Rajasthanis in America (ARA), titled *Rajasthan* (named for an Indian state), illustrates this phenomenon. Reaching members nationwide, it was compiled and Xeroxed by the organization's secretary, who resided in Illinois. A letter to readers opened: "Dear Rajasthani Bandhu [Brother]," and continued, "We are increasingly covering the Continent with this newsletter and our mailing list is increasing day by day." It profiled Indian immigrant community leaders who hailed from Rajasthan, listed upcoming Hindu festivals, and included matrimonial classified advertisements, items championing vegetarianism, and folktales in the Marwari Rajasthani dialect. An announcement of the upcoming "Annual Diwali Get-Together and Cultural Function" in Chicago noted: "If you are coming from a long distance and need overnighting, a lot of host families are available. You only need to call" (*Rajasthan*, fall 1991).

Members of Indian cultural groups began increasingly to meet face-to-face in weekend gatherings held in different parts of the country. In May 1996 one smaller, jati-based meeting, the sixth annual convention of the Somavaunshiya Sahasrajun Kshatriya Samaj of North America (SSKNA), was held in Washington, D.C. "While most of the 61 participants came from the East Coast, visitors from India also attended. . . . Following the meeting, the second day of the Convention consisted of a picnic at Black Hill Regional Park. The 1997 SSKNA convention is tentatively planned to be held in Detroit" (*India Abroad* 7/12/96). The larger regional organizational networks had started meeting in annual conventions in the 1980s, with locations rotating among cities where local Indian sponsors could coordinate these events. With their growing attendances, these national organization conventions began to converge on certain long weekends, and in 1996 so many chose the July Fourth weekend that *India Abroad* decided to do a special round-up feature on them (7/19/96):

> Thousands of Indian American families across the country gathered at conventions and conferences during the July 4 weekend. At least 12 such meetings took place, attracting over 20,000 Indian Americans. . . . Malayalis gath-

ered in Houston for their convention, at which the state Chief Minister, E. K. Nayanar, was present. About 4,000 people attended the American Telugu Association's national convention, while the Bengali conference drew about 3,500. . . . More than 300 were at the Assamese convention near Chicago. The 27th annual convention of the Orissa Society of North Americas, was held in Gaithersburg, Maryland. . . . Two conventions brought together more than 600 Jains and 300 members of the Zoroastrian community in San Francisco. The second conference of the National Association of Asian Indian Christians (NAAIC), in Allentown, Pennsylvania, attracted about 300. . . . The fourth annual convention of the Vokkaligara [caste] community ended in Cherry Hill, New Jersey, with a call by its spiritual leader to stand united. . . . The first Konkani conference was held in Hightstown, New Jersey, to celebrate the community's ancestry, heritage, and culture.

At these conventions, prominent figures from India were chief guests, awards were presented to members who excelled professionally and honored their community, distinctive Indian heritages were passed on to the next generation, and programs included opportunities for family outings. Although youth sections met, by and large the second generation did not take their regional or caste identities as seriously as did their parents. They attended mainly out of curiosity and to meet other youth from their own Indian cultural group; the vast cultural and historical content of their own backgrounds appeared puzzling to most.

The regional and caste associations did not necessarily fragment the Indian immigrant population. It was possible, and not uncommon, for leaders to participate in pan-Indian activities and also be members of regional, religious, and caste associations. Regional associations even formed within the national Association of American Physicians from India (AAPI). In 1996 *India Abroad* carried an announcement of a convention for "All Rajasthan Medical Graduates, Family & Friends" sponsored by the Chicago chapter of the Rajasthan Medical Association of Alumni from India, at the Nordic Hills Resort in Illinois, with a "Continuing Medical Education Seminar, Lake Michigan Dinner Cruise, Gala Banquet Dinner Dance, Talent Show & Cultural Program for Children, and Tennis, Golf, & Cricket Match"; it also featured an appeal to physicians from the Indian state of Assam to join an "Alumni Get-Together (Welcome All, Including Family)," organized by the American Association of Physicians from Assam at Bonnie Castle in Thousand Islands, New York (7/19/96).

The pan-Indian organizations and the cultural associations ignored or deemphasized the social service needs of the increasingly stratified immigrant population, especially that in New York. Charity was seen as an individual act, and affluent individuals might make large donations to a house of worship to mark a festival with instructions to distribute food or clothing to

[167]

the needy and poor. For the pan-Indian and regional organizations, famine, floods, or other natural disasters in India were the occasions to mobilize charity appeals. In the New York area, several charity organizations focused on needs in India emerged in the 1980s, including Share and Care, Heart and Handicapped, and Children of Hope. At a well-attended annual fundraiser in New Jersey for the Share and Care Foundation, which shipped clothes to the poor in India, a professional theater performance was preceded by a video of various Share and Care projects (*India Abroad* 10/16/87, 12/15/89).

Women's Organizations

In the 1980s three new women's organizations began to challenge the established, male-dominated pan-Indian organizations and their elite and India-focused agendas. These organizations were part of a wave of organizing by South Asian women all over the United States that heralded a new phase in community leadership (Vaid 1999/2000). The first women's organization in New York City was Asian Indian Women in America (AIWA), founded in 1980 by a group of well-educated and professionally employed immigrant Indian women. These women had been members of pan-Indian organizations like the FIA, but felt the need for a new group to address women's issues, and particularly those of Indian immigrant women struggling to adapt to American society. AIWA held job fairs for women and represented Indian women at various Indian and multiethnic forums in the city. Though AIWA was able to create a name for itself and to network with Indian women beyond the New York area, its leaders shared the upper-middle-class immigrant perspectives of the pan-Indian organization leadership. Indeed, through the 1980s AIWA continued to be a member of the FIA. AIWA intervened effectively in some cases in which Indian women professionals faced racial discrimination, but its links to immigrant women from lower educational and economic backgrounds were limited, and when such women's cries for help in cases of domestic violence started reaching the organization, it did not develop an effective response.

Later in the 1980s AIWA was overshadowed by Manavi, a women's organization founded in New Jersey in 1985. Initially the two organizations were linked, and some AIWA members claimed Manavi as a chapter, but Manavi perceived itself as independent, and also as the first organization for all South Asian women, one that simultaneously addressed service needs and offered new approaches. As Shamita Das Dasgupta, a cofounder of Manavi, explained:

In the 1970s, I was part of a mainstream feminist organization where we joined sit-ins and rallies. I was constantly asked to bring Indian women to join these activities arranged for freedom of women. I tried to include issues of colonialism and community traditions in this organization's debates on feminism, but was not successful in getting even attention, not to say anything about serious consideration. What was worse is that I was made to feel constantly sorry for my culture, for my people, and to almost be apologetic about their remaining in arranged marriages and families. After several years of trying to find common grounds, I gave up and walked out of this organization.

Discarding the security of the mainstream feminist movement was not easy. Neither was my conscious decision to wed my feminist agenda with my ethnic identity. Until then my relationship with my Indian community had been based only on my birth; now my relationship became an act of choice. As a symbol, I gave up wearing all western clothing. However, this was not enough. I had to develop a feminist agenda in the context of the South Asian community. I realized that I was not alone in my efforts. Serendipitously, I came together with five other Indian women, all runaways from mainstream feminism. (DasGupta and Das Dasgupta 1993, 126)

The early activities of Manavi included compiling a *Resource Directory for Asian Indian Women in America* and a self-help guide to assist in facing domestic violence, seeking temporary emergency shelter, dealing with rape or other sexual assaults, combatting workplace sexual harassment and discrimination on the basis of sex, race, or national origin, and locating a lawyer. Manavi members worked on cases of domestic violence and child custody disputes, and also sought to advance debate on feminist theory and international feminist issues. Though rooted in the needs of immigrant women, Manavi also was connected to women's issues in India. Its tenth-anniversary newsletter reported on Manavi's local activities as well as "Indian Women and National Identity" and "Beijing '95: A Global Referendum on the Human Rights of Women" (*Manavi Newsletter* 1995).

In the late 1980s another group of women—all graduate students and young professionals from India—met in New York to start a women's organization. After looking at the existing organizations and assessing the service and advocacy needs of South Asian women, they founded Sakhi, meaning a woman's female friend, in 1989. Within a short period the number of calls to their hotline, where battered women could seek help, grew rapidly. Sakhi's South Asian staff and volunteers connected their increasing caseload to appropriate local service agencies specializing in domestic violence intervention. Sakhi also mounted awareness-raising drives and demonstrations, including one in front of a male batterer's home in Jamaica, Queens, where placards read: "Is It Your Business If Your Neighbor Beats His Wife? You Bet Her Life It Is" and "Domestic Violence Destroys Our Communities."

[169]

As Sakhi's newsletter later reported, "We circled around the family house to the sounds of chants such as 'Wake up fathers, Wake up brothers. If you abuse, you will lose!' We also delivered a poster-letter to the family warning them to stop their terrorization of [the victim]. . . . [The victim] and Sakhi remain determined to bring [the perpetrator] to justice and warn families like his that they cannot get away with sheltering those who terrorize women" (*Sakhi Quarterly*, summer 1996).

Sakhi's public outcries against domestic violence shocked the Indian community, particularly its established elite leaders. Meanwhile, Sakhi broadened its agenda and sponsored film festivals, cultural performances, and fundraising programs presenting women artists and activists. In one Sakhi "Speak Out" night, several South Asian women told personal stories of love, anger, happiness, and bitterness; and several of Sakhi's film festivals screened acclaimed films made by and about South Asian women. By the early 1990s, Sakhi was one of the foremost progressive feminist organizations in New York City.

These new women's organizations backed their advocacy work with writings by scholars who were members or closely linked to them (Das Dasgupta 1986, 1995, 1998; Bhattacharjee 1992, 1997a, 1997b; DasGupta and Das Dasgupta 1993, 1996; Abraham 1998, 2000). One of them, Margaret Abraham, analyzes existing literature on domestic violence:

> There is a conspicuous gap in the literature concerning the structural and cultural factors that legitimate domestic violence among ethnic groups, especially recent immigrant groups. Focusing on gender alone . . . keeps women from looking at other structures of oppression and as such works to the advantage of the dominant groups. In the context of addressing domestic violence in a stratified society such as the United States, a contextualized feminism must explicitly acknowledge both the commonality and differences of experiences based on the intersection of ethnicity, gender, class, and citizenship. (2000, 6)

South Asian feminists also traced their lineage to contemporary and earlier generations of feminists in South Asia (Sangari and Vaid 1989; Das-Gupta and Das Dasgupta 1993; Kumar 1993). They reported on developments there in newsletters and forums, kept in contact with South Asian women's movements, and sponsored visits by women activists from South Asia. They also aligned themselves theoretically with Third World women's movements and with women of color in the United States (Mohanty 1991, 1993).

While domestic violence quickly became a leading issue for South Asian activists, the new women leaders were well aware that it was not the only problem facing South Asian women. In public forums Manavi and Sakhi leaders asserted that domestic violence was a strategic entry point to the broader feminist agenda facing South Asian women immigrants in America (Abraham 1995, 2000). In championing this agenda, these organizations joined progressive voices beyond the South Asian community. Sakhi coordinator Prema Vora, for example, opposed welfare reform provisions in the mid-1990s, stressing their implications for South Asian immigrant women: "The decision to leave an abusive husband or a partner is always a difficult one. . . . The decision to leave is perhaps even more difficult for an immigrant woman who speaks little English, is unfamiliar with her surroundings and, most [of all,] depends on her abuser for her immigration status" (*Newsday* 6/26/95).

When South Asian women confronting domestic violence did utilize mainstream social service agencies or shelters, they frequently faced cultural insensitivity ranging from language barriers to stereotyped and antagonistic understandings of Indian marriage and family relationships. In a number of instances, women leaders housed female victims of abuse at their own homes or in temporary shelters. After years of fundraising, Manavi opened its own shelter for South Asian women in 1997.

In the 1990s Indian immigrant professional mental health and social workers, both women and men, also began to address openly the social and service needs of the Queens Indian community. Several members of the Association of Indian Psychiatrists formed Helping Professionals to build links among its members working in existing organizations. In the mid-1990s its education and service section merged with Elmhurst-based Nav Nirmaan (New Construction), an organization concerned with "alcoholism and chemical abuse among persons of South Asian descent residing in the US as well as in India" (*Nav Nirmaan* n.d.). Other professionals at the Queens Child Guidance Center's Asian Clinic in Elmhurst focused on behavioral, emotional, and academic problems of children and their families, and counseled South Asian children and parents in Queens public schools. In 1994 an Indian female social worker launched a women's organization called Pragati (Progress) "to empower poor, unemployed and/or abused South Asian women" by providing English and health education classes, employment referral services, and cultural activities.

Situating immigrant women's issues in a space between the home country and mainstream America allowed these women's organizations and their successors to challenge the pan-Indian organizations' exclusive and dominant role in defining Indian American identity. Their practical emphasis on the everyday immigration context was coupled with severe critiques not only of mainstream American feminism but also of patriarchal hegemony in both India and the United States.

Youth Organizations

In 1987 the New York City Indian community received a wake-up call when a series of high-profile public episodes of anti-Indian violence occurred in neighboring New Jersey. Indians in Queens had already experienced racist name-calling, stone-throwing, and defacing of houses of worship for many years, and these incidents were widely discussed among themselves. Then in 1987 Indian immigrant Bharat Kanubhai Patel was beaten by men who broke into his house, and the *Jersey Journal* published a statement from the "Dotbusters" (referring to the bindi that women wear on their foreheads) who claimed responsibility, adding: "We will go to any extreme to get Indians to move out of Jersey City." On September 27, 1987, in Hoboken, New Jersey, a thirty-one-year-old Indian man, Navroze Mody, was beaten severely by a gang of white and Hispanic youth and died a few days later. Mody's immigrant parents pursued the case in court, public forums mobilized community concern, and a number of Indian organizations raised funds for the legal and political struggle (Misir 1996).

The anti-Indian violence in New Jersey put a spotlight on similar cases nationwide and made the younger generation of Indian Americans more aware of their racial minority status in the United States. South Asian students in the New York–New Jersey area formed Indian Youth Against Racism (IYAR) to support prosecution of the Mody case, but the group eventually became inactive.

In 1990 a small number of Indian American youth started South Asian Alliance For Action (SAAFA). As the original core grew, however, internal disagreements reflecting differences of class background and sexual orientation proved irreconcilable, and SAAFA lasted only a couple of years (Advani 1997). Other organizations of young South Asian progressives soon took its place, among them Youth Against Racism (YAR, a successor to IYAR), the South Asian Lesbian and Gay Association (SALGA), South Asian AIDS Action (SAAA), and Concerned South Asians (CSA). Although these groups addressed a variety of issues, their characteristics were similar. Because their members had grown up either in the United States with a sense of racial consciousness or in the South Asian progressive world, themes of racial and ethnic discrimination, social justice, and equality were integral to their agendas. Many in this small and intimate group of youth had arrived in New York City recently and hoped to fill what was a void in South Asian activism, aside from the recently founded Sakhi, which seemed a promising precedent and potential ally.

Common to all these organizations was an inclusive "South Asian" identity that rejected divisions of caste, religion, region, or national ancestry

(Women of South Asian Descent Collective 1993; Maira and Srikanth 1996). When members of the defunct organization IYAR regrouped in the 1990s, they dropped the label "Indian" and called themselves simply YAR, which means both "Youth Against Racism" and, in Hindi and Urdu, "buddy." "South Asian" also evoked progressive American values of equality regardless of gender, class, religion, or sexuality, and therefore was not a mere substitution for "Indian." However, the young progressive activists would find it a challenge to expand this pan–South Asian consciousness in a population dominated by first-generation immigrants, as some South Asian Americans themselves recognized (Islam 1993; Sinha 1998).

Most of the young activists in New York City had few longstanding contacts with the adult immigrant population or with Queens. Their organizations met in Manhattan, and most lived in Manhattan or Brooklyn, away from their families or relatives. These gaps were exacerbated by cultural differences with the immigrant generation, particularly over issues relating to gender and sexuality (P. Shah 1997). Often the South Asian progressives received more support from like-minded activists in other ethnic and racial groups than in their own. During the 1990s several young South Asians joined pan–Asian American organizations, including the Asian Pacific Islanders Committee on HIV-AIDS (APICHA), the Asian American Legal Defense and Education Fund (AALDEF), and the Asian American Federation, as staff or volunteers (Advani 1997; Sinha 1998). In 1990 several young South Asians also created a Leased Drivers Coalition (LDC) to organize South Asian cabdrivers under the umbrella of the pan–Asian American Committee Against Anti-Asian Violence (CAAAV). Salim Osman, who had worked as a cabdriver in New York City, and previously as a lawyer in Pakistan, was the first LDC staff person.

The second half of the 1990s saw concerted attempts at youth organizing. Responding to both the progressive youth concerns and the social issues spurred by the women's organizations, in 1996 a group of young South Asians founded SAYA! (South Asian Youth Action!) to serve the needs of New York's burgeoning South Asian youth population for mentoring, peer counseling, and community-based programs. It was launched under the aegis of a pan-Asian organization, the Asian American Federation of New York, which supported many Asian agencies in the New York area. Focusing on Queens, where a majority of New York's South Asian youth lived, in its first year SAYA! secured funding to conduct a career fair and several workshops and community forums. In 1997 SAYA! rented office and recreation space at a church in Elmhurst, where its programs attracted teenagers of diverse South Asian backgrounds. SAYA! reached out to local schools, offered year-round programs for developing self-esteem and awareness to South Asian youth from diverse socioeconomic backgrounds at its rented site, and presented public forums and performances throughout New York City, including Manhattan (Kiang 2001, 233). By the late 1990s its founder-director, Sayu Bhojwani, had also developed coalitions with many Asian American and youth service organizations.

In Manhattan, Youth Solidarity Summer, organized by progressive South Asians, brought youth from different parts of North America to the city for summer workshops. In 1998,

> They had come from Sugarland, Texas; from Guelph, Ontario; from Buffalo, New York. Across the map of North America, stories told by progressive youth sounded very similar. They were searching for a space in which to work together with others who shared their social vision, and for an ideological thread that would bind together their various activities. Some had been involved with pan-Asian student coalitions; some with queer, largely white, groups; several with feminist campaigns; and others with labor organizations. (Maira 1999/2000, 141)

Political Organizing

In 1986 the South Asia Forum was founded to air issues concerning South Asian immigrants. The topics of its monthly meetings ranged from South Asian literature, to communalism in South Asia, to women's and youth issues in U.S. communities. The members were mainly immigrants in the New York area, although one member produced its newsletter in Washington, D.C. Except for an annual public event, meetings took place in members' homes. The Forum, intended to remain informal, with minimal structure, produced provocative discussions among its Indian, Bangladeshi, and Pakistani participants.

In contrast to their active cultural life in their new surroundings, most Indians were not much involved in American political life until the 1990s. Before then a professional-dominated Indian American Forum for Political Education (IAFPE) had held annual conventions to which American political figures were invited, but it did not seek to disseminate political information to a larger group of Indians. Interest among Indian immigrants widened in the 1990s with growing participation in the presidential elections, and a handful even attended the Democratic and Republican conventions. A few Indians ran and lost in bids for national public offices—Ram Uppuluri in 1994 and Peter Mathews in 1998 for U.S. congressional seats from Tennessee and California, respectively. In 1998 two Indian candidates won reelection bids for state office—Kumar Barve from Maryland and Satvir Chaudhary from Minnesota (Srikanth 1998, 1999/2000). The newspaper *India Abroad* started an India Abroad Center for Political Awareness and opened an office in Washington, D.C., in the late 1990s, but it was the only Indian organization besides the Association of American Physicians from India to have an office in the U.S. capital. A few professional organizations started placing interns in congressional offices, but the foremost political activity of upper-class Indians was fundraising for candidates of Indian origin or for American politicians with a pro-India foreign policy record. Here the professional networks of upper-class Indian immigrants were tapped, even when contributors lived beyond a candidate's district.

In contrast to this growing involvement in national American politics, Indian community leaders in New York City ignored grassroots politics entirely and, unlike other Asians and immigrants, played no role during 1991–92 in city council and congressional redistricting hearings. However, Indians in New York did fundraise for U.S. Representative Stephen Solarz, beloved for his support of India, in a 1992 primary bid for his redrawn congressional seat; his Indian supporters built no coalitions with other voting groups in the district (which included several Queens neighborhoods) and were shocked when he lost the primary election to a female Puerto Rican candidate, Nydia Velasquez, who went on to win the seat.

Indians in the 1990s were conspicuous by their absence in grassroots neighborhood or citywide politics in New York City. Only a handful of Indians were appointed to any of the city's fifty-nine community boards, and these individuals were not perceived as leaders in the Indian community. This lack of political activism formed a striking contrast to that of other Asian immigrants, particularly Chinese and Koreans, who presented several community board appointees and elected local school board members and a handful of city council electoral contenders. (In New Jersey, Indian grassroots political participation was more visible.)

In urban India, apart from voting in national and state elections, civic participation at the grassroots level is practically absent. Neighborhood quality-of-life issues are not crucial to political organizing in India (Sanjek 1998), and to most Indian immigrants the word *political* suggested not civil rights or community issues, but corruption and nepotism. Indeed, politicians are not highly respected figures in India, especially those at the middle and lower strata, who are often viewed as good-for-nothings who did not concentrate enough on education or career-building. At higher levels, Indian cabinet ministers and members of parliament and state legislative assemblies are valued for their power to disseminate favors to their supporters. Therefore, Indian immigrant leaders often opted to deal with state or national figures at the upper layers of American political life; grassroots politics seemed undeserving of their attention or energies.

In 1996, for the first time, two South Asian immigrant men ran in a New

York City school board election, and both won. Morshed Alam, a Bangladeshi municipal worker, ran in mostly-black District 29 in southern Queens, and thereafter became active in the local Democratic Party. Alam's vote, the highest in the district, was based on his careful coalition-building with other groups, as well as support from fellow Bangladeshis. The victory of Sachi Dastidar, a college professor, in the predominantly white School District 26 was an outcome of the growing concentration of Indians in eastern Queens; as a longstanding member of the mainly-white Northern Bellerose Civic Association, a local homeowner group, he had been appointed to Community Board 13 in 1991. Following Dastidar's school board campaign, an organization called Indian/South Asians of Eastern Queens (ISAEQ) was formed to involve more Indian residents in local civic issues. Dastidar's campaign was managed by a handful of Indian volunteers who had to persuade Indian residents of the significance of the election and convince them to register to vote (Sinha 1998). Dastidar also received support from the Asian American Legal Defense and Education Fund (AALDEF) in a recount of the votes, which proved crucial to his victory (Sinha 1998, 158). Despite repeated appeals, Dastidar's candidacy received no fiscal, political, or moral support from established Indian organizations or elite leaders. When confronted about this, some organization leaders explained their lack of support as a desire not to be partisan; one leading pan-Indian spokesperson even defined his organization as "nonpolitical."

In organizing along class or cultural lines, New York City's Indian immigrants had long ignored the local American boundaries of community or school districts, or borough, city, or state electoral districts. Their pattern of organizing by Indian cultural region and religion was contradictory to overall representation as Indians or South Asians within such geographic areas of residence. Even though Indians were a large ethnic group in New York City, and definitely so in Queens, there was no single organization representing all Indians in Flushing, Elmhurst, or Queens, not to mention in the city at large. The Jackson Heights Merchants Association, founded in 1990, was the only exception, but it represented South Asian businesses in the 74th Street commercial area, and not Indian residents of Jackson Heights.

The India Day Parade of 1995 and Its Aftermath

During 1992 and 1993 several progressive South Asian organizations were present at the South Street Seaport fall Diwali festivals organized by the AIA and at the India Day parades staged each August by the FIA (Bhattacharjee 1992). The pan-Indian sponsor organizations did not approve of the radical politics of the new South Asian organizations, but at that time did not consider them to be a significant challenge to their leadership. Accordingly, Sakhi's contingent was permitted to march in the FIA's India Day Parades for several years.

In 1994, however, the Indian immigrant organization leadership decided that the progressive "South Asians" would not be tolerated any longer, and the FIA denied SALGA members permission to march. Sakhi, however, invited them to join its contingent, and two mainstream newspapers, the *New York Times* and *New York Newsday*, printed pictures with brief captions of marchers carrying SALGA banners.

In 1995 the FIA would not permit SALGA, Sakhi, or the SAAA to join the parade. The FIA's official reason was that "South Asia" had no place in a parade celebrating Indian independence (P. Shah 1997). The barred organizations formed a joint task force to protest their exclusion and to challenge the FIA's explanation, contending that the FIA really disapproved of progressives who served disadvantaged and underrepresented sections of the Indian community. The task force challenged FIA leaders to debate the issue, and on a live Indian television show one FIA official justified the decision by stating that the barred organizations were not serious about the "mother country of India" and its culture. The FIA refused to change its stance, and the task force publicized the dispute through the mainstream press, and obtained the support of Manhattan Borough President Ruth Messinger. When the August 1995 FIA event was held, the protestors, their friends, and supporters from progressive pan-Asian organizations appeared at the parade location and raised banners and shouted slogans drawing attention to the unfairness of the decision to bar them.

To most Indians who attended or watched the parade on television, this episode overshadowed the parade itself. To American mainstream media and politicians, the chief issue had become the exclusion of homosexuals, which resonated with a similar debate over the participation of Irish gays and lesbians in the St. Patrick's Day Parade. In the years following 1995, the India Day Parade continued to be a site of contestation between alternative definitions of Indian ethnic identity. In 1996 the organizers of both the India Day Parade and the Pakistan Day Parade excluded SALGA from marching (*New York Times* 8/4/96). While the established Indian immigrant leaders found new technical grounds to exclude the South Asian groups from marching, the progressive organizations continued to enlist the support of various city political and civil rights groups to seek permission to march.

The second half of the 1990s saw accelerated organizing efforts by younger South Asian progressive and social service groups at both the city and national levels (Mathew and Prashad 1999/2000; Abraham 2000). One forum for South Asian leftists and progressive views was *SAMAR (South*

Asian Magazine for Action and Reflection), a magazine and a radio program. The most acrimonious expression of these developments was the split
within Sakhi in 1997 when its Domestic Workers' Committee, claiming that
Sakhi was "dominated by middle-class women," separated to form a new organization called Workers' Awaaz (Voice of Workers). At the time of the
split, Workers' Awaaz members themselves were primarily not domestic
workers but ex-Sakhi members who, though coming from the middle and
upper classes, wanted to pursue an agenda of organizing South Asian domestic workers.[2] Sakhi's leaders, on the other hand, maintained that organizing household workers was a separate cause from working with survivors
of domestic violence, Sakhi's original mission (Chansanchai 1997; Aliani et
al. 1999/2000; Abraham 2000).

In 1998 South Asians led a strike of thousands of New York City cabdrivers to protest Mayor Rudolph Giuliani's new taxi fine and summons
policies (*Daily News* 5/14/98; Kazem et al. 1999/2000). Although forgoing a
day's earnings was a burden, the drivers hoped to impress the public with
the seriousness of their grievances. Described in the media as "a shocking
success," the strike pointed to pan–South Asian working-class solidarity
across home-country nationality divisions. Its organizers, who included
young South Asians, were members of the recently formed New York Taxi
Workers' Alliance (NYTWA), "an independent, non-profit organization that
fights for rights of taxi drivers against the combined interests of the city authorities, the garage owners, and the Police Department" (Kazem et al.
1999/2000, 171). One NYTWA organizer, Bhairavi Desai, a young U.S.-col-
lege-educated woman, described the struggle in these terms: "American
capitalism carves out roles for people in the economy depending upon their
ethnic background. The positioning of working-class South Asians into [an]
informal service sector as taxi drivers and their romanticization as independent businessmen explains the domination of the Yellow Cab industry by
South Asians in New York City" (Mathew and Prashad 1999/2000, 170).

Another direction in South Asian organizing in New York City was spot-
lighted in 1998 following the severe beating of Rishi Maharaj, a young Indo-
Trinidadian, by three white youths in South Ozone Park, Queens. For years
young South Asian leaders had emphasized shared issues and struggles between subcontinental and diaspora Indian groups (Sinha 1998), but it was
the Maharaj case that actually brought such an active alliance of diverse
young South Asian organizers and spokespersons. It also reinforced the
linkage of Asian American organizations, in particular the Asian American
Legal Defense and Education Fund, to South Asian communities in
Queens.

With the emergence of new political organizing, largely fostered by
younger South Asian Americans, the late 1990s also witnessed a dramatic

increase in use of media and technology. Cyberspace was perceived to be a more convenient area for building networks than were the geographical communities where various political and generational interests were more real. The noticeable growth in numbers of new Indian arrivals in the information technology (IT) industry also boosted this phenomenon, but the younger generation's use of new media technology was more widespread than that of older generation. This technology, more suited to the younger generation's need to create an identity separate from their parents, came to represent the private space so integral to their lives. Sharp change was also noticeable in the popularity of creative arts—movies, videos, music— which, though ethnic, sought a place in both the national and transnational arenas. By the late 1990s, creative writing in English became a favorite medium of expression for young South Asian Americans, who took keen interest in the emerging literature and literary figures.

As the new identities became more defined, their gap with those of an older generation of immigrants deepened. The India Day Parade in 2000 reflected many of these emerging issues in South Asian New York. Its organizer, the Federation of Indian Associations, continued the format of previous years, with attendance by invited Indian and American dignitaries, and FIA's immigrant leaders carrying India's national flag. Movie stars from Bombay's film industry were once again honored guests and the major draw for the Indian parade spectators. Cultural, regional, and religious organizations marched, among them Indian Christians and the American Federation of Muslims from India; South Asian youth were represented by university fraternities and clubs.

The South Asian Lesbian and Gay Association, whose inclusion in the parade had long been a cause of tension, this year had acquired permission from the local community board to march on its own. Their small contingent was placed at the very end of the parade, however, and marched by itself without other supporters. Their primary boosters were a group of young progressives organized by Youth Solidarity Summer, who from the sidelines proclaimed with placards: "South Asian Unity," "Smash Hindu Nationalism," "I Don't Want To Be A Doctor, We Are Not A Model Minority." SALGA attracted some attention from others in the crowd and from reporters, but the larger audience ignored them in their rush to see the Bollywood movie stars and other dignitaries. At the end of the parade route, scores of organizations and businesses had set up information tables and food stalls, among them media firms and dot.com businesses, reflecting the expanding technological terrains of the South Asian communities (Rai 1995). Social service groups, including Nav Nirmaan, SAYA!, and the New York Immigration Hotline, offered flyers and information in English and South Asian languages.

[179]

For most Indian Americans the chief reason for attending the parade continued to be pride in their national heritage. At the parade, as at the Diwali celebration at the South Street Seaport, they cherished the celebration of their identity in a public space, particularly in Manhattan, and the mass gathering of Indians and South Asians (AIA 2000). Food and other cultural symbols epitomized their presence in New York and the United States, and the presence of Bollywood movie stars captivated them.

To the many progressives who had drawn battle lines with the FIA over defining the boundaries of the Indian community, the parade, however, was a dull affair (Prashad 2000a). Like those who preferred to overlook ethnic politics at the India Day Parade, they continued their activities within the broader Indian/South Asian communities of the New York area.

For all, there was by now more than one way of being Indian in the United States.

Notes

Introduction

1. The term *Indian* is used in this book for immigrants from India. I use the term *South Asian* only when the population being discussed includes other South Asian groups as well.

2. According to the U.S. Census, the Asian Indians in New York City numbered 46,708 in 1980, 94,590 in 1990, and 170,899 in 2000. These growing numbers accounted for a significant share of the Indians in the total U.S. population: 361,531 in 1980, 815,447 in 1990, and 1,678,765 in 2000.

3. The "Asian and Pacific Islander" category, introduced in the 1980 Census, was replaced by "Asian" in the 2000 Census.

4. For documentation and analysis of different aspects of this community, see Mazumdar 1984; Gibson 1988; Jensen 1988; La Brack 1988; Leonard 1992.

5. Among works on the early post-1965 Indian immigrants, Saran and Eames's *New Ethnics: Indian Immigrants in the United States* (1980) and Fisher's *Indians of New York City* (1980) portray life in the 1970s, when the population was still relatively small and homogeneous (see also Chandrasekhar 1982; Saran 1985); a later study of these affluent immigrants is the Helwegs' *An Immigrant Success Story* (1990). There are also a number of dissertations by Indian/South Asian graduate students focused on Indian/South Asian communities in towns and cities where these students lived (Jain 1964; Gupta 1969; Hasan 1978; Datta 1979). In the 1980s scholars directed their attention to the religious activities of Indian immigrants: Williams's *A New Face of Hinduism* (1984) analyzed the Hindu Swaminarayan sect, and his *Religions of Immigrants from India and Pakistan* (1988) was a comprehensive volume on various South Asian religions (see also Williams 1992, 1996); Fenton's *Transplanting Religious Traditions* (1988) focused on the beliefs and activities of Indian immigrants in Atlanta, Georgia (see also Fenton 1995). Singh's annotated bibliography, *South Asians in North America* (1988), has proved invaluable to many scholars.

In the 1990s American social scientists continued to publish their research, including Lessinger's *From the Ganges to the Hudson* (1995) and Bacon's *Life Lines* (1996). But there were also new trends in Indian and South Asian American studies. South Asians themselves began doing research and compiling anthologies about their own communities. A first step was Agarwal's *Passage from India* (1991), which focused on young Indian Americans. Several anthologies followed, including *Our Feet Walk the Sky* (Women of South Asian Descent Collective 1993), *Contours of the Heart* (Maira and Srikanth 1996); *A Part, Yet Apart* (Shankar and Srikanth 1998), and *Satyagraha in America* (Mathew and Prashad 1999/2000). These represent the emergence of a new generation of Indian Americans, and included poetry, photographs, and stories, as well as scholarly articles.

Chapter 1. The Landscape of South Asian New York

1. Parmatma Saran, a scholar of Indian immigration and himself an immigrant to the United States in the 1950s, pointed out this distinction between students and immigrants early on in my research.

2. The 1990 U.S. Census counted 4,955 Bangladeshis in New York, which to South Asians seemed an obvious undercount. Their population continued to grow: the 2000 Census counted 19,148 Bangladeshis in New York City. The majority of them resided in Queens neighborhoods such as Astoria, Woodside, Jackson Heights, Elmhurst, Corona, and Fresh Meadows. Pakistanis, the other large South Asian group, had significant numbers in both Brooklyn and Queens. In the 2000 census, however, the Pakistani population of Queens was larger than that of Brooklyn, and was concentrated in neighborhoods such as Astoria, Long Island City, Jackson Heights, Elmhurst, Corona, Flushing, and Fresh Meadows (New York City Department of City Planning 1996; for 2000 data, www.nyc.gov/html/dcp/html/popstart.html).

Chapter 2. Transplanting Indian Culture

1. Movie theaters in India are many times larger than in America and are packed seven days a week. The theater is divided into three or four sections of varying ticket price, and all seats are numbered. Going to the movies in India is a community experience shared by families and couples, and usually viewers make advance reservations.

2. On similar processes among Indian populations in Trinidad and Britain, see Vertovec 1995.

3. See Kelly 1988 on the gradual ascendancy of Diwali over Holi in Fiji.

Chapter 3. Worship and Community

1. The issue of hate speech and hate crimes against South Asians in the period immediately following September 11, 2001, should be viewed from this perspective.

Chapter 4. Building Careers, Encountering Class

1. Such statements were frequently made by Indians, both formally and informally, in New York City, but were emphasized more in interactions with other Americans than within the Indian immigrant community itself.

Chapter 5. Family and Gender

1. On extended family networks comprising two or more households of persons living under one roof, see Chen 1992, 52–54.

Chapter 7. The Evolution of South Asian Organizations

1. These five Kerala associations were the Kerala Samajam of Greater New York, the Kerala Association of New Jersey, the Kerala Cultural Association of North America, the Hudson Valley Malayalee Association, and the Westchester Malayalam Association.

2. This information is based on my conversation with Margaret Abraham.

References

Abraham, Margaret. 1995. Ethnicity, Gender, and Marital Violence: South Asian Women's Organizations in the United States. *Gender and Society* 9(4):450–468.

———. 1998. Speaking the Unspeakable: Marital Violence against South Asian Women in the United States. *Indian Journal of Gender Studies* 5(2):215–241.

———. 2000. *Speaking the Unspeakable: Marital Violence among South Asian Immigrants in the United States.* New Brunswick, N.J.: Rutgers University Press.

Advani, Anuradha G. 1997. Against the Tide: Reflections on Organizing New York City's South Asian Taxicab Drivers. In *Making More Waves: New Writing by Asian American Women*, ed. Elaine H. Kim, Lilia V. Villanueva, and Asian Women United of California, 215–222. Boston: Beacon.

Agarwal, Priya. 1991. *Passage from India.* Palos Verdes, Calif.: Yuvati.

AIA (Association of Indians in America). 1991. Glimpses of . . . History, Achievements, Objectives. Organization pamphlet.

———. 2000. Diwali Souvenir. Program booklet.

Aliani, Shahbano, Shehenshah Begum, Rokeya Mollah, Sushila Patel, and Biju Mathew. 1999/2000. Loud and Clear: A Conversation with Workers' Awaaz. In Mathew and Prashad, eds., 183–193.

AT&T. 1990. *Handbook for Asian Indians in the U.S.A., 1992–1993.* Pittsburgh: Spindle.

Bacon, Jean. 1996. *Life Lines: Community, Family, and Assimilation among Asian Indian Immigrants.* New York: Oxford University Press.

Baird, Robert D. 1978. Religion and the Legitimization of Nehru's Concept of the Secular State. In *Religion and the Legitimization of Power in South Asia*, ed. Bardwell J. Smith, 73–87. Leiden: Brill.

Bald, Vivek Ranjan. 1996. Taxi Meters and Plexiglass Partitions. In Maira and Srikanth, eds., 66–73.

Barot, Rohit. 1987. Caste and Sect in the Swaminarayan Movement. In Burghart, ed., 67–80.

Barrows, John Henry, ed. 1893. *The World's Parliament of Religions*. 2 vols. Chicago: Parliament.

Barth, Frederick, ed. 1969. *Ethnic Groups and Boundaries*. Boston: Little, Brown.

Basu, Rekha. 1989. American Born Confused "Desis." *India Today*, August 18.

Baumann, Gerd. 1996. *Contesting Cultures: Discourses of Identity in Multiethnic London*. Cambridge: Cambridge University Press.

Bhachu, Parminder. 1985. *Twice Migrants: East African Sikh Settlers in Britain*. London: Tavistock.

Bhatt, R. V., J. M. Soni, N. F. Patel, and P. S. Doctor. 1976. Migration of Baroda Medical Graduates, 1949–72. *Medical Education* 10(4):240–242.

Bhattacharjee, Anannya. 1992. The Habit of Ex-nomination: Nation, Woman, and the Indian Immigrant Bourgeoisie. *Public Culture* 5(1):19–44.

———. 1997a. The Public/Private Mirage: Mapping Homes and Undomesticating Violence Work in the South Asian Immigrant Community. In *Feminist Genealogies, Colonial Legacies, Democratic Futures*, ed. Jacqui M. Alexander and Chandra Talpade Mohanty, 308–329. New York: Routledge.

———. 1997b. A Slippery Path: Organizing Resistance to Violence against Women. In Shah, ed., 29–45.

Borden, Carla M., ed. 1989. *Contemporary Indian Tradition*. Washington, D.C.: Smithsonian Institution Press.

Bowen, David. 1987. The Evolution of Gujarati Hindu Organizations in Bradford. In Burghart, ed., 15–31.

Brooks, Douglas, Swami Durgananda, Paul E. Muller-Ortega, Constantina Rhodes Bailly, and S. P. Sabharathnam. 1997. *Meditation Revolution: A History and Theology of Siddha Yoga Lineage*. South Fallsburg, N.Y.: Agama.

Burghart, Richard, ed. 1987. *Hinduism in Great Britain: The Perpetuation of Religion in an Alien Cultural Milieu*. London: Tavistock.

Burki, Shahid Javed, and Subramanian Swamy. 1987. South Asian Migration to the United States: Demand and Supply Factors. *Economic and Political Weekly* 22(12):513–517.

Center for India Studies. 2000. *Languages and Writings in India*. Stony Brook: State University of New York at Stony Brook.

Chandrasekhar, Sripati, ed. 1982. *From India to America*. La Jolla, Calif.: Population Review.

Chansanchai, Athima, 1997. Maid in the U.S.A. *Village Voice*, October 7.

Chatterjee, Nilanjana, and Madhulika S. Khandelwal. 1995. Culture and Identity in Ethnic Festivals: Indian Immigrants in New York City. Unpublished manuscript.

Chen, Hsiang-shui. 1989. A Changing Congregation: Taiwanese, Tamils, and Americans in a Queens Church. In *Worship and Community: Christianity and Hinduism in Contemporary Queens*, ed. Roger Sanjek, 19–22. Flushing: Asian/American Center, Queens College, City University of New York.

———. 1992. *Chinatown No More: Taiwan Immigrants in Contemporary New York*. Ithaca: Cornell University Press.

Chopra, P. N., ed. 1982. *Religions and Communities of India*. Atlantic Highlands, N.J.: Humanities.

Danta, Rosalia. 1989. Conversion and Denominational Mobility: A Study of Latin

American Protestants in Queens, New York. M.A. thesis, Queens College, City University of New York.

Das, Veena, ed. 1990. *Mirrors of Violence: Communities, Riots, and Survivors in South Asia*. Delhi: Oxford University Press.

Das Dasgupta, Shamita. 1986. Marching to a Different Drummer? Sex Roles of Asian Indian Women in the United States. *Women and Therapy* 5(2/3):297–311.

———. 1995. Negotiating Safe Space. *Little India*, December, 58–61.

———, ed. 1998. *A Patchwork Shawl: Chronicles of South Asian Women in America*. New Brunswick, N.J.: Rutgers University Press.

DasGupta, Sayantani. 1999. *Her Own Medicine*. New York: Fawcett Gold Medal.

DasGupta, Sayantani, and Shamita Das Dasgupta. 1993. Journeys: Reclaiming South Asian Feminism. In Women of South Asian Descent Collective, eds., 123–130.

———. 1996. Women in Exile: Gender Relations in the Asian Indian Community in the United States. In Maira and Srikanth, eds., 381–400.

Datta, Mukul. 1979. Acculturation of Indian Immigrants in an Urban Metropolitan Area. Ph.D. diss., New York University.

Davis, Richard H. 1995. Introduction. In *Religions of India in Practice*, ed. Donald S. Lopez, 3–52. Princeton: Princeton University Press.

DeCamp, Suzanne. 1991. *The Linguistic Minorities of New York City*. New York: Community Service Society.

Depoo, Tilokie, ed. 1993. *The East Indian Diaspora: 150 Years of Survival, Contributions, and Achievements*. Flushing: Asian/American Center, Queens College, City University of New York.

Dickey, Sara. 1993. *Cinema and the Urban Poor in South India*. Cambridge: Cambridge University Press.

Dugger, Celia W. 1996. Queens Old-Timers Uneasy as Asian Influence Grows. *New York Times*, March 31.

Eade, John. 1990. Bangladeshi Community Organization and Leadership in Tower Hamlets. In *South Asians Overseas: Migration and Ethnicity*, ed. Colin Clarke, Ceri Peach, and Steven Vertovec, 317–329. Cambridge: Cambridge University Press.

Edel, Matthew. 1989. The New York Fiscal Crisis: Lessons for Latin America. In *Cities in Crisis: The Urban Challenge in the Americas*, ed. Matthew Edel and Ronald G. Hellman, 67–90. New York: Bildner Center for Western Hemisphere Studies, Graduate School and University Center, City University of New York.

Embree, Ainslee T. 1989. Brahmanical Ideology and Regional Identities. In *Imagining India: Essays on Indian History*, ed. Mark Juergensmeyer, 9–27. Delhi: Oxford University Press.

Farber, Jim. 1997. Concert for Bhangra—Dance! *Daily News*, July 13.

Fenton, John Y. 1988. *Transplanting Religious Traditions: Asian Indians in America*. New York: Praeger.

———. 1995. *South Asian Religions in the Americas: An Annotated Bibliography of Immigrant Religious Traditions*. Westport, Conn.: Greenwood.

Fisher, Maxine. 1980. *Indians of New York City*. New Delhi: Heritage.

Fornaro, Robert J. 1980. American-Hindu Acculturation: Reaction and Regression. *Eastern Anthropologist* 33(2):107–121.

Friedman, Daniel, and Sharon Ginsberg. 1997. *Miss India Georgia*. Film.

References

Ganesan, Indira. 1994. Resisting My Family History. *Glamour*, September, 124.
Gans, Herbert J. 1962. Urbanism and Suburbanism as Ways of Life: A Re-evaluation of Definitions. In *Human Behavior and Social Processes: An Interactionist Approach*, ed. Arnold M. Rose, 625–648. Boston: Houghton Mifflin.
Gehr, Richard. 1993. Bhangra the Bass. *Village Voice*, July 6.
Gibson, Margaret A. 1988. *Accommodation without Assimilation: Sikh Immigrants in an American High School*. Ithaca: Cornell University Press.
Gopinath, Gayatri. 1995. Bombay, U.K., Yuba City: Bhangra Music and the Engendering of Diaspora. *Diaspora* 4(3):303–321.
Gordon, Alastair. 2000. Raj Style Takes the Silk Road to the Suburbs. *New York Times*, January 27.
Gordon, Leonard A. 1989. Bridging India and America: The Art and Politics of Kumar Goshal. *Amerasia Journal* 15(2):69–87.
Gosine, Mahin, ed. 1990a. *Caribbean East Indians in America*. New York: Windsor.
———, ed. 1990b. *Dot-Head Americans: The Silent Minority in the United States*. New York: Windsor.
Gregory, Steven, and Roger Sanjek, eds. 1994. *Race*. New Brunswick, N.J.: Rutgers University Press.
Guo, Zibin. 2000. *Ginseng and Aspirin: Healthcare Alternatives for Chinese Elderly in New York*. Ithaca: Cornell University Press.
Gupta, Santosh. 1969. The Acculturation of Asian Indians in Central Pennsylvania. Ph.D. diss., Pennsylvania State University.
Gupte, Pranay. 1987. Big Money on Cheap Rock. *Forbes*, August 7, 64–67.
Hanson, R. Scott. 1997. Sri Maha Vallabha Ganapati Devasthanam of Flushing, New York. Paper presented at International Conference on the Hindu Diaspora, Concordia University, Montreal, August 22–23.
———. 1999. Intra- and Extra-Religioethnic Encounters: Responses to Plurality among [Two] Hindu Temples on Bowne Street in Flushing, New York. Paper presented at Association of American Religions annual meeting, Boston, November.
Hasan, Muhammad. 1978. The Social Geography of South Asians in Syracuse, New York. Ph.D. diss., Syracuse University.
Helweg, Arthur W., and Usha M. Helweg. 1990. *An Immigrant Success Story: East Indians in America*. Philadelphia: University of Pennsylvania Press.
Holloway, Lynette. 1995. The Cop in Little India. *New York Times*, April 9.
Husain, S. Yasir. 1997. South Asian Muslims in New York City: Sketches from Organizations and Communities. Paper, Neighborhood Studies Project, Asian/American Center, Queens College, City University of New York.
India International Centre Quarterly. 1995. Special issue, Secularism in Crisis. Spring.
India Sari Palace. 1993. *Reflections of Indian Americans: Twelve Award Winning Articles*. Jackson Heights, N.Y.: India Sari Palace.
Islam, Naheed. 1993. In the Belly of the Multicultural Beast I Am Named South Asian. In Women of the South Asian Descent Collective, eds., 242–245.
Jain, Usha R. 1964. The Gujaratis of San Francisco. M.A. thesis, University of California at Berkeley.
Jayawardena, Chandra. 1980. Culture and Ethnicity in Guyana and Fiji. *Man* 15(3):430–450.
Jensen, Joan M. 1988. *The Passage from India*. New Haven: Yale University Press.

Juergensmeyer, Mark. 1991. *Radhasoami Reality: The Logic of a Modern Faith.* Princeton: Princeton University Press.

Kakar, Sudhir. 1988. *Intimate Relations: Exploring Indian Sexuality.* Chicago: University of Chicago Press.

Kale, Madhavi. 1995. Projecting Identities: Empire and Indentured Labor Migration to Trinidad and British Guiana. In van der Veer, ed., 73–92.

Kapferer, Bruce. 1988. *Legends of People, Myths of State: Violence, Intolerance, and Political Culture in Sri Lanka and Australia.* Washington, D.C.: Smithsonian Institution Press.

Karatzas, Daniel. 1990. *Jackson Heights: A Garden in the City.* New York: n.p.

Kazem, Mohammed, Rizwan Raja, Biju Mathew, Kevin Fitzpatrick, and Dominique Esser. 1999/2000. Reorganizing Organizing: Immigrant Labor in North America. In Mathew and Prashad, eds., 171–181.

Kelly, John D. 1988. From Holi to Diwali in Fiji: An Essay on Ritual and History. *Man* 23(1): 40–55.

Khandelwal, Madhulika S. 1992. Indians of New York City: Patterns of Growth and Diversification, 1965–1990. Ph.D. diss., Carnegie-Mellon University.

———. 1995. Indian Immigrants in Queens, New York City: Patterns of Spatial Concentration and Distribution, 1965–1990. In van der Veer, ed., 178–196.

———. 1996a. Caste and Social Networks: Asian Indians in New York City. In *Immigrants and Immigration Policy: Individual Skills, Family Ties, and Group Identities,* ed. Phanindra Wunnava and Harriet Duleep, 115–131. Washington, D.C.: JAI.

———. 1996b. Issues of Diversity and Inclusion: Reflections on Race and Ethnicity. In *Asian Americans: The Year 2000 and Beyond,* conference proceedings, ed. Jenn-Yun Tein and Thomas K. Nakayama, 73–85. Tempe: Arizona State University.

———. 1997a. Community Organizing in an Asian Group: Asian Indians in New York City. *Another Side: Journal of the Michael Harrington Center* 5(1):23–32.

———. 1997b. Defining Community and Feminism: Indian Women in NYC. *Race, Gender, and Class: Asian American Voices* 4(3):95–111.

———. 1997c. In Step with Times? *India Today* (North American Supplement), January 3.

———. 1998. Reflections on Diversity and Inclusion: South Asians and Asian American Studies. In *Teaching Asian America: Diversity and the Problem of Community,* ed. Lane Ryo Hirabayashi, 111–122. Boulder: Rowman and Littlefield.

Khurana, Swati, and Leith Gill-Murgai. 1997. *Desi Dub.* Film.

Kiang, Peter Nien-chu. 2001. Asian Pacific American Youth: Pathways for Political Participation. In *Asian Americans and Politics,* ed. Gordon Chang, 230–257. Stanford: Stanford University Press.

Kibria, Nazli. 1993. *Family Tightrope: The Changing Lives of Vietnamese Americans.* Princeton: Princeton University Press.

———. 1996. Not Asian, Black, or White? Reflections on South Asian American Racial Identity. *Amerasia Journal* 22(2):77–86.

Knott, Kim. 1987. Hindu Temple Rituals in Britain: The Interpretation of Tradition. In Burghart, ed., 157–179.

Kotkin, Joel. 1993. *Tribes.* New York: Random House.

Kumar, Radha. 1993. *The History of Doing: An Illustrated Account of Movements for Women's Rights and Feminism in India, 1800–1990.* New York: Verso.

References

La Brack, Bruce. 1988. *The Sikhs of Northern California, 1904–1975: A Socio-Historical Study*. New York: AMS.

Lahiri, Jhumpa. 1999. *Interpreter of Maladies*. Boston: Houghton Mifflin.

Leonard, Karen. 1992. *Making Ethnic Choices: Punjabi Mexican Marriages in California*. Philadelphia: Temple University Press.

Leonard, Karen, and Chandra Tibrewal. 1993. Asian Indians in California: Occupations and Ethnicity. In *Immigration and Entrepreneurship: Culture, Capital, and Ethnic Networks*, ed. Ivan Light and Parminder Bhachu, 141–162. New Brunswick, N.J.: Transaction.

Lessinger, Johanna. 1989. The Tyranny of the American Dream: New York's Indian Immigrants as Workers and Investors. Paper presented at American Anthropological Association meeting, Washington, D.C.

——. 1995. *From the Ganges to the Hudson: Indian Immigrants in New York City*. Boston: Allyn and Bacon.

Maira, Sunaina. 1999/2000. Ideologies of Authenticity: Youth, Politics, and Diaspora. In Mathew and Prashad, eds., 139–149.

Maira, Sunaina, and Rajni Srikanth, eds. 1996. *Contours of the Heart: South Asians Map North America*. New York: Asian American Writers' Workshop.

Mangru, Basdeo. 1987. *Benevolent Neutrality: Indian Government Policy and Labour Migration to British Guiana, 1854–1884*. London: Hansib.

——. 1993. *Indenture and Abolition: Sacrifice and Survival on the Guyanese Sugar Plantations*. Toronto: Tsar.

Mathew, Biju, and Vijay Prashad, eds. 1999/2000. Satyagraha in America: The Political Culture of South Asian Americans. *Amerasia Journal* 25(3):viii–279.

Mazumdar, Haridas T. 1986. *Asian Indians' Contribution to America*. Little Rock: Gandhi Institute of America.

Mazumdar, Sucheta. 1984. Colonial Impact and Punjabi Immigration to the United States. In *Labor Immigration under Capitalism: Asian Workers in the United States before World War II*, ed. Lucie Cheng and Edna Bonacich, 316–336. Berkeley: University of California Press.

——. 1989. Race and Racism: South Asians in the United States. In *Frontiers of Asian American Studies: Writing, Research, and Community*, ed. Gail M. Nomura, Russell C. Leong, Stephen H. Sumdia, and Russell Endo, 25–38. Pullman: Washington State University Press.

Melwani, Lavina. 1996. Living on the Edge. *India Today* (North American Supplement), May 15.

Min, Pyong Gap. 1996. *Caught in the Middle: Korean Communities in New York and Los Angeles*. Berkeley: University of California Press.

Misir, Deborah N. 1996. The Murder of Navroze Mody: Race, Violence, and the Search for Order. *Amerasia Journal* 22(2):55–76.

Mogelonsky, Marcia. 1995. Asian-Indian Americans. *American Demographics* (August), 32–39.

Mohan, Radhey, ed. 1990. *Secularism in India: A Challenge*. New Delhi: Dr. Zakir Husain Educational and Cultural Foundation.

Mohanty, Chandra Talpade. 1991. Cartographies of Struggle: Third World Women and the Politics of Feminism. In *Third World Women and the Politics of Feminism*, ed.

Chandra Talpade Mohanty, Ann Russo, and Lourdes Torres, 1–47. Bloomington: Indiana University Press.

——. 1993. Defining Genealogies: Feminist Reflections on Being South Asian in North America. In Women of South Asian Descent Collective, eds., 351–358.

Mukhi, Sunita S. 2000. *Doing the Desi Thing*. New York: Garland.

Naim, C. M. 1989. Being a Muslim in India: The Challenge and the Opportunity. In Borden, ed., 57–66.

Nair, Rajamohan. 1997. South Asians in Two Neighborhoods of Eastern Queens. Paper, Neighborhood Studies Project, Asian/American Center, Queens College, City University of New York.

Nandan, Yash, and Edwin Eames. 1980. Typology and Analysis of the Asian Indian Family. In Saran and Eames, eds., 199–215.

Narayan, Shoba. 2000. I Wonder: Was It Me or Was It My Sari? *Newsweek*, March 13.

Narayanan, Vasudha. 1992. Creating South Indian Hindu Experience in the United States. In Williams, ed., 147–176.

New York City Department of City Planning. 1992. *Demographic Profiles*. New York.

——. 1993. *Downtown Flushing Plan*. New York.

——. 1996. *The Newest New Yorkers, 1990–1994*. New York.

Omi, Michael, and Howard Winant. 1986. *Racial Formation in the United States*. New York: Routledge and Kegan Paul.

Park, Kyeyoung. 1989. "Born Again": What Does It Mean to Korean Americans in New York City? *Journal of Ritual Studies* 3:287–301.

——. 1997. *The Korean American Dream: Immigrants and Small Business in New York City*. Ithaca: Cornell University Press.

Peterson, Jon A. 1987. *A Research Guide to the History of the Borough of Queens*. Flushing: Department of History, Queens College, City University of New York.

Prashad, Vijay. 2000a. Bored out of Our Ethnicity. *Little India*, September, 33.

——. 2000b. *Karma of Brown Folk*. Minneapolis: University of Minnesota Press.

Rai, Amit S. 1995. India On-line: Electronic Bulletin Boards and the Construction of a Diasporic Hindu Identity. *Diaspora* 4(1):31–57.

Ramanujan, A. K. 1990. Is There an Indian Way of Thinking? In *India through Hindu Categories*, ed. McKim Marriott, 41–58. New Delhi: Sage.

Richardson, E. Allen. 1988. *Stranger in This Land: Pluralism and the Response to Diversity in the United States*. New York: Pilgrim.

Ricourt, Milagros, and Ruby Danta. 2002. *Hispanas de Queens: Latino Panethnicity in a New York City Neighborhood*. Ithaca: Cornell University Press.

Robb, Peter. 1995. Introduction: South Asia and the Concept of Race. In *The Concept of Race in South Asia*, ed. Peter Robb, 1–76. Delhi: Oxford University Press.

Roland, Alan. 1986. The Indian Self: Reflections in the Mirror of American Life. In *Tradition and Transformation· Asian Indians in America*, ed. Richard Harvey Brown and George V. Coelho, 43–52. Williamsburg, Va.: Department of Anthropology, College of William and Mary.

Roy, Mahaswetha. 1994. Return of the Natives. *NRI Today*, August.

Sangari, Kumkum, and Sudesh Vaid, eds. 1989. *Recasting Women: Essays in Colonial History*. New Delhi: Kali for Women.

Sanjek, Roger. 1988. The People of Queens from Now to Then. Flushing: Asian/American Center, Queens College, City University of New York.

——. 1994a. The Enduring Inequalities of Race. In Gregory and Sanjek, eds., 1–17.

——. 1994b. Intermarriage and the Future of Races in the United States. In Gregory and Sanjek, eds., 103–130.

——. 1998. *The Future of Us All: Race and Neighborhood Politics in New York City.* Ithaca: Cornell University Press.

Sanjek, Roger, Hsiang-shui Chen, Madhulika S. Khandelwal, and Kyeyoung Park. 1989. *Chinese, Indian, and Korean Elderly: Backgrounds and Issues for the Future.* Flushing: Asian/American Center, Queens College, City University of New York.

Saran, Parmatma. 1985. *The Asian Indian Experience in the United States.* Cambridge, Mass.: Schenkman.

Saran, Parmatma, and Edwin Eames, eds. 1980. *The New Ethnics.* New York: Praeger.

Sengupta, Somini. 1994. Out of India. *New York Newsday,* September 19.

——. 1995. Kanu Chauhan's Christmas Spectacular. *New York Times,* December 24.

——. 1996. To Be Young, Indian and Hip. *New York Times,* June 30.

——. 1997. The New Indo Chic. *New York Times,* August 30.

Sethi, Rita Chaudhry. 1994. Smells like Racism: A Plan for Mobilizing against Anti-Asian Bias. In *The State of Asian America: Activism and Resistance in the 1990s,* ed. Karin Aguilar-San Juan, 235–250. Boston: South End.

Shah, Purvi. 1997. Redefining Home: How Community Elites Silence Feminist Activism. In Shah, ed., 46–56.

Shah, Sonia, ed. 1997. *Dragon Ladies: Asian American Feminists Breathe Fire.* Boston: South End.

Shankar, Lavina Dhingra, and Rajini Srikanth, eds. 1998. *A Part, Yet Apart: South Asians in Asian America.* Philadelphia: Temple University Press.

Singh, Jane, ed. 1988. *South Asians in North America: An Annotated and Selected Bibliography.* Berkeley: Center for South and Southeast Asian Studies, University of California at Berkeley.

Sinha, Sumantra Tito. 1998. From Campus to Community Politics in Asian America. In Shankar and Srikanth, eds., 146–167.

Slymovics, Susan. 1995. New York City's Muslim World Day Parade. In van der Veer, ed., 157–177.

Smith, Christopher. 1995. Asian New York: The Geography and Politics of Diversity. *International Migration Review* 29(1):59–84.

Sridhar, Kamal. 1988. Language Maintenance and Language Shift among Asian Indians: Kannadigas in the New York Area. *International Journal of Social Languages* 69:73–87.

——. 1997. The Languages of India in New York. In *The Multilingual Apple: Languages in New York City,* ed. Ofelia Garcia and Joshua A. Fishman, 257–279. Berlin: Mouton de Gruyter.

Srikanth, Rajini. 1998. Ram Yoshino Uppuluri's Campaign: The Implications for Pan-Ethnicity in America. In Shankar and Srikanth, eds., 186–214.

——. 1999/2000. Identity and Admission into the Political Game: The Indian American Community Signs Up. In Mathew and Prashad, eds., 59–82.

Steinberg, Stephen. 1981. *The Ethnic Myth: Race, Ethnicity, and Class in America.* Boston: Beacon.

Sterba, James P. 1987. Immigrant Saga. *Wall Street Journal*, January 27.

Thapar, Romila. 1966. *A History of India*. Harmondsworth: Penguin.

Thomas, Annamma, and T. M. Thomas. 1984. *Kerala Immigrants in America: A Sociological Study of the St. Thomas Christians*. Cochin, India: Simons.

Tinker, Hugh. 1977. *The Banyan Tree: Overseas Immigrants from India, Pakistan, and Bangladesh*. New York: Oxford University Press.

Vaid, Jyotsana. 1999/2000. Beyond a Space of Our Own: South Asian Women's Groups in the U.S. In Mathew and Prashad, eds., 111–126.

van der Veer, Peter, ed. 1995. *Nation and Migration: The Politics of Space in the South Asian Diaspora*. Philadelphia: University of Pennsylvania Press.

Vatuk, Sylvia. 1975. The Aging Women in India: Self-Perceptions and Changing Roles. In *Women in Contemporary India*, ed. Alfred de Souza, 142–163. Delhi: Manohar.

——. 1980. Withdrawal and Disengagement as a Cultural Response to Aging in India. In *Aging in Culture and Society*, ed. Christine L. Fry, 126–148. New York: Praeger.

——. 1989. Making New Homes in the City: Urbanization and the Indian Family. In Borden, ed., 187–202.

Vertovec, Steven. 1995. Hindus in Trinidad and Britain: Ethnic Religion, Reification, and the Politics of Public Space. In van der Veer, ed., 132–156.

Visweswaran, Kamala. 1997. Diaspora by Design: Flexible Citizenship and South Asians in U.S. Racial Formations. *Diaspora* 6(1):5–29.

Waldinger, Roger. 1986. *Through the Eye of the Needle: Immigrants and Enterprise in New York's Garment Trades*. New York: New York University Press.

Williams, Raymond Brady. 1984. *A New Face of Hinduism: The Swaminarayan Religion*. Cambridge: Cambridge University Press.

——. 1988. *Religions of Immigrants from India and Pakistan: New Threads in the American Tapestry*. Cambridge: Cambridge University Press.

——, ed. 1992. *A Sacred Thread: Modern Transmission of Hindu Traditions in India and Abroad*. Chambersburg, Pa.: Anima.

——. 1996. *Christian Pluralism in the United States: The Indian Immigrant Experience*. Cambridge: Cambridge University Press.

Women of South Asian Descent Collective, eds. 1993. *Our Feet Walk the Sky: Women of the South Asian Diaspora*. San Francisco: Aunt Lute Books.

Wong, Morrison G., and Charles Hirschman. 1983. The New Asian Immigrants. In *Culture, Ethnicity, and Identity: Current Issues in Research*, ed. William C. McCready, 381–403. New York: Academic.

Index

Index

The Anthropology of Contemporary Issues
A Series Edited by Roger Sanjek